Lost in Translation

Lost in Translation

The Book of Revelation Through Hebrew Eyes

by John Klein and Adam Spears
with Michael Christopher

The Book of Revelation Through Hebrew Eyes

Published by Covenant Research Institute, Inc.
© 2009 by John Klein, Adam Spears, and Michael Christopher

International Standard Book Number: 978-58930-237-2

Cover by Ross Chandler, Chandler Photography, Bend, Oregon

Unless otherwise indicated, all Scripture quotations are from
New American Standard Bible® (NASB) Ó 1960, 1977, 1995
by the Lockman Foundation. Used by permission.

Additional Scripture quotations are from:

The Amplified Bible (AMP)
© 1965, 1987 by Zondervan Publishing House

The Holy Bible, New International Version (NIV)
© 1973, 1984 by International Bible Society,
used by permission of Zondervan Publishing House.

The Holy Bible, King James Version (KJV)

The Holy Bible, The New King James Version® (NKJV)
Copyright © 1979, 1980, 1982, Thomas Nelson, Inc., Publishers

The Holy Bible, English Standard Version®, copyright © 2001 by Crossway
Bibles, a publishing ministry of Good News Publishers. Used by permission.
All rights reserved.

Complete Jewish Bible (CJB)
© 1998 by David H. Stern. Published by Jewish New Testament Publications, Inc.
All rights reserved. Used by permission.

Printed in the United States of America
ALL RIGHTS RESERVED

No part of this publication may be reproduced, stored in a retrieval system, or
transmitted, in any form or by any means—electronic, mechanical,
photocopying, recording, or otherwise—without prior written permission.

For information:
Covenant Research Institute
P.O. Box 8224
Bend, OR 97708
www.lostintranslation.org

To our children. May this book be a dependable source of knowledge and understanding in the months and years ahead. And may it also be both a comfort and an inspiration.

Acknowledgment

The authors wish to thank Jodi Klein for her assistance in the preparation of this manuscript. Without her commitment, perseverance, and boundless enthusiasm this book might still be sitting on the launching pad.

Contents

Foreword   xi
Introduction   xv

1 — Revelation Revealed 19
2 — The Master Menorah 41
3 — Meat on the Bones 63
4 — The Seven Letters 83
5 — Shamash to the Seven Seals 127
6 — The Seven Seals 145
7 — Shamash to the Seven Trumpets 175
8 — The First Trumpets 205
9 — The Seven Thunders 249
10 — The Final Trumpets 279
11 — Coming to a Close 297

Appendix A — God's Incredible Consistency 311
Appendix B — The Seven Rules of Hillel 319
Endnotes 325
Bibliography 335
Recommended Reading 337

Foreword

In the foreword to Volume 1 of this three-volume series[1] I talked about learning to shave without slicing my face off. I spoke of cutting against the grain, of dragging the razor backwards in spite of all the nicks I got when I started.

My main intent was to find an appropriate metaphor to help introduce a complex subject. Ironically, that original metaphor is every bit as suitable here in Volume 2 as well, for a very simple reason. This time out our two co-authors spend even more time dragging themselves backwards against the grain of conventional thought. And, they're still depending for many of their insights on the ancient Hebrew customs and understandings that were common knowledge thousands of years ago.

But beyond all that, much of what God has shown them about the book of Revelation is probably even less "conventional" than what they've said so far. How much "less conventional"? Let me give you a little personal background before I try to answer that.

A few years ago, my wife and I moved to a new city and stumbled into a class on the book of Revelation, taught by two Messianic Jewish rabbis. At the time I had no idea what that term meant, but it didn't take long to find out.

They were both Jewish by birth, but neither one had known it for more than a decade or so. Both were raised in the Christian church, and both had become staunch, traditional "Christian believers" in their teenage years. And yet, at some point both men began to sense at a visceral level that something huge was missing. It turned out to be their Jewish heritage, plus the cultural understandings that are so often taught almost from birth to traditional Jewish children.

John Klein had been told that he came from German stock, which was true but was not the whole story. Adam Spears was adopted into an Irish-American family and discovered almost by accident that his birth parents were Jewish. They hadn't wanted to "burden" him with that knowledge when they signed his birth certificate before giving him up for adoption.

Soon after he found this out via his first-ever telephone conversation with his birth mother, like so many others who feel called by God into Messianic Judaism, Adam began rabbinical studies but remained a believer in Yeshua (i.e., Jesus Christ). Thus he assumed the somewhat ungainly title of *Messianic Jewish Rabbi-in-Training*, which was once extremely rare but is slowly becoming more and more common.

For my wife and me, Adam's story strikes very close to home. Patricia had an Austrian grandmother who never told the folks in her family of their true Jewish heritage out of fear for their future. Imagine Trish's surprise, a few months after we joined Adam's congregation in Bend, Oregon, when she finally learned the truth. No wonder we felt such a strong pull that went even beyond the delight of finally finding teachers who seemed to understand vast portions of the Bible at a far deeper level than most.

For that is the point of this book, after all. We hear much in this modern age about people around the world who have been called by God and given particular pieces of the Revelation "puzzle." Except that it's not a puzzle; it's a classic Hebrew text, revealed by a Hebrew God, written down by a Hebrew believer, structured ac-

Foreword

cording to Hebrew thought patterns, phrased in Hebrew idioms, and delivered first to people intimately familiar with ancient Hebraic concepts.

As a result, you don't have to be a Hebrew to understand it but until you learn to think within that frame of reference you won't get much more than what's on the surface. This is one of the main messages of John Klein and Adam Spears, and it's a message that has found a welcome home all over the country. As so many readers have told us, the first volume in this series was both revelationary and revolutionary, and this volume promises much more of the same.

All this is especially ironic because – in contrast to what so many modern believers seem to think – Revelation is absolutely full of some of the most hopeful, helpful material to be found anywhere in our entire Bible. But it wasn't written by Greek philosophers and it doesn't follow Western literary conventions. Most important of all it's not irrelevant, which is what so many Christians have been taught to believe about everything in the Bible except the Gospels and the Pauline letters.

As both John Klein and Adam Spears keep repeating over and over, the Bible is one complete, unified whole, from cover to cover. The proof lies dead ahead.

Michael Christopher
Bend, Oregon – 2009

Introduction

In Volume 1 of this three-volume series we laid plenty of groundwork. Now it's time to incorporate the things we've already talked about into an ordered, logical, step-by-step discussion of the specific words given by God Himself to the apostle John, in the book of Revelation.

Our method will be twofold.

First, we will strip Revelation to its bare bones, talk briefly about the skeleton itself, then fit each of Revelation's chapters, concepts, and events into its proper place on the underlying framework.

"Bones without flesh" do not make a living creature. And, except for some of the least complex organisms within God's handiwork, "flesh without bones" is no more viable a combination. Only when the two are brought together, in the perfect harmony that only God could create, can the result live and breathe as Revelation was meant to do.

Second, even as God breathed His own Spirit into Adam's nostrils and thus made man unique, God has made Revelation unique by breathing the very essence of His own holy covenant into its pages.

The nature of God is love. The desire of God is for man to love Him in return. The nature of the love relationship that God desires to have with man is embodied within the marriage covenant that

Introduction

He outlined Himself in the first 65 books of the Bible. And even as the first five books represent God's marriage contract (an ancient *ketubah*[2]) with His own people, Revelation explains the final events leading up to the wedding, identifies the participants, and reveals the details of the marriage ceremony itself.

And by the way, chapters 5 and 6 of Revelation clearly identify the formal ketubah (the "little scroll"). It then makes reference to its seven seals (the seven official signatures on every ancient ketubah), and identifies the only participant in the marriage ceremony who is legally authorized to open the scroll.

Why this image and these connections? Because the whole purpose of God's plan is for man to enter back into a marriage relationship with Himself, and that's what we're seeing in the last book of the Bible.

Unfortunately – and here's where that business of "scraping against the grain of conventional thought" comes back into the picture – relatively few modern believers seem to approach the book of Revelation looking for that kind of understanding. They sometimes don't seem to recognize that Revelation represents the fulfillment of God's entire plan. This is its sole purpose. Since the fall of man God's desire has always been to restore mankind back to a right relationship with Himself – back to Garden of Eden levels so He could lead us gradually and gracefully into marriage.

Instead, we sometimes seem to approach all of Scripture from a disjointed perspective, as though it were a series of 66 separate books with each of the parts only vaguely connected and just barely supporting each other – if they did so at all. And therefore we don't realize that Revelation literally pulls together everything that has gone before, and adds the ultimate climax.

Just as often, modern readers often seem to concentrate on the New Testament only. How many times have you heard someone

Introduction

say that since we are "not under the law" anymore we don't really need to pay much attention to anything that happened before Christ came to save us by grace? Because, all that matters is what's happened *since* He was born.

The reason for all this is quite simple. Long ago the branch of Judaism that was known as the "sect of the Nazarene"[3] was largely taken over by Greek scholars thinking Greek thoughts, concentrating on Greek culture, and thereby interpreting the world's pre-eminent Hebraic book as though it were written in ancient Athens by Greek philosophers. The obvious result is a huge disconnect with God's ongoing plan. Given such a worldview, He's no longer a Hebraic God and His book is no longer a Hebraic book. Likewise, His plan is no longer the ultimate Hebraic plan for a Hebraic groom, a Hebraic bride, and a Hebraic marriage involving a long period of preparation (an ancient Hebraic custom) that required total commitment from the very beginning.

Sometimes we treat "marrying God" as though we could live our lives any way we please, then rush off to Vegas and "do the deed" when we finally can't avoid it any longer. But that's not quite the way the Bible – *including the book of Revelation* – lays it out for us.

So . . . to pull the two main aspects of our own approach to Revelation back together again, when we are familiar with the basic structure we can fit the individual pieces into a coherent whole. Or, to return to the metaphor we started with above, when we understand how the skeleton fits together we can fit the internal organs, the muscles, the sinews, the blood, and the skin back into their proper places and have a whole body that we can recognize once again.

In other words, when we are familiar with the larger story – and when we understand where all of God's Word was intended to take us – we can logically resolve most remaining questions of *who*, *what, when, where, why,* and *how* without having to make any gigantic, illogical leaps.

The God we serve is not a God of ambiguity. The "revelation" of Revelation is always right in front of us. The key lies in what tools of understanding we have in our toolbox.

If that makes no sense to you, before you look with us into Revelation, please read (or re-read) Volume 1 in this series, listed in the very first endnote at the back of this volume as *Lost in Translation: Rediscovering the Hebrew Roots of Our Faith*. That volume can stand on its own, but it will be even more valuable to you as an introduction to Volumes 2 and 3.

And now . . . let's get started!

John Klein and Adam Spears

1

Revelation Revealed

A FEW YEARS AGO, before the British Isles were wired for electricity, many poor villagers in Scotland used to buy what were known as "farthing dips." A farthing dip was a short length of common thread, dipped in whale oil and sold for a fourth of a penny.

Once lit, a farthing dip burned slowly and gave off a little light, but barely enough to read by. It's probably a safe bet to assume that those who could only afford farthing dips did not spend much time reclining in bed, studying the book of Revelation.

In the modern era we have no such excuse. So we make up others instead. "It's too hard to understand," we say. "And most of it won't apply to us anyway. We'll all be raptured out of here before anything bad begins."

We find only two things wrong with the above. First, Revelation is *not* too hard to understand. On the contrary, if you can read a roadmap you can understand Revelation.

Second, and much more important, we believe that a lot more of the information given to us in Revelation will apply to a lot more people than is commonly assumed.

Quite frankly, no matter what their theological/seminary training might be, those who try to interpret Hebrew idioms and Hebrew metaphors from a Greco-Roman perspective have spread tremendous misunderstandings throughout the modern body of believers. And such misunderstandings have been made all the more popular because they encourage wishful thinking.

Even worse, they engender attitudes and assumptions that could cause all kinds of trouble for all kinds of people in the years ahead. And they discourage actions that could do the exact opposite. If you sincerely believe that you'll never go through a hurricane you'll never dig a storm cellar. If you sincerely believe that you'll never go through a flood you'll never build a boat. And if you sincerely believe that you'll never have to endure any of the catastrophic, cataclysmic, calamitous events of Revelation you'll never dig a cellar, build a boat, or prepare yourself in any other way.

It's so much easier to convince ourselves that the coming storm will hit only our neighbor's house than it is to board up our own windows.

Likewise, if you sincerely believe that you were never intended to have an ancient Hebraic marriage relationship with God, involving total purity, total commitment, and total focus on Him, you won't be getting ready for that, either.

We do not say these things to frighten or confuse anyone. On the contrary, the real purpose of Revelation is not to scare God's people; it's to get us excited in a positive way, to help us prepare for what's coming.

Thus our goal is to make our study of Revelation so inviting and so invigorating that you'll want to read it again and again, over and over, to test the truth of what we have to say. And we'll give you the tools to do that.

1 - Revelation Revealed

God Takes Care of His Own

God will take care of His own, but that doesn't mean that modern, end-times believers, alone among all the servants of God since the days of Adam, won't be around when things get tough. Neither does it mean that we'll all be "rescued" in exactly the same way, at exactly the same time, to exactly the same reward. Consider what God says in Revelation 12:10–11:

> [10]Then I heard a loud voice in heaven, saying, "Now the Salvation, and the power, and the kingdom of our God and the authority of His Christ have come, for the accuser of our brethren has been thrown down, he who accuses them before our God day and night. [11]*And they overcame him because of the blood of the Lamb and because of the word of their testimony, and they did not love their life even when faced with death.* (italics added)

Who is God talking about here? Well, martyrs like Peter and Stephen, who put their lives on the line, come immediately to mind. So do the stories of Noah and Lot, the first of whom was warned, was obedient, and was therefore allowed to prepare by conforming to God's plan. The second one became passive and missed all the signs, yet still got a chance to run before the fire and brimstone fell. Nevertheless, because of his slack response he lost his wife and his children turned reprobate.

In the same vein, Paul's second letter to the Thessalonians contains a reference that often seems to be overlooked:

> [1]BUT RELATIVE to the coming of our Lord Jesus Christ (the Messiah) and our gathering together to [meet] Him, we beg you, brethren,
> [2]Not to allow your minds to be quickly unsettled or disturbed or kept excited or alarmed, whether it be by some [pretended] revelation of [the] Spirit or by word or by letter [alleged to be] from us, to the ef-

fect that the day of the Lord has [already] arrived and is here.

³Let no one deceive or beguile you in any way, for that day will not come *except the apostasy comes first* [unless the predicted great falling away of those who have professed to be Christians has come], and the man of lawlessness (sin) is revealed, who is the son of doom (of perdition),

⁴Who opposes and exalts himself so proudly and insolently against and over all that is called God or that is worshiped, [even to his actually] taking his seat in the temple of God, proclaiming that he himself is God. (2 Thessalonians 2:1–4, AMP, italics added)

It's hard to read verse 3, above, and still claim (as so many do) that we'll see a huge end-times revival. Indeed, other translations even call this coming apostasy a "great falling away," which probably makes the point even more plainly. Likewise, many other portions of Scripture talk about an end-times apostasy but none talk about an end-times revival.

The book of Revelation is a book of instructions intended to prepare God's people physically, mentally, and spiritually for what's coming – but only if they heed His words and get ready. As we are told in Revelation 1:3:

> Blessed is he who reads and those who hear the words of the prophecy, and heed the things which are written in it; for the time is near.

Thus Revelation provides a clear picture of what's coming so we can take steps to protect ourselves, even as we trust in Him and make absolutely sure that our relationships with Him are exactly as they ought to be.

That, in fact, is the exact purpose of Revelation, as stated by Yeshua[4] (i.e., Jesus) Himself in the first and last chapters. Yet many people disregard Revelation because they believe it's directed mostly to the Jews and the unbelievers "left behind" after the Rapture takes place. However, the book of Revelation opens with seven letters to seven congregations in Asia, not Israel. The people who attended those congregations were both Jews and Gentiles. Clearly, God was giving eternal instructions to *all* his people, not to a specific group who lived only in that time and place. Add to this the whole concept of "grafting Gentiles in" to the nation of Israel, as explained so well by Paul in the eleventh chapter of the book of Romans, and you should begin to get the concept.

What a slap in God's face to deny the value of His last book! Literally, that book explains what has been His hope, His dream, and His promise for the last 6,000 years. Yet we seldom see God as someone "in love." And, though we often talk about being part of the Bride we seldom see ourselves in an engagement period leading up to a marriage. Worse yet, we never see ourselves in that sacred period of final preparation between the signing of the marriage contract and the actual ceremony itself.[5]

Perhaps equally telling, you could take many books out of the Bible and, even though you might seriously diminish Scripture (as we believe the church did when it outlawed the book of Enoch[6]), the loss would not be fatal to an understanding of God's eternal plan. If you took away any of the Gospels you'd still have a fairly complete accounting of Yeshua's life on earth. If you took away Psalms, the Bible would be infinitely less rich but no less comprehensible in most respects. Likewise, if you took away Esther, or Ruth, or Job, or some portions of the Pauline epistles, you might not lose anything utterly essential to understanding the rest of the text.

But that's not true of Revelation. You can't take it away. You can't ignore it. You can't overlook it. And you can't possibly allow yourself to believe that what it has to say is not important.

On the contrary – with one significant exception that we'll come back to in a moment – of no other book in the Bible does God tell us that we will get a special blessing if we read it and apply it to our lives, as He explained in Revelation 1:3 as quoted above.

At the very end of Revelation He also says:

> And behold, I am coming quickly. *Blessed is he who heeds the words of the prophecy of this book.* (Revelation 22:7, italics added)

What's more, in this passage the word interpreted as "heeds" really means "guards" or "shepherds." It also means to "apply" and to "do" what we've learned. This is therefore an especially powerful passage and gives us added responsibility, because it basically circles back to the essence of His desired God/mankind relationship by encompassing the principles that a bride must follow to be a responsible Hebraic marriage partner.

At the same time, in no other book of the Bible are we threatened with having our names removed from the Book of Life, as in Revelation 3:5. And nowhere else are we told that we will receive the plagues described in Revelation if we add to or subtract from the text, as in Revelation 22:18–19.

In fact, beyond what Yeshua Himself said about not changing a single jot or tittle (Matthew 5:18; Luke 16:17), in only one other place in the Bible does it talk about adding or subtracting from any of the instructions that God gives us, and that happens in Deuteronomy 12:32. Isn't it interesting that the book of Revelation shares the same standard that God gave His people to live by in the first five books of the Bible, known to Jews both ancient and modern as the *Torah*?

What Is a Ketubah?

Beyond all the above, as we explained in Volume 1, the Torah itself takes the form of a classic Hebrew ketubah, as detailed in this short extract from Volume 1:

> *Ketubah*[7] is the Hebrew word for *marriage contract*. As indicated above, the terms of the contract were worked out between the two families during the meal they shared together. When both sides were satisfied they brought in a scribe or a rabbi to write the actual document itself, which had five parts.
>
> - First came a combined family history of the bride and groom, which included detailed family trees and anecdotes.
> - Second came a personal and family history of the bride, with a detailed family tree and anecdotes.
> - Third came a personal and family history of the groom, also with a family tree and anecdotes.
> - Fourth came the story of how the bride and groom met, with related anecdotes.
> - Fifth came a final section detailing both the bride's and the groom's responsibilities before and after the wedding.
>
> Let us pause for another moment and look at some more significant parallels to the marriage contract itself, one from the beginning of Scripture and one from the very end. We would not be the first researchers to point out that the first five books of the Bible correspond to the five parts of the ancient Hebrew ketubah.
>
> - Genesis provides the combined family history of the Bride and Groom.
> - Exodus gives the personal and family history of the Bride.

- Leviticus provides the history of God's "family," the Levites.
- Numbers tells of God's love affair with His people in the wilderness and records His joys and sorrows as He reaches out to His Bride.
- Deuteronomy specifies the responsibilities that both Bride and Groom must fulfill.

So what are we saying? That the first five books of the Bible are written as a marriage contract between God and His people. We're not even talking "analogy" here – that's what they *are*.

When all these details and conditions of the coming marriage were recorded in writing, the ketubah required seven signatures, seven "seals." These came from the bride and the groom, the two fathers, a scribe (or, in later times, a rabbi), and two witnesses.

In our opinion, in the Torah those seven signatures come from seven major players. Remember [that] our covenant patriarchs . . . play a very important role in this ketubah, this marriage contract. Figuratively, they become the signatories as follows:

- Adam and Noah were the two witnesses.
- Abraham, the father of many nations, was also father of the groom.
- Jacob was the father of the bride.
- Moses was the scribe (he wrote down the Torah as God dictated).
- David, often called God's beloved, was the bride.
- Yeshua, representing salvation, was the groom.

At the end of the Bible, in the book of Revelation, we encounter the whole concept of the "seven seals" once again, in a very big way. To some researchers the references seem mysterious and difficult to understand, but in reality they refer directly to a classic Hebrew marriage ketubah.

About Hebrew Hermeneutics

One more very important thing. You need to realize that this book might not resemble very much of what you're likely to read in some of the more popular end-times theology books that dominate the shelves in bookstores. Ironically, in many ways we respect and admire the authors of those works. We believe they have done extremely well, given their preconceptions. But many of those preconceptions arise from a Greco-Roman or Western view of the text – cultural, economic, moral, and religious – rather than from the viewpoints of the authors of the Bible themselves, which were thoroughly Hebraic.

Thus many such preconceptions simply have to go. Other preconceptions have to be re-aligned and re-adjusted to reflect the far richer, far deeper, far more cohesive reality that God has built into the book of Revelation. In a moment we want to graphically demonstrate what we're talking about. But first, a little more background and review.

To re-establish a major point from Volume 1 in this series, the Scriptures that believers put their faith in, whether we call them, collectively, a Tanakh and a B'rit Hadashah[8] or an Old Testament and a New Testament, were written down, under the inspiration of God, by ancient Hebrew authors. There's not an American, a European, an Asian, a Nordic, or an Eskimo anywhere in the bunch. Which is not intended as a denigration of anyone – just a simple statement of fact.

And, following logically on the above, as we have demonstrated elsewhere,[9] up to 92 percent (or more) of those same Scriptures was written down first in Hebrew. This was the native language of the authors, who also used the Hebrew idioms and metaphors that were common at the time.

Likewise, modern authors use modern idioms and expressions to resonate with modern readers. If you met a friend on the street you might say, "Hey man – what's up?" If your friend took your question literally he might feel obligated to list every airborne object within a fifty-mile radius. But of course he would not do that, not even if he were an air traffic controller.

Unless he were totally obtuse he would know immediately that "What's up?" was simply your way of saying, "Hi! How are you? What have you been doing lately?"

Or, can you imagine what a literal-minded, slang-deprived person might think if you said, "When he saw me come in late he really hit the ceiling!" Or, "Watch out or something awful is gonna' hit the fan!"

Someone who knew absolutely nothing of American English idioms and expressions would be totally mystified.

Hebrew Metaphors and Idioms

With that in mind, let's look at several examples of idiomatic Hebrew expressions taken directly from Scripture.

1) In Matthew 5:17–18, Yeshua said: "Do not think that I came to abolish the Law [in Hebrew, *Torah*] or the Prophets; I did not come to abolish but to fulfill. For truly I say to you, until heaven and earth pass away, not the smallest letter or stroke shall pass from the Law until all is accomplished."

   How many times, in churches all over the world, have believers been taught that, by "fulfilling" the Law, Yeshua meant that he was effectively terminating our need to observe it? After all, according to Western thought, if you fulfill a contract you "finish it off" so it's no longer in force.

In *Understanding the Difficult Words of Jesus*,[10] David Bivin and Roy Blizzard present a detailed explanation of what Yeshua actually meant here. We urge you to read the whole book for yourself, but here are just a few paragraphs explaining what the above verses actually mean:

> It is unnecessary to repeat all of what was said above [i.e., what was on page 92 of the *Difficult Words* book] about the Hebrew idiom "I have come," an idiom denoting intent or purpose. One thing, however, must be emphasized again. When Jesus says "I have come" he is not referring to his Incarnation.
>
> Undoubtedly, in trying to understand this passage, everything hinges on the meaning of the words "destroy" and "fulfill" in verse 17. What does Jesus mean by "destroy the Law" and "fulfill the Law"?
>
> "Destroy" and "fulfill" are technical terms used in rabbinic argumentation. When a sage felt that a colleague had misinterpreted a passage of Scripture, he would say, "You are destroying [abolishing] the Law!" Needless to say, in most cases his colleague strongly disagreed. What was "destroying the law" for one sage was "fulfilling the law" (correctly interpreting Scripture) for another.
>
> What we see in Matthew 5:17 is a rabbinic discussion. Someone has accused Jesus of "destroying" the Law. Of course, neither Jesus nor his accuser would ever think of literally destroying the Law. Furthermore, it would never enter the accuser's mind to charge Jesus with intent to abolish part or all of the Mosaic Law. What is

being called into question is Jesus' system of interpretation, the way he interprets Scripture.

When accused, Jesus strongly denies that his method of interpreting Scripture "destroys" or weakens its meaning. He claims, on the contrary, to be more orthodox than his accuser. For Jesus, a "light" commandment ("Do not bear hatred in your heart") is as important as a "heavy" commandment ("Do not murder").[11] And a disciple who breaks even a "light" commandment will be considered "light" (have an inferior position) in Jesus' movement (Matthew 5:19).
"Never imagine for a moment," Jesus says, "that I intend to abrogate the Law by misinterpreting it. My intent is not to weaken or negate the Law, but by properly interpreting God's written Word I aim to establish [bring into being or prove] it, that is, make it even more lasting. I would never invalidate the Law by effectively removing something from it through misinterpretation. Heaven and earth would sooner disappear than something from the Law. Not the smallest letter in the alphabet, the *yod*, nor even its decorative spur will ever disappear from the Law."

(Editor's Note: The small spur projecting from the yod's upper edge is commonly called a "tittle.")

To supplement the above, the word that Yeshua actually used is the Hebrew word *malah*,[12] which is generally interpreted as "fulfill." However, *malah* has a number of possible meanings. These include "to do anything fully, thoroughly, strongly; to be fulfilled; to be filled to overflowing." The idea here, in this context, is to thoroughly and correctly interpret Torah. It is not, as many have proposed, "to complete, to thereby end, or to terminate the applicability of Torah in our lives."

This last function ("to do anything fully") would, of course, be the proper office of the High Priest. Thus the word *malah* would be rendered more accurately as "interpret." Therefore, Yeshua was saying that He had come to show the world exactly how the Law applied to their lives, and how it should be observed day by day. He was also saying that He had come to correct their understanding of all matters pertaining to the Torah – that is, to clear out the forest of complicated, convoluted, but basically false interpretations that had grown up around it. And that is exactly why he railed so often against the Sadducees, and certain Pharisees (but especially the Sadducees), for using the Torah as a weapon for beating others into submission to their own precepts, not the precepts of God.

In fact, on one level these verses actually provide a study in contrasts. But sadly, rather than seeing what happens when man subverts or adds to God's Torah, we often use these verses instead to support the notion that we in the modern age have no responsibility to follow any of those "old laws" at all. As such thinking must inevitably conclude, Christ has somehow freed us from the same laws that prohibit murder, incest, and thievery, since we are supposedly under no obligation whatsoever except, perhaps, to follow our own interpretation of the "Golden Rule" as we wander untethered and unconnected to God in any significant way throughout our lives here on earth.

To quote again from Volume 1 in this series:

> . . . some . . . "wrong answers" have subtly contaminated our understanding of certain Scriptures for hundreds of years. Thus, thousands of people today read Matthew 5:17 ("Do not think that I came to abolish the Law or the Prophets; I did not come to abolish but to fulfill.") and believe that we're completely freed from observing those nasty, outdated "laws" of the Old Testament because Yeshua came to "ful-

fill" and thereby cancel the law, rather than coming to "interpret" it as the Scriptures really say.

Indeed, in this particular passage, because we also get the meaning of "law" wrong (Hint: The word translated as "law" is actually "Torah" and refers to all of the Old Testament Scriptures, not just to the 10 commandments and the 603 principles for [righteous] living), we fail to understand that He was *fulfilling prophecies*, not *canceling divine principles*. His life on earth was meant to illuminate the Holy Scriptures that had pointed toward Him and promised His coming for centuries. He came, literally, to show us how to live holy lives. In the process He obliterated nothing.

For another example, consider Revelation 16:15:

> "Behold, I am coming like a thief. Blessed is the one who stays awake and keeps his clothes, so that he will not walk about naked and men will not see his shame."

How often have you heard anyone explain that the "nakedness" this verse refers to has only to do with a lack of physical garments? On the contrary, it has everything to do with the protective covering provided to Adam and Eve, representing an eternal covenant with the God who created that very concept. But because we depend on Greek translations and Greek insights we miss out on what "naked" really means. We also think that coming "like a thief in the night" refers to some kind of soundless, sly, cat-burglar infiltration. On the contrary, this is a Hebrew idiom meaning that He will come boldly, like an armed intruder who kicks in the door and makes sure everyone in the neighborhood knows he's there (cf, 1 Thessalonians 5:2).[13]

2) Another phrase that sometimes seems problematic to some readers, even though it should not, occurs in Paul's letter to the Romans. Romans 10:4 says: "For Christ is the end of the law for righteousness to everyone who believes." Contrary to what some teach, the word "end" does not mean "termination," "conclusion," or "finalization" – it means "focus" or "goal." Thus the above verse would be more correctly rendered as "The whole purpose of Torah (i.e., the 'law') is to lead you to Yeshua so you can achieve true righteousness through Him."

Also, the word commonly translated here as "end" (the Greek *telos*) is used forty-two times in the New Testament, and thirty-seven times it's interpreted as *goal*. Five times it is interpreted as *fulfill*, all of which strongly suggests that it does *not* mean "end" or "termination" in this setting, as so many, so often, seem to believe.

Furthermore, Yeshua Himself tells us precisely when the law will be terminated in the passage from the fifth chapter of Matthew that we mentioned above: "For truly I say to you, until heaven and earth pass away, not the smallest letter or stroke shall pass from the Law [Torah] until all is accomplished" (Matthew. 5:18). This then links up directly with what John said near the end of the book of Revelation, in 21:1: "Then I saw a new heaven and a new earth; for the first heaven and the first earth passed away, and there is no longer any sea."

And by the way, most assuredly this doesn't sound like something that happened when Yeshua died on the cross, yet that is what we are often taught in many churches today. On the contrary, this passage references a time *after the completion of the thousand-year reign.*

3) Genesis 30:22 uses another common Hebrew idiom: "Then God remembered Rachel, and God gave heed to her and opened her womb." This one is commonly understood, but it's still worth

noting that it does not indicate prior forgetfulness on God's part. In this context, "remember" means to do a favor for someone; to intervene on their behalf. The same word is used again in Genesis 40:14, where Joseph asked the butler to intercede on his behalf: "But when all goes well with you, remember me and show me kindness; mention me to Pharaoh and get me out of this prison"(NIV). Some translations replace the word "remember" with a paraphrase; the NIV does a little bit of both, resulting in a very clear rendition of the "sense" of that word in that context.

We find expressions like these throughout the Bible. And sadly, those who try to interpret the words literally, by using a word-for-word translation, will never get the actual meaning until they understand the Hebraic nature of the passage and deal with it accordingly.

With respect to almost one hundred percent of the Tanakh (the Old Testament), the original language was ancient Hebrew. No biblical scholars seriously question this, although most believe that short sections of the books of Daniel and Ezra, amounting to less than one percent of the Tanakh, were written first in Aramaic, a local language directly related to Hebrew.[14]

Also a Hebraic Origin

But contrary to popular opinion, with respect to the B'rit Hadashah, much of the original language was also ancient Hebrew.[15] In addition to extensive arguments presented in such books as *Understanding the Difficult Words of Jesus* (see bibliography and numerous endnotes), consider three simple arguments.

1) First, despite probable fluency in other languages, all the authors spoke Hebrew in their daily activities and affairs. Given the last sixty years of archeological findings, including the Dead Sea Scrolls, most of the arguments in support of the idea that Greek and/or Aramaic were the languages used almost exclusively in Yeshua's

day have fallen by the wayside. Is it logical, therefore, to suggest that any biblical authors would suddenly switch over and write the most important work of their lives in Greek only, especially in books that were targeted primarily to ancient Hebrews?

2) Second, as we demonstrated in Volume 1 of this series, many (or even all) of the recurring "difficult words" scattered throughout the first three gospels, and the first fifteen chapters of Acts, become perfectly clear when redacted back into what were common Hebrew idioms.[16] Yet the notion that the entire B'rit Hadashah was communicated first in Greek still persists. Worse, many so-called experts claim that Hebrew was no longer spoken in Yeshua's time, despite abundant evidence to the contrary. For example:

- It was the custom of that era to write personalized messages to the deceased on ossuaries. These were heavy boxes, often made of stone, in which the bones of the dead were re-buried in the earth (or placed in tombs), to keep them together after the flesh was completely gone. Hundreds of these have been excavated and almost all of those poignant messages were written in Hebrew, by ordinary people.

- Most of the manuscripts among the Dead Sea Scrolls were written not in Aramaic or in Greek, but in Hebrew. Yet most of them were written in the century preceding the destruction of Qumran in AD 70 – many of them during Yeshua's lifetime. Even the few remaining items that preceded Yeshua were also written in Hebrew. Many of these were letters to families and personal manuscripts of that sort. In other words, they were not technical documents; they were just everyday communications.

- As everyone knows, the words "King of the Jews" appeared on a sign placed over Yeshua's head on the cross (Luke 23:38; John 19:19–20).[17] That sign was written in three languages:

Hebrew, Latin, and Greek. Aramaic was not among the three, even though several otherwise reliable translations of the Bible mistakenly claim that it was Aramaic in their footnotes. Which begs the question: If Aramaic really was the language everyone spoke, why was that language not on the sign?[18] Conversely, if Hebrew was not the common language of the day, why was it included?

- Another excellent example would be Acts 26:14, which quotes Paul himself: "And when we had all fallen to the ground, I heard a voice saying to me in the Hebrew dialect, 'Saul, Saul, why are you persecuting Me? It is hard for you to kick against the goads.'"

This was the voice of Yeshua Himself, speaking to Paul in Hebrew, as several popular translations affirm – including KJV, NKJV, AMP, ESV, ASV, and others. Among the translations most commonly used, only the NIV takes the liberty of "interpreting" the Greek text's use of "Hebrew" and changing it to "Aramaic." Interestingly, the NIV also changes the John 19 reference to Aramaic. Is the NIV selling a particular viewpoint, or what?

3) Third, when a rational person realizes that the Greek of the so-called original text is actually "translator's Greek,"[19] he simply has to wonder why. Translator's Greek was a form of the Greek language that was not spoken but, instead, was used specifically to translate non-Greek documents into Greek writings. Sometimes it's referred to, by scholars, as "sloppy Greek."[20] The claim that Matthew, Mark, and Luke all spoke impeccable Greek seems like a huge contradiction. Logically, you can't have it both ways – wouldn't they also write Greek that was at least as literate as what they supposedly spoke?

Remember, also, that the ancient Hebrews had developed a culture steeped in commerce, involving trade with nations from all

1 - Revelation Revealed

over the known world. As we mentioned in Volume 1, most of the major trade routes of that era went through Israel. The Jews of that day facilitated their trading by becoming fluent in the languages of the people they traded with. It was common even for average, sparsely educated Jews to know three, four, and even more languages. Certainly, in Yeshua's day, most Jews knew Hebrew, Aramaic, Greek, and Latin.

Beyond what we've established above, and especially considering how much space we devoted to Hebraic culture and customs in Volume 1, except for a few footnotes and other review materials we have elected not to go into exhaustive detail in this book. For that reason alone, once again we urge you to read Volume 1 before you read any farther in this one.

However, we would like to include the following quote, from Volume 1 of this series, because it leads into several important points that bear directly on our upcoming discussion of Revelation:

> When the ancient Greek philosophers translated Hebrew writings, of both the Old and the New Testament, they mistakenly believed that the text "worked" on one of two levels only, the literal and the allegorical – and never both at the same time. Have you ever heard someone say, "Oh – that passage should be taken 'spiritually,' not literally?" Comments like that reflect the Greek hermeneutics approach.
>
> Second, because they had developed their methods by working on Greek mythological texts, they were crippled by their assumption that the Hebrew text would also, automatically, reflect 75 percent creative imagination and only 25 percent truth. That left a lot of room for them to interject their own biases.
>
> By contrast, Hebrew hermeneutics . . . is a rigorous system of logic used for detailed interpretation of the Hebrew Scriptures. It recognizes that about 98 percent of those Scriptures operate on four levels simultaneously: (1) p'shat – direct, simple; (2) remez – hinting; (3) darash – commentary, com-

parison; and (4) sod – deep, hidden.[21] Hebrew hermeneutics also require the interpreter to agree to a moral standard of unbiased translation. Nothing can be added or subtracted; to the Hebrew mind, Scripture is 100% true, exactly as written. The goal is to recognize and understand that truth, wherever the hunt might lead.

Why do you suppose you can get something brand new out of a passage that you've already read a hundred times? It's not by accident; it's by design.

On What Level Does Revelation "Work"?

In the end, whether Revelation was first written down in Hebrew, Aramaic, or even Greek is not the main point here. Our God is the only true God of the universe, and He is also, without question, a Hebrew God. Thus Yeshua spoke to His human transcribers in Hebrew metaphors. And John was a Hebrew man who understood things from a Hebraic perspective. Therefore it's not surprising that "Revelation's 404 verses contain as many as 278 quotes, or allusions to, the Old Testament [Tanakh], especially Psalms, Isaiah, Ezekiel, Daniel, and Zechariah."[22]

In other words, exactly as we said in Volume 1, 68.2 percent of Revelation either *absolutely is* – or *absolutely contains* – Hebrew Scripture.

Therefore, Revelation is a Hebrew book in every important way. And given its overarching importance to the whole of Scripture, more than any other book, Revelation is heavily weighted to the "sod" (hidden) level. On the whole, that means it requires deeper, more orderly study.

In Closing . . .

When we two co-authors first began researching and studying together we considered ourselves ordinary students of biblical prophetic material. Even so, by the time we came together we had

1 - Revelation Revealed

both realized that – unless we were willing to focus on the Hebrew roots of Scripture, from which perspective the apostle John wrote – we would never get beyond the most basic understandings. Otherwise, Revelation would seem like mass confusion. Worse, we would never cancel out our own preconceptions.

It's not hard to find examples of what happens when we interpret Scripture – and even current events – according to our own preconceived ideas. Sadly, this is not a modern phenomenon. Many of the ancient Hebrews had their own set of preconceptions about what Messiah would be like.

1) Many expected a glorious king coming in worldly splendor amid claps of thunder and bolts of lightning. Instead they got an anonymous baby, born in a stable to the most "ordinary" woman. He spent His first night on earth in a feeding trough used by camels and donkeys.

2) Another school of thought, which included most of the laity and some of the scribes and Pharisees, believed in two separate comings. They believed that Messiah would first come as a suffering servant, and second as a glorious king.

The Sadducees held the first view, which leaned more toward glory and less toward suffering. Eventually they took that perspective to an extreme and didn't even recognize Messiah as God. Others believed that Messiah would come only once, would suffer, and would then triumph. Still others expected two separate messiahs, as in #2 above, but assumed one to be the son of Joseph (descendant of Jacob) and another to be the son of David (descendant of Jesse).

Over the centuries, most religious leaders had gradually combined the two prevailing concepts. So, by the time Yeshua actually arrived on the scene the leaders had discounted and even ignored the suffering servant prophecies for so long that they'd effectively forgotten the suffering aspect altogether. They fervently believed that Messiah would win the freedom of the Hebrew nation and eliminate forever the tyranny of so many centuries. He would be a Conquering Hero from the moment He first identified Himself.[23]

Contrary to all the above, even though many of the people of Yeshua's day actually got it right, we still have to remember that the Hebrews had suffered under Assyrian, Babylonian, Medo-Persian, Greek, and Roman tyranny for a long time, the latter even prevailing during Yeshua's day. For that reason we can easily understand the Hebrew leaders' motivation for emphasizing the prophetic passages that talk about the triumphal return of their King. Undoubtedly they had developed a deep need for those prophetic portions to be fulfilled – to see their Messiah coming as a liberator and giving them their freedom.

Certainly the last thing in the world they wanted to hear, after centuries of anticipation, was that Yeshua had come only to die. Thus, however we look at the situation, Yeshua didn't fit the images they held in their imaginations. Because of poor scriptural exegesis all those years ago, the ancient Hebrews were looking for the wrong thing and most of them missed Him completely.

The question is, are we doing the same thing today?

We'll leave that for you to answer as we go along. Our main goal, here and now, is to point out what could be a very significant parallel. To repeat: Many people who attempt to interpret the book of Revelation do so according to their own sets of preconceptions and presumptions. Many of these preconceptions, in turn, are based on other misunderstandings that overlay each other and somehow "coalesce together" into a mishmash of faulty deductions – entire cathedrals resting on a few quivering bricks, standing on edge.

2

The Master Menorah

THINK BACK TO YOUR HIGH SCHOOL classes in geometry. Or, if you somehow managed to avoid that subject altogether, think in terms of one of its most basic principles, familiar to almost everyone:

Three points determine a plane.

To say the same thing in more visual terms, if you set three stacks of books on the floor and rest a piece of plywood on them, the plywood will not wobble. Two points of support and it will fall. Or, as anyone who has ever tried to build a chair or a table will understand, four points of support and they'll all have to be at precisely the same height for the plywood to be stable.

But three points determine a plane. That's why we use tripods (i.e., "three feet") for cameras, telescopes, and surveyors' instruments. You could never be sure that a "quadpod" (four feet) or a "quintpod" (five feet) would establish a stable base wherever you put it, especially on uneven ground.

God has also seen fit to anchor His own rock-solid identity on three fundamental truths about Himself. Even as God is always one, at the same time He comprises Father, Son, and Holy Spirit.[24] Likewise, because we are made in His image we are body, spirit, and soul. And each of our souls comprises three parts as well – intellect, emotion, and will.

It should also go without saying that a successful marriage requires three foundational parts, too: a husband, a wife, and the constant presence of God Himself. In metaphorical terms these are the "three cords" that are so hard to break in a marriage, just as three actual cords – wound together – gain more strength than the sum of their parts. Indeed, as we are told in Ecclesiastes 4:12: "A cord of three strands is not quickly torn apart."

So it is that both God and His noblest creation are identified and even defined by the critical balance between the three pillars that support them and make them unique. The God of the Bible would not be complete, and certainly not the same God we all know, if either the Son or the Holy Spirit went missing. And as the aberrations we are now seeing in modern society clearly demonstrate, neither can men and women be completely functional, in the glorious ways that God intended, when they fail to nurture and develop any of the critical aspects of their basic natures.

Three Solid Supports

So what's the point of all this? Our goal is to show you, in graphic terms, how the book of Revelation rests on three solid supports as well. When you see that foundation and understand how the pieces fit together, your ability to comprehend both the individual elements and their relationships to each other will be vastly increased. Only then will Revelation be readily comprehensible.

Here are the three supports.

1) **First,** the book of Revelation is a thoroughly Hebraic text and therefore communicates on four levels at the same time (see

chapter 1 of this volume, and chapter 1 of Volume 1 as well). But to the student who is looking at the text through Hebrew eyes, the words of Revelation also communicate other far deeper and more intimate understandings.

2) **Second**, in terms of its actual construction, the book of Revelation arrays itself naturally onto a very simple, solid, structural foundation,[25] based on the menorah. God has taken an image that was thoroughly familiar to the ancient Hebrews and expanded it as only He can do, to serve as an underlying framework.

This particular image is no longer familiar to most modern, non-Hebraic audiences, and is therefore not usually part of any teachings on how to diagram and understand Revelation. And yet, once you put that framework in place you can hang every major event in Revelation in its appropriate spot and thereby see exactly where every major event fits in relation to every other major event.

In addition, the beauty of Revelation is that every end-times biblical prophecy can *also* be hung on the same framework, such that you now see this detailed, chronological panorama of biblical eschatology laid out with breathtaking clarity. It all comes together in Revelation.

Books such as Daniel and Zechariah, end-times prophecies as old as those in Deuteronomy and Genesis, and all the late-dated prophecies as well can be overlaid on this structure. Thus Revelation itself provides a brief outline and some details about the events that lead up to the second coming of Messiah. Meanwhile, other biblical prophecies embellish these events along the way, so you get a much more detailed description – when you overlay them on the menorah – of other events that lead to the big one.

To repeat, that structural foundation – which we have also called its *structural metaphor* – is based on the menorah, which we'll begin diagramming in a moment.

3) **Third,** an accurate understanding of Revelation requires an understanding of the basic types of covenant. As we've said so many times already, if you don't know covenant you don't know Scripture. However, to fully understand Revelation you must be especially familiar with the ultimate covenant that God desires all of mankind to enter into with Him – its mechanics, its terms, and all of its standard requirements.

The primary *conceptual metaphor* on which Revelation rests is the ancient Hebrew marriage covenant.

The Structural Foundation

To summarize what we've said so far, Revelation rests on three solid pillars of support and can only be understood by considering each one of those underpinnings in context with the other two. These three are (1) its essential Hebraicness, (2) its structural linkage to the menorah, and (3) its conceptual linkage to all four forms of Hebraic covenant – with special emphasis on betrothal covenant – which represents what has always been God's individual goal for each one of us.

Revelation also functions like a *roadmap*, a *timetable of events*, and a *traveler's guide* all rolled into one. It shows you *where you are*, *where you're going next*, and *what you should be watching for* as you journey from the present day to the time of Yeshua's return. Revelation does all that by giving you a list of milestones that have to be passed, in the proper order, before you can move from one spot to another on the map – or, on the timeline.

Even so, many serious biblical scholars miss certain events entirely. Or, they concentrate on surface issues and miss the layered

2 - The Master Menorah

meanings behind these events, leaving out the context entirely even though this is often what God uses to communicate deeper truths. Or, they get some of the "coming events" right but – as we will show in upcoming chapters – they still have separate and distinct events occurring at the same time, or in a faulty sequence.

In other words, to repeat what we've said earlier, this happens because many students of the Bible try to fit things into a preconceived Western or Greek schematic. And such formulaic approaches sometimes have little or nothing to do with the way God actually laid things out, with a distinctly Hebraic cultural context always in the background. Imagine trying to illustrate the battles of the American Civil War on a topographical map of Europe and you'll get the point.

Fortunately, God Himself, the Master Builder, has once again provided the structural framework. He gave part of it to the craftsman Bezalel way back in the wilderness, when he commissioned him (Exodus 35:30–33; 37:17–24) to hammer the first menorah from a 90-pound lump of gold. He expanded the concept for Ezekiel when he showed him the "wheels" of chapters 1 and 10, and for the apostle John when He showed him the seven golden lampstands (menorahs) of Revelation 1:12–20. We have talked briefly about both of these passages in Volume 1, and we will examine both of them at greater length elsewhere in this volume.

Imagine This

Let us now consider that God-given "master framework" in the clearest possible visual terms. To see how it works for yourself, grab a pencil and paper and draw a standard, seven-branch temple menorah. For many years this image has been the official symbol of the State of Israel, on which many millions of people have gazed without realizing what they were actually seeing. So – if the word "menorah" doesn't bring a clear image to mind, think of the Israeli symbol.

However, keep your version simple and make it large enough to spread out across your paper. But leave plenty of room at the top, and also leave lots of space between each of the branches, as shown in Figure 2-1.

Now, once you have that much on paper, starting with the farthest branch to the right, draw a smaller menorah directly on top of that branch, with the upward-pointing branch of the larger menorah extending directly into the shamash (the central branch) of the smaller menorah, which we will call a "mini-menorah" from now on. Essentially, the rightmost branch of the larger menorah "becomes" the shamash of the first mini-menorah.

Next, add a similar mini-menorah to the top of each of the remaining two branches on the right side of the larger menorah. Leave the center, for a moment, but pay special attention to one more important detail as you work. Starting with the first mini-menorah on the right, make sure that its leftmost branch merges into the central branch of the mini-menorah on its left, as shown in Figure 2-2. Do the same with the next two mini-menorahs.

Finally, at the very center, draw mini-menorah number four, with all of its seven branches extending straight up but, again, with the shamash of the original menorah extending directly into the shamash of the small one, as shown in Figure 2-3. And, most important, with the leftmost branch of the mini-menorah to its right merging into its shamash.

Congratulations! You're a little more than halfway done. Now, do exactly the same thing in reverse by drawing three more mini-menorahs on top of the remaining three branches on the left side of the original menorah. Start on the extreme left and create a mirror image of what you've done so far.

When you're finished, the composite drawing you've created should resemble Figure 2-3. At that point you'll have a total of

2 - The Master Menorah

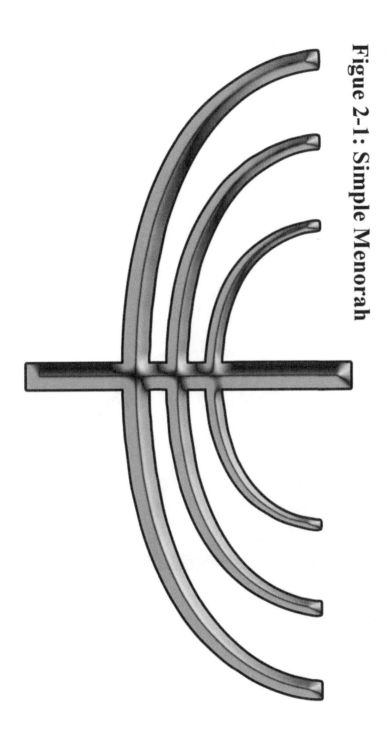

Figue 2-1: Simple Menorah

The Book of Revelation Through Hebrew Eyes

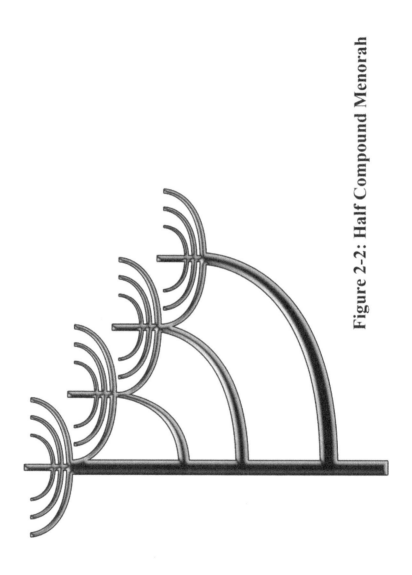

Figure 2-2: Half Compound Menorah

seven mini-menorahs, resting on the six branches and the central shamash of the original menorah, all connected together as shown in Figure 2-3.

The Master Menorah

The master menorah[26] has forty-nine lights, arranged in seven groups of seven. Each of the events listed in Revelation fits somewhere in one of those seven groups. And once you begin to put them in their proper places you immediately begin to see patterns that were not apparent before.

Essentially, the master menorah is the roadmap that we've already mentioned, which groups related events together and arranges them more or less in chronological order. It also separates them, visually, and allows us to see a very clear distinction between each grouping.

Also, just as each separate light on God's original menorah was lit from the shamash, in order, from right to left, the events of Revelation, on the right side of the master menorah, will occur in the same sequence, from right to left.

Each One Leads into Another

Finally, as you will note if you look closely at the complete drawing of the master menorah, starting on the right side, the left branch of each mini-menorah leads directly into the shamash of the next mini-menorah. Thus, the last event in each group of seven "serves notice" to the next group of seven that it's time for them to begin.

Perhaps the most dramatic example of what happens on the right side occurs in the first two verses of chapter 8 of Revelation, where the seventh seal flows seamlessly into the seven trumpets:

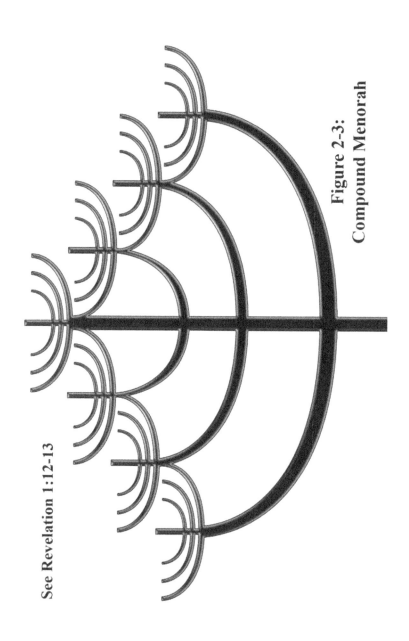

2 - The Master Menorah

> When the Lamb broke the seventh seal, there was silence in heaven for about half an hour. ²And I saw the seven angels who stand before God, and seven trumpets were given to them. (Revelation 8:1–2)

As always, the Bible provides its own best example, with this text graphically demonstrating how the mini-menorahs are linked. In this example, after the thirty-minute silence that follows the opening of the seventh seal (see chapter 8 in this volume), we see seven trumpets revealed.

What could be clearer than that?

More "Three-isms" in God's Creation

Numerous triads of foundational supports can be found in God's creation. For example, on the first day God created three things – time, space, and matter, which are often referred to as the "time-space-matter continuum." Each one of these can then be best understood by recognizing that it is defined by three separate "aspects" or parts:

1) Space is defined by height, width, and depth.
2) Time is defined by past, present, and future.
3) Matter is defined by the three forms in which it occurs – liquid, gas, and solid.

God is the *fourth* "aspect" that binds all the above together.

It's interesting that He also created four elementary forces that hold everything together on a physical level, on both the smallest and the largest playing fields – (1) gravity, (2) electro-magnetic attraction, and (3) the greater atomic force, which keeps the nucleus of atoms together, and (4) the lesser atomic force, which keeps the atoms of creation in an orderly state.

What Are "Shamash" Chapters?

Before we conclude this chapter let's put a few more things in place. First, as shown in Figure 2-4, the seven mini-menorahs represent seven different groups of related events. These seven groups are delineated by the text of Revelation itself. However, because Revelation is an ancient Hebrew book reflecting ancient Hebrew thought patterns and writing styles, the seven "groups" are not arranged in what our Western orientation would consider a perfect sequence. But from a Hebraic orientation it all makes perfect sense.

Starting from right-to-left, in order, those groups are:

- The Letters
- The Seals
- The Trumpets
- The Thunders
- The Bowls
- The Angelic Proclamations
- The Evil Kingdoms

The main portion of Revelation is basically organized into seven sections. Each section has an introductory portion (shamash) and a portion that describes the seven events that fit onto its corresponding mini-menorah. Each of the seven sections of Revelation, including their introductions as well as the seven events, will therefore require separate chapters (or more) in Volumes 2 and 3 in this series.

In contrast to the above, for many decades, various expositors have viewed Revelation as a disorganized batch of confusion. But again, that's not true from a Hebraic perspective.[27] Ironically, many people think the same thing about the prophetic books of Isaiah, Ezekiel, Joel, and others. However, even though not everyone in-

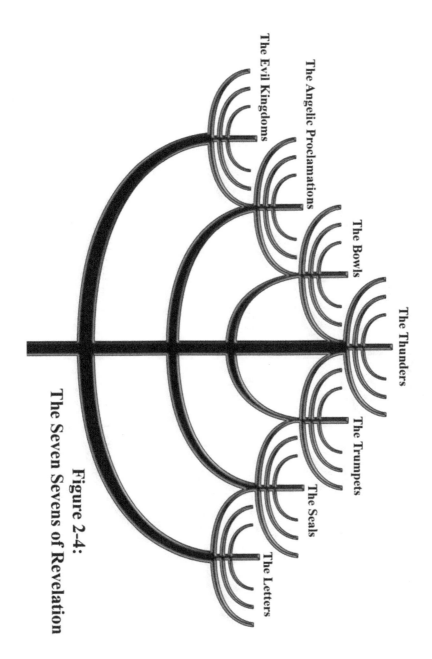

Figure 2-4:
The Seven Sevens of Revelation

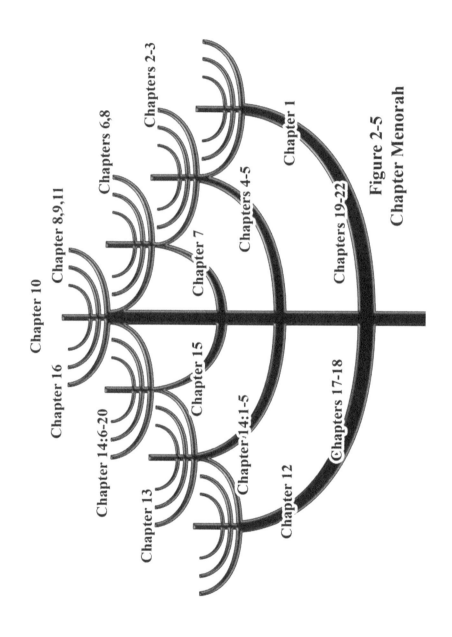

Figure 2-5
Chapter Menorah

stantly recognizes or perceives a prophetic and chronological flow, this does not make these books "random."

On the contrary, all these books do have a logical chronology, and so does Revelation. But again, you have to understand "order" as defined from a Hebraic perspective. Thus, as shown in Figure 2-5, all 22 chapters of Revelation can be overlaid directly onto the master menorah. But only when you position those chapters in their proper places can you truly see how they all relate to and interact with each other.

Why is this true? Well, to repeat what we have already said several times, because Revelation is a Hebrew book it doesn't proceed from start to finish without seeming to go sideways once in a while. Hebrew authors liked to insert additional commentary relating to the events they'd already described or were about to bring up, and Revelation is no exception. Indeed, if you've ever read *Moby Dick* you'll remember that Herman Melville did exactly the same thing . . . and he wasn't even Jewish!

So, the numbers *above* the mini-menorahs in Figure 2-5 identify the chapters that directly correspond to – and describe – the events in each mini-menorah. On the right side, as you will soon see, they represent the events as they occur in chronological order. At the same time, the numbers *below* the mini-menorahs represent the introductory, expository chapters that we are referring to when we talk about shamash chapters. These are the preparatory chapters (or portions of chapters) that contain explanations and elaborations relating to the corresponding mini-menorah events.

To quote briefly, once again, from Volume 1 in this series:

> The center lamp [of the menorah] was referred to as the *ner tamid* or "eternal light" (Leviticus 24:2). This particular light is also called the *shamash*, or "servant light," because it was used to rekindle the remaining six lights on the menorah whenever

they were trimmed. The Hebrew word for "sun" is also shamash, and the sun is considered the servant light to the natural world. The sun was created on the fourth day, just as the shamash holds the fourth position on a menorah.

Ancient Hebrew rabbis have suggested that this shamash position represents Messiah. The shamash is also called the plumb line (Zechariah 4:1–14). A plumb line is used in construction as the true level for establishing the foundation of a new building, just as Messiah's life should be the true and correct foundation for our lives. Yeshua is the source of strength and light from which we glorify the Father.

In other words, shamash chapters provide introductions, give background information, and set the scene for us so we can better understand the seven events that follow each one. How do they do that? Well, that's where it begins to get exciting.

To Keep the Story Going

In addition to all that we've said about them up to this point, shamash chapters also give us a whole series of mini-revelations that are sometimes slightly understood and sometimes misunderstood completely, but are almost never seen for what they really are. Even as the mini-menorah "action" chapters of Revelation detail the end-times events that will be going on, one by one, in chronological order, the shamash chapters introduce us to the main players and participants in an entirely different Big Event that will soon be going on as well. At first it's happening somewhat behind the scenes, but eventually it winds up out in the open, front-and-center, with no competition at all.

In fact, maybe we could compare Revelation to a movie that uses both flashbacks and cutaways to tell *parallel stories,* by giving you chunks of information that only begin to make sense once you've accumulated enough to see the big picture. From a storytelling per-

2 - The Master Menorah

spective, the goal of many movie makers is to keep you in suspense even as they also try to keep you reaching out for more information. The book of Revelation does almost exactly the same thing, except that we seldom realize it's playing out that way. We don't fully recognize the information we're being given, and therefore we don't always track the parallel-but-separate threads that will finally merge at the end of the story.

The Big Event that starts out in the background of Revelation is what's commonly called the Wedding of the Lamb. And the shamash chapters that introduce us to it, beginning with Revelation 1, 4, and 5, do so by introducing us to the main players in a very logical, organized way, beginning with the Groom and his Father and extending eventually to the Bride. Along the way, these chapters provide some fascinating information that normally slides under the radar. This happens because the background info doesn't seem to make any sense, given what everyone sees in the foreground, which are the mini-menorah events under which the world is reeling.

All of this makes the shamash chapters much more exciting than they might seem to be at first glance. It's a little like the sales pitch you might hear at a major league ballpark – "If you want to know the players you gotta' get a program!" Or, at the very least, you've gotta' open up the one you have.

Is It a Harvest or a Rapture?

The term "Rapture" is not used anywhere in the Bible. Nor does it show up in any known Christian writings before the year 1830. Neither do its basic tenets, involving two separate end-times visitations by Yeshua during which He (1) first comes invisibly and "Raptures" His church away, to allow them to escape the Tribulation that will soon be affecting everyone else still alive on earth, and then (2) comes one more time, visibly, to bring justice to the nations and end the age.

> None of this is clearly taught in Scripture. It has been generated by inductive reasoning by various commentators, stringing several verses together to come to their desired conclusion. At the same time, in dealing with the absence of any mention of the Rapture as noted above, most such commentators tend to suggest that teachings about the Rapture ceased completely after the Apostolic Age, giving us more than seventeen centuries of total silence regarding what many consider one of the most important doctrines to be extrapolated from the Bible. In other words, during those seventeen centuries some of the most brilliant theologians who ever lived somehow missed it completely.
>
> In our opinion, it makes much more sense to use the modern word "Harvest," which actually occurs in the book of Revelation. Oh – and there are *three* harvests, by the way, all of which we'll deal with at considerable length in Volume 3 of this series.

Further Evidence

Before we finish introducing the master menorah and actually begin using it to diagram and clarify the book of Revelation, please allow us to show you just a few places in the Bible in which the master menorah itself is introduced.

For example, in Volume 1 we've already mentioned that it's possible to use the Septuagint as a template to redact the Greek words of the Old Testament back into the original Hebrew words on which those Greek "equivalents" were based. And in every case, redacting Greek back to Hebrew always takes the text back to the original Hebrew thought, and often to the precise Hebrew itself.

We can also do the same thing with the New Testament, which is exactly what's already happened. Today it's no trick at all to buy a *Hebrew New Testament* that has been created via that process, using the Hebrew equivalents of what most people accept as the original Greek words of the New Testament.

2 - The Master Menorah

So, when we open the *Hebrew New Testament*[28] and go to the Hebrew word from which comes the Greek word that gives us the English word "lampstands" of Revelation 1:12–13, that original Hebrew word (Surprise!) is *menorah*. But not just one menorah in this particular passage – we're talking about *seven* menorahs, which is precisely how many we have on the master menorah that was given us by God.

> [12]Then I turned to see the voice that was speaking with me. And having turned I saw seven golden lampstands[13] [i.e., menorahs] and in the middle of the lampstands I saw one like a son of man, clothed in a robe reaching to the feet, and girded across His chest with a golden sash. (Revelation 1:12–13)

This is reinforced by Zechariah 4:2–3:

> [2]He said to me, "What do you see?" And I said, "I see, and behold, a lampstand [i.e., a menorah] all of gold with its bowl on the top of it, and its seven lamps on it with seven spouts belonging to each of the lamps which are on the top of it; [3]also two olive trees by it, one on the right side of the bowl and the other on its left side."

Much More Than One War

A lot of commentators have tried to superimpose a kind of "arbitrary order" on Revelation by using their own Greek and Western methods, which are distinctly non-Hebraic. But those methods simply do not work. If you try to deal with events in Revelation without understanding their unique placement and duration in time, you cannot deal with them coherently.

For example, whenever some see a passage about a war that occurs in the end times they might define it as "Armageddon." And, since so many also assume that we'll all be raptured out before anything the least bit problematic begins, why worry? But actually there are four separate wars in Revelation, specifically delineated as individual conflicts, from the first seal onward.

In Closing . . .

When it comes to understanding Revelation, perhaps the ultimate irony is that many of us would never dream of trying to get from Atlanta to San Diego by using a map of China. Neither would we try to build a house without erecting a proper framework first. But for some reason, that's exactly what many people tend to do with Revelation.

In contrast to that approach, we really need to look no further than what God Himself has given us. Once we begin to see how His very own creation, the master menorah, functions as both a foundational and structural metaphor, and a definitive roadmap of end-times events, a clear chronology begins to emerge. And, you will gradually realize that you can also overlay every other end-times, yet-to-be-fulfilled prophetic statement found in the Bible right over the top of the master menorah as well.

Doesn't matter whether the statement or description comes from Joel, from Daniel, from Yeshua Himself in the twenty-fourth chapter of Matthew, from Ezekiel, or from anyone else in the Bible. Joel, for example, provides a huge collection of details; he just doesn't show us where they fit. Indeed, it's only when you *do* interweave all the end-times prophecies from Scripture together, on the framework exposed and revealed by the book of Revelation (and on which Revelation itself is also built), that you can see the full design of this detailed tapestry of events that God has given to mankind.

For example, Joel is an embellishment of trumpets 6 and 7 – but more about that in Volume 3.

2 - The Master Menorah

To reiterate, Revelation's origin is Hebraic, its framework is a master menorah, and its essence is covenant. Thus the real picture is a multi-layered, multi-dimensional mosaic of information given by God to warn, encourage, and bless mankind. It most assuredly is not a simple line drawing.

In addition, the master menorah, paired up with the events described in Revelation, provides a foundational structure for the end times that is simply not found anywhere else *except in the Bible itself*. The rest of the Tanakh and the B'rit Hadashah provide wonderful descriptions of small portions – highlights – of some of these events. But again, Revelation shows their proper position on the roadmap, their proper order in the timeline, and often their proper duration as well.

The master menorah also reveals the proper connection of all the details of all these events to elements of the betrothal covenant, the conceptual metaphor that also underlies the whole of Revelation itself. In other words, the master menorah shows you where everything fits. It uses a divinely inspired design to show us how to organize what would otherwise be a confusing profusion of facts and concepts.[29] And, at that point, an understanding of betrothal covenant helps you understand what all of the above actually *means*.

In other words, almost the entire purpose of the book of Revelation is to show you what everything is, where everything fits, and what it all means. That's the literal definition of the word "revelation," in fact – to *reveal* something.

What? Are we talking about reinforcement here?

Ahem . . . how many times have we pointed out that God is a God of logic and order, of harmony and accord? He is also a God who communicates clearly, almost relentlessly, using repetition, different kinds of substantiations, repeated corroborations, and clear confirmations of all kinds to make sure we get the point and get it right. Therefore, it makes perfect sense that everything He has told us about the ultimate destiny of this world would fit together harmoniously onto one Master Pattern.

That Master Pattern is the master menorah.

3

Meat on the Bones

WE COME NOW TO THE THIRD LEG OF THE STOOL, the book of Revelation's metaphorical foundation. Let's begin with a quote from Ezekiel:

> [3]He said to me, "Son of man, can these bones live?" And I answered, "O Lord GOD, You know." [4]Again He said to me, "Prophesy over these bones and say to them, 'O dry bones, hear the word of the LORD.' [5]Thus says the Lord GOD to these bones, 'Behold, I will cause breath to enter you that you may come to life. [6]I will put sinews on you, make flesh grow back on you, cover you with skin and put breath in you that you may come alive; and you will know that I am the LORD.'" (Ezekiel 37:3–6)

The above passage contains a great number of intriguing "rabbi trails." For example, this is the primary reference to the Resurrection in the Old Testament (*Tanakh*). Indeed, it's quite possible that no one in the last 4,000 years has yet unraveled all its prophetic implications, considered in context with the verses that surround it.

But we leave that to another time and place. For now, we want to link up our own text with the indelible image that Ezekiel provided. Because, it's all about putting muscles and meat on the bones of the structure we've already shown you.

Beginnings Again

The book of Revelation, in typical Hebraic fashion, gives us a broad view and then a narrow view. Then it gives us a narrower view, and then a still narrower view. It concerns itself almost exclusively with end-times events, but it unfolds those events as though God had walked out to the night sky, shown us everything in the heavens, then brought in a gigantic telescope and focused on just one galaxy. He then focused on just one star, and then on one planet, and then on one event on that chosen planet.

The same pattern holds true through the metaphor of the master menorah. If you put all the events in their proper positions on the master menorah you get an amazingly clear picture of their sequence in time and their overall relationships one to another. And then, as you zoom in on one "galaxy" (i.e., just one of the mini-menorahs referencing seven events), and then on one event, you begin to pick up the details that expand on each event and explain how they all work together.

As you work your way up the master menorah, each mini-menorah then gives you more details about the end of The End. Thus the master menorah exposes a divine order to end-times events that no other system of interpretation seems able to reveal so clearly. And through the years we've investigated more "systems" than we can hope to remember, mostly to no avail. That's undoubtedly why we were so relieved when God began to show the master menorah pattern to us several years ago, and then began to show us how the meat fit on the bones. Apparently, God does not always reveal either Himself or His truths until most of the alternatives have bit the dust first.

Maybe that's also why the master menorah made such total sense from the first time God revealed it to us, even though no one we've ever met or heard about had ever proposed anything like it before. In truth we specifically remember the awe we felt at how *much* sense it made. This wasn't only a case of suddenly seeing something that had been there for thousands of years; it was also a case of seeing and sensing the divine origin of something that only God could originate and reveal.

No amount of human study could possibly make any difference except to prepare our hearts and minds. Also, the master menorah didn't come to us all at once, but in stages, step by step, moving from the general to the specific so we never lost our sense of where everything fit.

Most amazing of all, nothing of what God has shown us has contradicted anything else. On the contrary, absolutely every new thing God has shown us has reinforced every old thing, and thereby made the overall picture more and more clear. Just as the simple menorah reveals God's pathway to intimacy with Him through relationship, via all the separate details and levels of covenant, so the lights of the master menorah reveal the order and chronology of Revelation.

As we shall see, it also reveals the deceptively packaged strategies that Satan will counter with as an alternative, for those not in close covenant with God and thus susceptible to Satan's wiles.

The Covenant Overlays

The same ancient Hebrew covenants that we explained in Volume 1 (i.e., blood, salt, sandal, and the marriage covenant itself) all fit onto the master menorah without a trace of dissonance. And as you would expect, given multiple references throughout Scripture to the "mighty right hand of God," the "hand of honor," and the God-ordained custom of lighting the menorah from right to left, we therefore see all the godly covenants overlaying the menorah on the right side, to the right of the throne in the temple.

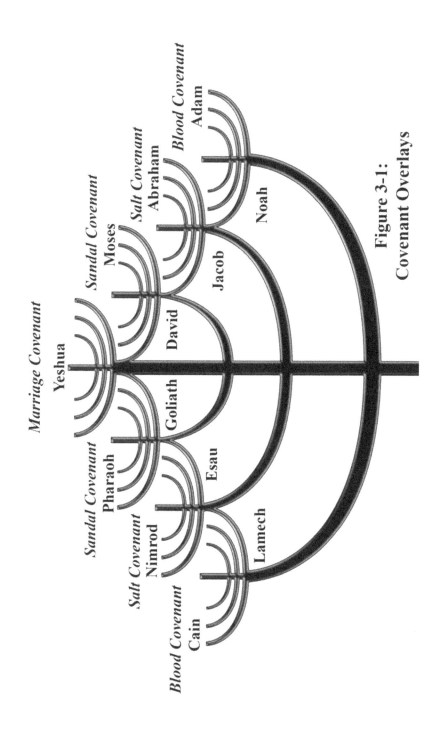

Figure 3-1: Covenant Overlays

3 - Meat on the Bones

As shown in Figure 3-1, blood covenant overlays the first mini-menorah to the extreme right. The ancient Hebrew patriarchs (see Table 2-1 in Volume 1) first associated with blood covenant are Adam and Noah. Adam received God's first initiative; God created Adam and Eve, gave them the Garden of Eden, and asked them to serve Him. When they failed, God shed the blood of an animal to cover their sin and clothed them with the skin of that same animal in what the book of Genesis refers to in Hebrew as a *katanot*. This word refers to an inner garment worn next to the skin, also corresponding to the first layer of bridal garments.

Responding, Expanding, and Extending

In other words, even as God gave Adam and Eve the symbol of service (blood), He also revealed his endgame by clothing them in the first bridal garment. However, there's something even more fascinating going on here as well. Each of the three Hebrew patriarchs who responded to God's initiatives in positive ways built on what the preceding patriarch had done. Thus, in each of those three responses we see the ultimate modeling in terms of what God wants to see in each of us. Each one "made the whole thing better" by accomplishing what God desired; to wit:

- **Noah** responded back to God's offer of covenant by offering his own blood sacrifice after he and his family had been preserved in the ark and returned to solid ground. Thus Noah modeled obedience to God in the face of ridicule from the people around him. How often was Noah scorned, laughed at, and ostracized for building that boat, anyway? If that's not service in spite of opposition, what is?

- **Jacob** responded by wrestling with God and refusing to take second place. Jacob wanted God's best, come hell or high water, clearly demonstrating that God is more than comfortable with those who risk everything and fight for His best – even with Him.

- **David** repeatedly battled on God's behalf, promoting and protecting godly things. He was patient, he did not try to force things to happen, and he honored God by refusing to harm or take revenge on anyone God had chosen to lead His people. He left "things of God" to God and focused on his *own* responsibilities.

Noah is also the "linking" patriarch leading into the second-from-the-right mini-menorah, over which the salt (friendship) covenant overlays. Abraham received God's next initiative when God sent Yeshua and two angels, whom Abraham then invited to break bread with himself. At that point God gave Abraham an unconditional promise of eternal friendship (salt covenant). Two generations later, Jacob took the next patriarchal step toward God by wrestling with Him for a specific renewal of God's original blessing as it applied to Jacob himself, now renamed "Israel," and to his descendants.

Like Noah, Jacob serves as the next "linking" patriarch leading into the next mini-menorah, over which sandal (inheritance) covenant overlays. In this case, Moses received God's initiative when God invited him to approach the burning bush and take off his sandals. At that point God promised to deliver Israel from bondage. Years later, David took the next significant patriarchal step toward God by serving God faithfully in spite of his own sins. In truth he paid a steep price for those sins, but he still retained his place of honor within the inheritance covenant by holding up his end of both the service and friendship covenants.

Salvation Has a Signature

As you make bigger commitments in your own life, to serve God and to war against everything that causes chaos in your own soul, God draws you closer and closer to Himself. And, as he draws you closer He gives you greater responsibility and authority. Thus the

> whole range of our potential relationship to God is pictured in the menorah, by the proximity of the players to the Groom (Shamash).
>
> For example, both Adam and Noah were asked to serve God. When they responded He gave them greater responsibility and authority. On the other hand, God gave David a lot more of practically everything. David was the apple of God's eye and was in an extremely close relationship with God. Therefore David got tremendous responsibility and ever-increasing authority all the way through his life.
>
> David also became the final "linking" patriarch leading into the mini-menorah at the very top of the diagram, which itself represents the ultimate covenant of marriage between Yeshua and His Bride.
>
> Many people today want to start off being the Bride. But covenant with God doesn't begin anywhere near there; it starts with being a servant. Likewise, some people think that once you get your ticket to heaven, via "salvation," you're free to do whatever you want. This also is not true, and anyone who teaches such a philosophy has little or no understanding of what the Scriptures actually say.
>
> On the contrary, James said, "I will show you my faith by my works" (James 2:18). We need to operate by the same standard. Faith is not just a warm fuzzy feeling – it's an active force that essentially "proves" the salvation that lies within you, which constantly rises to the surface.
>
> Or doesn't.

The Four Cups of Betrothal

The four cups of betrothal also overlay the master menorah in exactly the same sequence. Starting again at the right side (see Figure

3-2), the first cup of wine, drunk by the intended bride and groom and their families, corresponds to blood covenant and represents the very beginning of a committed service relationship between the bride and groom and their families, in preparation for marriage as explained in Volume 1.

The second cup, drunk by the intended bride and groom and their fathers, corresponds to salt covenant and represents the friendship level in the betrothal process. This is a point of deepening commitment, by which time both the bride and groom and their families have essentially pledged eternal linkage to each other.

The third cup, drunk only by the intended bride and groom, corresponds to sandal covenant and represents total commitment between the bride and groom at the inheritance level. At this point in the ancient Hebrew betrothal process, for all intents and purposes the bride and groom are legally married. If either one should die before the formal ceremony and consummation of the marriage, the survivor would still inherit the deceased party's estate.

The final cup of betrothal, drunk only at the wedding itself and only by the bride and groom, signifies their final coming together into a state of perpetual unity, as represented on the master menorah by the mini-menorah at the very top.

Colors of Covenant

When you overlay the colors of covenant onto the master menorah (see Figure 3-3), it's easy to see how they all combine to produce the pure white of betrothal between Yeshua and His Bride. But it is important to remember that the color of the Bride is not white because she is saved from sin on her own volition. She has become pure only because she has responded by demonstrating her willingness to actively walk in covenant with God Himself – and then has done so, for even willingness by itself is not enough. She didn't earn her white garments when God initiated a covenant with her;

3 - Meat on the Bones

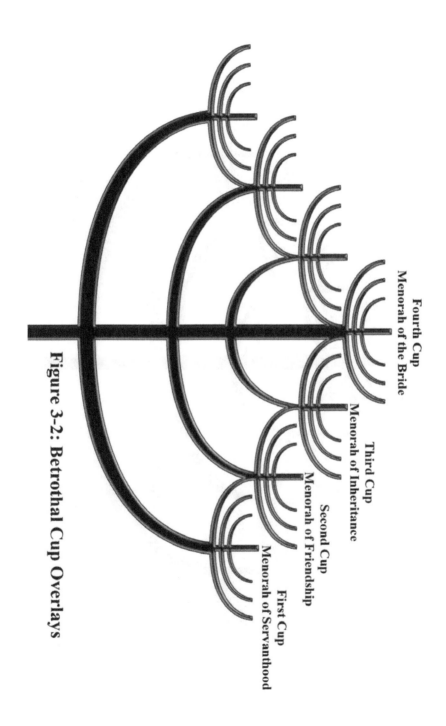

Figure 3-2: Betrothal Cup Overlays

The Book of Revelation Through Hebrew Eyes

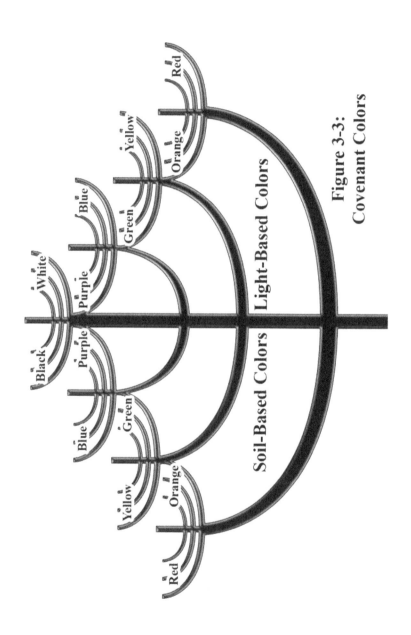

Figure 3-3: Covenant Colors

she earned them by responding back correctly. She has drunk the cups of betrothal as an outward sign, but inwardly she has paid the price (Revelation 19:7-8) and has made herself ready to put on the white garments of marriage.

Thus the eventual marriage of the Bride to Yeshua is not about salvation alone. Salvation is only the door leading onto the pathway; true marriage is about relationship. Granted, we don't earn our salvation by works but by accepting the free gift of God, just as a proper offer of marriage should be a free gift of love and not a business transaction.

Even so, a certain "What do I do and what do I get?" element eventually enters the arrangement. In ancient times, part of this was understood and part of it was specified, in considerable detail, within the marriage contract (ketubah) itself.

Yet the main point remains the same. Once you accept God's offer of salvation He intends for you to begin the process of deepening your covenant with Him, by which you enter into increasingly intimate levels of relationship and responsibility. And along the way, even as we ourselves are not sources but are merely conduits of light, as we deepen our relationship with God we reflect more and more of His light (color) into the world.

The experience of Moses on Mount Sinai, when his earthly body was so bathed in the light of God's glory that his face shone for days afterward, graphically demonstrates this whole point. How much more will we reflect God's glory in our heavenly bodies, even as Yeshua himself did on the Mount of Transfiguration (Matthew 17:2)?

The Satanic Overlays

In Volume 1 we presented detailed examples of how Satan establishes counter-covenants in direct conflict with the covenants established by God. Ironically, as though to illustrate his own pathetic lack of originality, even as Satan opposes God he attempts to copy Him at the same time, using unwitting men and women as pawns in a colossal chess game that he can never possibly win. In a way that further highlights the difference between Satan's relationships and those of the true God, Satan's counter-covenants overlay onto the mini-menorahs on the left side of the master menorah instead.

Seen on the diagram, the contrast could not be more stark. Godly covenant is about freedom while satanic covenant is about bondage. Yet Satan never seems to have any trouble in recruiting eager men and women to his side of the conflict. As it has for centuries, simple "pride of the flesh" continues to lead mankind astray in the vain hope of gaining personal power of one kind or another. Satan's false promises of money, sex, and influence over others seem to be just as attractive today as the deceptions He used to mislead Adam and Eve.

The earliest satanic counterparts of blood covenant involved Cain and Lamech, counterparts of Adam and Noah, who both drew the blood of innocent people. The story of Cain and Abel is familiar to all. As we noted in Volume 1, Cain basically asserted his allegiance to Satan and probably responded with words like this when he killed Abel, ignoring God's attempts to guide him into covenant with Himself: "Fine! You want a sacrifice? I'll give You one!"

Likewise Lamech, a contemporary of Noah, might be somewhat less familiar than Cain but he was no less willing to draw blood, even bragging to his wives about slaying a man for accidentally wounding him, and a young boy for accidentally striking and perhaps bruising him.

The earliest satanic counterparts of salt covenant (those of Abraham and Jacob) involved Nimrod and Esau. The former is best remembered for attempting to challenge God by building a tower that would reach into heaven "in the face of God." Nimrod was well-known among Babylonian mystics as a high sorcerer. Esau, who clearly rebelled against God's commandments and forsook the responsibilities that should have been his by virtue of his firstborn status, sealed his covenant with Satan by marrying Judith and Basemath of the Hittites, a tribe tainted with the curse of Canaan as recorded in Genesis 26:34.

The earliest satanic counterparts of sandal covenant involved (1) Pharaoh and Korah, both acting in direct opposition to Moses, and (2) Goliath and Saul, both acting in direct opposition to David. Sandal covenant was especially significant, which is probably why Satan established two counter-covenants in direct opposition to the two ancient Hebrew patriarchs.

The message in all this seems very clear. God is saying "Watch out!" There will always be internal and external opposition to His plans. And, the higher you go the tougher and more devious that opposition gets.

One more huge parallel seems striking. All the main participants in each of the counter-covenants listed above were alive at the same time as their counterparts who participated in covenants with God. This suggests that Satan usually reacts to God's major initiatives within a fairly short time. Thus Cain was the son of Adam, and Lamech was contemporary with Noah. Likewise, Nimrod and Abraham were contemporaries, as were, of course, the twin brothers Esau and Jacob. Finally, Pharaoh resisted Moses' entreaties for freedom in Egypt, while Korah was one of the original children of Israel led out of bondage by Moses. Likewise, both Goliath and Saul tried their best to kill David before he became king.

Counter-Color Overlays

Because Satan's goal is to make man into God (or, to be more precise, to deceive man into thinking he can become a god), Satan's counter colors imitate those of God but come from another source entirely. The colors of godly covenant come from God Himself, from the light He created to radiate outward from Himself as the source. Indeed, the Bible tells us that God *is* light (1 John 1:5).

But Satan has no way to create light on his own, so even as he depends on men made from the dust and clay of the earth[30] to worship him and elevate him to the status of the true God, Satan uses soil-based colors to imitate the light-based colors God creates out of nothing. Granted, it's possible to mix certain soil-based pigments to create red, yellow, and blue. But when you mix all the soil-based colors together, rather than pure, brilliant, white light you get the exact opposite – a muddy, dull, gray-black that could not possibly be more distant from the clarity and radiance associated with God.

Thus, even as God's covenant people radiate the true Light of the World, Satan's people reflect the pathetic darkness of sin. They also reflect a depressing truth about any association anyone can ever have with Satan. He always slips a little bit of truth into everything he's selling, but it's never more than a pale shadow of anything that originates with the true God of the Universe.

Counter-Covenant Overlays

As God makes very clear throughout the Bible, we must all choose whom we will serve, both in this life here on earth and in the eternity that follows. Despite what so many modern people seem to believe, to the effect that we can all play around with a little "white magic," can tell a few "white lies," and can quietly embrace any or all of the various perversions (sexual and otherwise) so common to this age, in truth we can serve only one master. And that will either be the One who originates truth or the one who perverts it.

Naturally, Satan would like to be in charge of your life. That's why he has devised a step-by-step counter-covenant path for you

3 - Meat on the Bones

to follow that corresponds roughly to the path laid out by God, and even includes the false allure of godhood. Satan does not offer four cups of wine, leading to formal marriage, but he does try very hard to lead us into four levels of counter-covenant with himself.

In the process he offers four cups of vinegar. Romans 6:23 tells us that the "wages of sin is death," but those "wages" usually involve a lot of suffering before the ultimate payment arrives.

One of the differences, of course, is that God offers intimacy with Himself in a spirit of honesty and love, while Satan offers false intimacy with himself in a spirit of deception and hate. But a far more important difference is that God offers everlasting life through eternal union with Himself as the ultimate goal, while Satan offers union with himself but then delivers the exact opposite of eternal life. It's called everlasting death.

The best way to visualize the satanic counter-covenants, leading to eternal destruction, is to overlay the three levels of sin, according to ancient Hebrew understanding, on the three mini-menorahs on the left side of the master menorah, leading toward the fourth mini-menorah at the top. To do this we need only recall the definitions we introduced in Volume 1. Here's what we said there:

1) *Avon* (ah-vone) is the Hebrew word for iniquity. Iniquity is the weakness or tendency to fall under temptation in specific areas. However, avon is not sin in the generally understood sense. It manifests itself in various ways by bringing thoughts and emotions into our lives that we know are evil. But it does not involve taking action in a condoning way, based on those thoughts.

2) *Chatah* (khah-tah) is the Hebrew word for transgression. Transgression is more than the weakness of iniquity; it is the action of violating God's principles. Thus, chatah carries with

it the idea of making a mistake, of violating God's principles then picking yourself up, repenting, seeking God, and trying to restore covenant with Him. In contrast to avon, chatah involves taking action on what we thought or felt, but we still don't identify with it. When we commit a transgression of the chatah type, then correct ourselves and repent, God applauds us. To fight the good fight is honorable.

3) *Peshah* (peh-shah) is the Hebrew word for sin. Peshah means, literally, "to defect; to go over to the other side." In other words, as we would put it, it means "to enter into counter-covenant with evil." Peshah is deliberate sin, consciously choosing to violate God's principles and identifying with the principles of evil. It is a clear act of rebellion – when you are "in peshah" you are no longer struggling against your sin as you do in transgression (chatah).

Ironically, when Paul called Satan the "lawless one" in 2 Thessalonians 2:8, the Hebrew word he uses here is *peshah* (i.e., "the peshah one"), which also could have been translated as "the rebellious one."

But rebelling against what? Against Torah, which makes him "the lawless one" or "the Torah-less one." This could also be translated[31] as "the rebellious one who has violated the Law," or as "the covenant breaker." All of which, of course, brings up the obvious question. If the Law expired on the day of Yeshua's crucifixion, as many modern Christians believe, why is God (via the words of Paul) still calling Satan "lawless" for violating a standard that no longer applies? Why is violating Torah *still* the definition of someone who has fallen away?

In any case, the major difference here, between chetah and peshah, is that the sinner now says "I no longer recognize and subscribe to your standard. I now honor a different standard – that of the enemy." In *chetah* you're still trying to shoot your bow in the right direction; in *peshah* you don't even pick up the bow in the first place, for now you're in relationship with someone else.

For example, how many times have you heard someone say, as a justification for their misbehavior, "Hey, that's just who I am; take it or leave it!" That's what God calls rebellion, and that's what Yeshua was referring to when He said, "Be ye therefore perfect, even as your Father which is in heaven is perfect" (Matthew 5:48 KJV). He was saying, "Stop your rebellion against God and his principles."[32]

> **What Was Adam's Sin?**
>
> The "original sin" that most commentators assign to Adam would probably best be described as a combination of *avon* and *chetah*. Adam embraced iniquity (*avon*) and became a transgressor (*chetah*) against both God and all the future generations of man. But as far as we know he didn't take the final step, reject God altogether, and enter into rebellion (*peshah*).
>
> He did not go over to the other side. Or, to put it another way, he did not give up trying to "hit the mark," which is one of the lesser-known meanings of the word *Torah*. Adam was afraid of God because of his sin, but he also seemed repentant as well, not defiant. Clearly he wanted to stop transgressing, and undoubtedly he spent most of the rest of his earthly existence just like all of God's people, fighting the good fight to remove transgression from his life.

Figure 3-4 illustrates how the preceding "sin" definitions overlay the left side of the master menorah. It also provides a graphic demonstration of how all sin, commonly downplayed throughout our culture as "something all flesh is heir to" and therefore not so bad, represents some level of covenant with Satan and leads inevitably to death. And as you can see, at the very top of the diagram all deceptions are revealed and Satan comes into direct conflict with

The fates arising from the two streams of covenant are exposed in the end.
Those in covenant with God receive life everlasting; those in covenant with Satan receive eternal damnation.

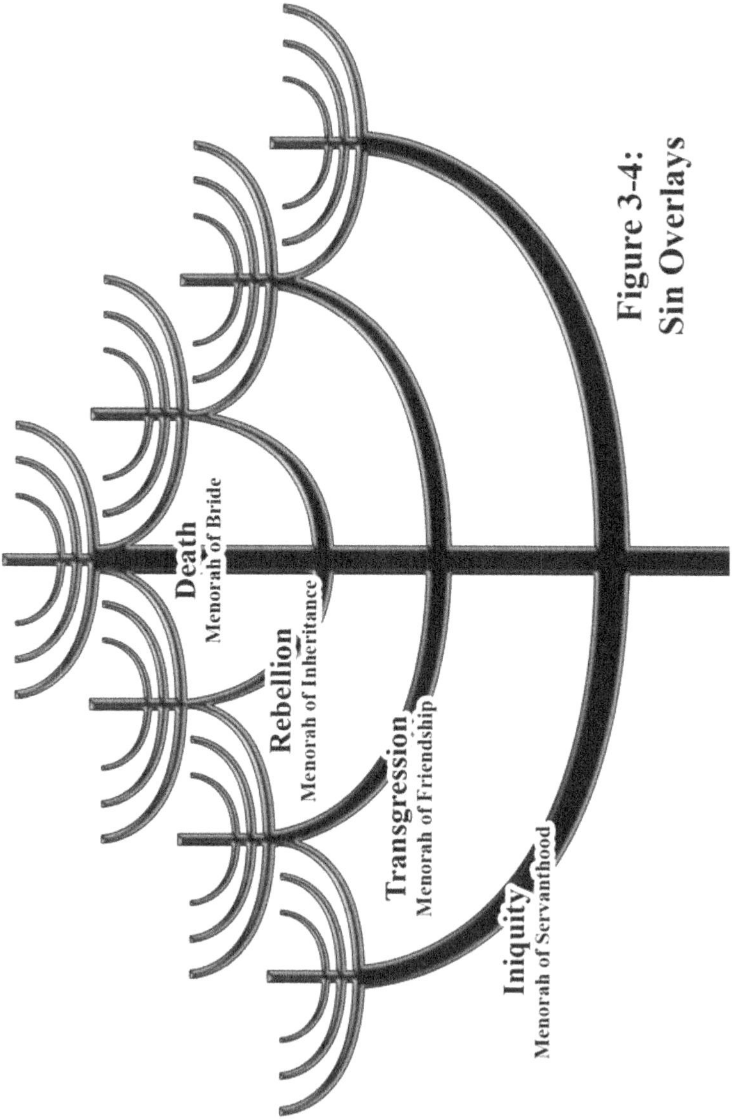

Death
Menorah of Bride

Rebellion
Menorah of Inheritance

Transgression
Menorah of Friendship

Iniquity
Menorah of Servanthood

**Figure 3-4:
Sin Overlays**

God, along with all his followers. What a horrific fate, to be in covenant with Satan at that moment.

In Closing . . .

Our use of the master menorah as a conceptual metaphor for the book of Revelation might seem unique – and it definitely is. To our knowledge, despite how logical it seems, until now the master menorah has never been used to show how everything in Revelation fits together.

But this interpretation does not come from us, which will become clear as we move forward. It comes directly from God's own Word, from the sacred text of Revelation itself, which provides its own interpretation. We are only reporting what Revelation reveals when we look at it from a Hebraic perspective.

Yet that's not all. Revelation also reveals the unique perspective that God has on his entire relationship with man. It encompasses everything from the creation to the Second Coming, and reinforces all that we've learned so far.

Thus, even as God reveals the superstructure that explains the end-times chronology, He also gives us the survival tools we'll need. And, He tells us over and over what He values most. Only those who are in an intimate relationship (covenant) with Him will have those tools, and only their ability to focus on what God Himself considers important will enable them to withstand the trials that will come as the events of Revelation unfold.

God has given us a multi-faceted image of the pathway man needs to walk, together with the means to do so. Covenant, relationships, covenant, betrothal, covenant, marriage, covenant, partnership with God – these concepts have been overlaid again and again throughout the Scriptures.

They all come together one final time in Revelation. To return to the verses from Ezekiel with which we started this chapter, the details of Revelation are like the muscles and sinews that Ezekiel spoke of, laid upon the dry bones that eventually rose up to become an army of God. Revelation comes alive just as those bones did in the vision God gave Ezekiel. We can also come alive – and move eventually into our promised inheritance of eternal life – even as those dry bones rose from the dust.

To God it's not about the end-times events; it's about His people being ready to walk with him *through* those end-times events. And it's about giving us the means by which we can walk that pathway successfully.

God illustrates His underlying message by using a unique visual display, which he ordered the Israelites to create from solid gold according to His unique design 3,500 years ago. In Revelation He incorporates that image into a final, colossal communication to us that literally brings everything in Scripture together.

It's like God Himself stands atop the Mount of Olives, waving His arms and saying over and over: "This is not a time for noncommitment! Enter into covenant with Me! Let my strength become yours; let my values become yours; let my spirit animate yours!"

That's what Revelation is all about.

4

The Seven Letters

FOR ANYONE BORN AFTER 1980 it's probably very hard to imagine a world without computers. For with computers came email and the Internet, giving millions of people the ability to find or create, copy, and send – to anyone else in the world – almost anything that can be put on paper, pasted into a sound recording, or captured in a video. And all within a matter of seconds.

But it wasn't always this way, of course. Those who came of age fifty years earlier had to write all their love letters in longhand. In fact, even after typewriters became available almost everywhere, until the 1980s it was still considered slightly gauche to use a machine to do a man or a woman's ultra-personal work. And though it was okay to type business letters, marketing experts were very careful *not* to use the fancy proportional fonts in sales letters for several years after *those* became generally available, too. It wasn't smart to look too slick and insincere in a world that still valued the personal touch even into the 1990s.

It's unclear what a person would have to do, here in the 21st century, to deliver a message in a truly "personal" manner, but there's no question that the oldest ways of all still work. And quite frankly, no letters ever written have ever been as effective – or resonated so powerfully throughout history – as the seven letters that the apostle John wrote down by hand to begin the book of Revelation.

John used chapter 1 to set the stage for the seven letters of Revelation, which then appear in chapters 2 and 3. For that reason, chapter 1 is what we call a shamash chapter as defined earlier in this volume. But before we examine any of these chapters individually, let's back up for a moment and put things in a broader context.

In typical Hebraic fashion, the book of Revelation gives us a panoramic view of how God has worked with mankind from the beginning to the end. God always starts off with an overview; that way the reader will understand where the specifics fit into the larger picture. Then, the Great Communicator will focus on the details.

In the same way, as we focus on each mini-menorah we zero in on smaller and smaller sections of time. And, as we proceed from the right side toward the shamash in the center, the sequencing constantly moves toward the end of The End.

Introduction to the Letters

The year is AD 92 and John the Apostle, the one Yeshua called "the Beloved," is on the Roman penal island of Patmos. Patmos is located in the Aegean Sea between the modern countries of Turkey and Greece, and John has been imprisoned there for his faith (Revelation 1:9).

Now – before we go any farther let's deal with something else that often comes up right about here. Here's a short extract from Volume 1, chapter 1 in this series:

> What most scholars now call the *Mattityahu Document* (i.e., the *Matthew Document*) containing Matthew, Mark, Luke, and Acts 1:1–15:35, was originally written on one scroll, in

4 - The Seven Letters

Hebrew. Later on these were broken out into separate scrolls. It's difficult to be as certain about the other New Testament books, but many signs also indicate that the original text of Revelation, if not written in Hebrew, might have been recorded first in Aramaic, an ancient dialect of Hebrew.

Contrary to what we just said, some people believe that Revelation came into being around AD 60–65. Their basis for this speculation is that the earliest copy of Revelation that we have was written in Greek that was not as refined as what John used in his other New Testament books – the Gospel of John and the three letters: 1 John, 2 John, and 3 John.

This suggested "progression of refinement" in John's writing itself is interpreted to mean that the book of Revelation was not actually written when he was on the Isle of Patmos near the end of his life, as John claims. On the contrary (so the story goes), it was actually his first effort at writing in Greek and therefore must have been written much earlier.

However, the suggestion of an earlier date for Revelation is not difficult to rebut, via one of the most often celebrated "exegetical" methods in use today, called "internal consistency." The very text of Revelation itself specifically supports the following suggestion:

> To this [i.e., the claim that John wrote Revelation in AD 92] it is objected that the style of Greek used in Revelation is far rougher and more Hebraic than that of the other four books, which all resemble each other. One possibility is that the fisherman from the Galil, for whom Greek was a second or third language, wrote the visions of Revelation himself, as commanded, and did not permit alterations; whereas for the Gospel and his letters he had a native Greek-speaker to help edit and translate."[33]

Since John was imprisoned on Patmos and no longer had access to fluent Greek transcribers, the above would make perfect sense. Meanwhile, the main reason for which many people wish to place the writing of Revelation at an earlier date is that such a date allows them to then proclaim that the prophecies contained in Revelation have already been fulfilled. In such a scenario, the primary agent for fulfilling these prophecies would therefore be the Romans' attack, dispersion, and destruction of the nation of Israel, coupled with the destruction of the temple, in AD 70.

The problem with this hypothesis is that the events surrounding the Roman destruction of the nation and the temple are never mentioned or prophesied in the book of Revelation at all. In reality, Revelation prophesies the exact opposite.

- The temple is not destroyed; it is rebuilt.

- The people are not dispersed; they're regathered.

- The nation is not destroyed; it is reborn and restored.

- In the book of Revelation the Antichrist (False Messiah) doesn't destroy the temple, but uses it to help him establish his false godhead. At the end the temple remains but the False Messiah is destroyed, and the true King comes and establishes peace over the entire earth.

The earliest version of the book of Revelation that we still have was written in "sloppy Greek."[34] However, as we have already explained in chapter 1 of this volume, if it is true that the original document the apostle John created was written in Hebrew or Aramaic, that's all the more reason to believe that it was not written in AD 65.

Nor should the increase in technology of the modern age, including the manifold advancements in medicine, agriculture, communications, transportation, living standards, and life expectancy, be interpreted as a moral and physical advancement toward the goal God wants us to reach for. In other words, what's happening now does not prove that we're already in the Age of Messiah, more commonly known as the millennial kingdom.

Beyond all that, the climax of the book of Revelation is all about the return of the King, and He has not returned yet. This is undoubtedly the most important point of all and is a major reason why we know that John wrote the book on Patmos exactly when he claimed. This would place the date of the writing close to AD 92.[35] And, because John was in prison at the time, he would not have had access to the Greek scribe (or scribes) who had helped refine his earlier writings.

One More Vital Point

As indicated above, Greek was John's second or third language. But what was his primary language – his fundamental linguistic and culture-based perceptual orientation? As we know from the gospel texts, John grew up as a Hebrew in a Hebrew culture, with a Hebraic perspective on just about everything. All that he relates to us in Revelation was thus filtered through a Hebraic lens. Therefore, as we will soon see, the metaphors he uses are Hebraic, his worldview is distinctly Hebraic, and his religious references are completely Hebraic. Thus his familiarity and high level of comfort with all things Hebraic is explicitly obvious throughout the entire book.[36]

Some others claim that the book of Revelation is the least important of all sixty-six books in the Bible and is even a complete waste of time. This opinion derives from the assumption that all believers will be raptured (i.e., taken out) prior to the Tribulation and will avoid all the cataclysmic end-times events. In such a scenario, because the book of Revelation deals almost exclusively with events that occur after all believers will supposedly be gone, some scholars claim it's unimportant.

This view, in light of even the limited insights we've laid out so far in Volume 1 and this text as well, is truly a gamble. To risk so much on one very narrow understanding of the text seems at least a little bit foolish. That's why we believe that the text speaks for itself, at the direction of a God who doesn't lie.

Starting Revelation

Here is how the book of Revelation begins:

> ¹The Revelation of Jesus Christ, which God gave Him to show to His bond-servants, the things which must soon take place; and He sent and communicated it by His angel to His bond-servant John, ²who testified to the word of God and to the testimony of Jesus Christ [Yeshua the Messiah], even to all that he saw. ³Blessed is he who reads and those who hear the words of the prophecy, and heed the things which are written in it; for the time is near. (Revelation 1:1–3)

The Hebrew word for the book of Revelation is *Kheezahon*, which means "revelation." The root word is *khazon*, which means a *divine vision*, especially a vision from God respecting future events, a prophetic vision, an oracle. Pictographically the Hebrew letters mean "the protecting weapon that manifests the covenant of life."

As we have also learned already (see Volume 1 of this series), the shamash of the menorah represents Messiah, the Groom and King. In chapter 1, which is the first shamash chapter, that very same Messiah specifically tells us about his own identity:

> "I am the Alpha and the Omega," says the Lord God, "who is and who was and who is to come, the Almighty." (Revelation 1:8)

4 - The Seven Letters

> **The Aleph and the Tav**
>
> As explained below, Yeshua actually called himself the Aleph and the Tav, but that's not our point here. This statement flies in the face of those who want to metaphorically "mysticize" the actual events of Revelation. Revelation *uses* metaphors, and it can certainly *seem* mystical to those who see mysticism in every corner. But on the contrary, our God is not into mysticism and never will be. He is a God of truth and clarity, even if it sometimes takes a little effort for us to understand what He's saying. And in this particular statement He is going out of His way to identify Himself so He cannot be misunderstood. No one else in the universe could make such a claim.
>
> Likewise, Revelation itself presents to us a series of prophetic events that God wanted us to study carefully so we could understand what lies ahead. It is not impossible to comprehend, it is not meant to be taken as pure metaphor alone, and it is not irrelevant in any way whatsoever.

At the same time, through the vision given to the apostle John, God makes it very clear that He wasn't talking about the Father only:

> [17]When I saw Him, I fell at His feet like a dead man And He placed His right hand on me, saying, "Do not be afraid; I am the first and the last, [18]and the living One; and I was dead, and behold, I am alive forevermore, and I have the keys of death and of Hades. (Revelation 1:17–18)

Clearly this is a vision of Yeshua, the Son, as verse 18 establishes with no wiggle room whatsoever. Thus, even as He claims to be the Alpha and the Omega, from His own Hebraic perspective he was actually saying that he was the *Aleph* and the *Tav*, which are the first and the last letters in the Hebrew aleph-bet. (The second letter is *bet*. And that, of course, is where we get aleph-bet.)

On the surface, when this passage is read from a western cultural perspective, the typical reader understands that Messiah is claiming to be the beginning and the end, which is exactly what the text says. And this is correct. However, from a Hebraic point of view, much more is being conveyed.

Recall what we've learned about the nature of Hebrew letters. As with all the letters in the Hebrew aleph-bet, the aleph and the tav represent *concepts* along with *sounds*. Thus the pictograph for aleph means "first, strong," while the pictograph for tav means "sign of the covenant" or "sign of the cross."[37] In fact, the ancient tav was even drawn in the shape of a cross, just like the one on which Messiah died. Likewise, on the first Passover, when the ancient Hebrews marked the posts and the lintels of their doorways in the blood of the Passover lamb, they were actually drawing the letter tav.

But let's go back to pictography. The reference to aleph and tav represents an unmistakable claim that Messiah is the "first strong sign of the covenant." Meanwhile, as we also explained in Volume 1, the Old Testament was given its name by God: *Torah*. And the Hebrew pictographs for this name tell us, "Behold the man nailed to the sign of the covenant (cross)."

But that's not all. In the first sentence in the book of Genesis we learned that "In the beginning, God created the heavens and the earth." These verses in Revelation actually link directly to the first verse in the book of Genesis. By using this language, God is describing Himself (i.e., "doing a wrap") as *the beginning and the end*, just as He referred to Himself in the opening verse of Genesis.

How does that work? Well, the fourth word of the first verse of Genesis just happens to be composed of two Hebrew letters, aleph and tav, pronounced as "et." But there is no English translation for this word, and very little corresponding concept of its function in English as well. However, in Hebrew it acts as a "linking word" connecting to the word that precedes it – in this case, *Elohim*, which means "God." Thus the text in Genesis, at a deeper level, also says: "In the beginning, the 'et' God, the God who is the first and the last, the beginning-and-end God, created the heavens and the earth." And that's exactly who Yeshua is claiming to be – i.e., *the beginning-and-end God*.

> **A Little Word with a Big Story**
>
> The rabbis believe that God used Hebrew to speak the universe into existence, and the very first sentence of the Bible provides quite a bit of evidence. Genesis 1:1 consists of seven Hebrew words, the fourth of which is the Hebrew word *et*, formed by the first and last letters of the Hebrew aleph-bet, *aleph* and *tav*. This little word strongly suggests that God is identifying Himself in the very first sentence of His Word as the *controller of the beginning and the end and everything in between*. Just as many linguists now believe that Hebrew is the true forerunner of all other languages, Hebrew also appears to be God's native language as well – His Mother-Father tongue.
>
> In Revelation 1:8, Yeshua reinforced all this when He said, "I am Alpha and Omega." Except, of course, that He was not a Greek, so He undoubtedly said, "I am Aleph and Tav." He is the same *et* who shows up in the shamash position (the fourth word) of the very first sentence of your Bible – which just happens to be seven Hebrew words long. How fitting. The shamash is the servant candle of the seven-branched menorah, used to light all the others, just as He is the greatest servant of all – and the only one who can literally "light up our lives" and make us lights for the world. The six candles – three on either side of the shamash – represent man. Thus Yeshua is the plumb line, surrounded by His people.
>
> If you look at any Hebrew Interlinear Bible you will see that *et* never gets translated. Why does this word have no English equivalent? Because *et* is a grammatical marker which functions like a road sign to tell the reader that *a definite direct object lies just ahead*.

> For example, "I ate the apple" in Hebrew would be "I ate *et* the apple." "I hit the ball" would be "I hit *et* the ball."
>
> How interesting that the author of the Hebrew language would place within the grammar of the language itself an indispensable word like *et,* whose very presence continually reminds us that He should be the ultimate *definite direct object* of all our words and all our actions. Whatever we do, in word or deed, should be done unto Him.
>
> He couldn't possibly make it more obvious.

The First Language in All of Creation

To go one step farther, from a Hebraic perspective it's also understood that God created the Hebrew language itself. Here's another short quote from Volume 1 in this series, dealing with that very subject:

> In addition, that same word [i.e., "et"] also means "the beginning and the end and everything in between." Thus, on another level, God could have been saying that He created the aleph and the tav, and all the letters in between – in other words, that He created the Hebrew language even before He created the physical world.

> Another significant indicator is that all the names of pre-flood individuals, in Genesis, have a distinct meaning in Hebrew. But not all the post-flood names do. This suggests that, prior to the flood, there was only *one* language and it was Hebrew. In addition, many modern linguists now believe that the language that lies at the core of every language on earth is Hebrew. No matter who analyzes the origin of any word in any language, it winds up being a Hebrew word at its ultimate root.[38] Granted, not all linguists have realized this yet, and some simply won't ever do so for various reasons, but many highly respected linguists maintain that it's true.

Meanwhile, one of the ultimate ironies of the modern age is that Hebrew isn't even on a lot of the evolutionary language trees, even though many highly trained, experienced linguists maintain that Hebrew is the ultimate source. Some have suggested that maybe that's because it truly is the root, and roots are usually kept out of sight.

One God in All Places

Sadly, some scholars still claim that Yeshua the Messiah never claimed to be the same God for whom the Hebrew word *Elohim* was used in Genesis 1:1. However, these two passages in Revelation and Genesis directly contradict this mistaken belief and tell an entirely different story. In Revelation 1:8, Messiah is saying with absolute clarity that He Himself is the same *Elohim* who created the universe in Genesis.

This is confirmed by other passages in the Old Testament, such as Isaiah 49:26:

> I will make your oppressors eat their own flesh;
> they will be drunk on their own blood, as with wine.
> Then all mankind will know
> that I, the LORD, am your Savior,
> your Redeemer, the Mighty One of Jacob." (NIV)

Yet even this translation doesn't quite reveal the true identities. In Hebrew it says "*Ki ani, Yahweh Moshiach, v'go alech, ahvir Ya'acov*" – meaning "*I alone, Yahweh, am your Messiah, your kinsman redeemer, the mighty One of Jacob.*" This passage equates Yahweh, which is interpreted as LORD here in the NIV, with the Messiah.

Also, Exodus 15:2–3 says:

> ²The LORD [*Yah*, a very personal expression for the name of God] is my strength and song, And He has become my salvation [*Yeshua*]; This is my *God* [*El*], and

> I will praise Him; My father's *God* [*El*], and I will extol Him. ³"The LORD [Yahweh] is a warrior; The LORD [Yahweh] is His name. (italics and brackets added)

This verse equates El with Yeshua, as well as the personal name of God, which is Yahweh. The word *Yeshua* means "salvation." And, in verse 3, the word *LORD* is actually *Yahweh*. God is therefore claiming in this verse that His name is Yahweh, but He is also El, the God who is the Savior, the Messiah.

So, in effect, both Elohim and Yahweh claim to be the Savior, the Messiah. This links Yahweh, El, and Yeshua, directly with salvation – but that's not all. We also find similar descriptions of God in other passages in the Bible, such as Exodus 34:29, Daniel 10:6 and 7:9, Revelation 1, and Ezekiel 2. Obviously, these are some of the ways in which He chose to represent Himself.

The First Vision

Revelation 1 then continues:

> ⁹I, John, your brother and fellow partaker in the tribulation and kingdom and perseverance which are in Jesus, was on the island called Patmos because of the word of God and the testimony of Jesus. ¹⁰I was in the Spirit on the Lord's day, and I heard behind me a loud voice like the sound of a trumpet, ¹¹saying, "Write in a book what you see, and send it to the seven churches: to Ephesus and to Smyrna and to Pergamum and to Thyatira and to Sardis and to Philadelphia and to Laodicea."
>
> ¹²Then I turned to see the voice that was speaking with me. And having turned I saw seven golden lampstands [menorahs]; ¹³and in the middle of the lampstands I saw one like a son of man, clothed in a robe reaching to the feet, and girded across His chest with a golden

> sash. ¹⁴His head and His hair were white like white wool, like snow; and His eyes were like a flame of fire. ¹⁵His feet were like burnished bronze, when it has been made to glow in a furnace, and His voice was like the sound of many waters. ¹⁶In His right hand He held seven stars, and out of His mouth came a sharp two-edged sword; and His face was like the sun shining in its strength.
>
> ¹⁷When I saw Him, I fell at His feet like a dead man. And He placed His right hand on me, saying, "Do not be afraid; I am the first and the last, ¹⁸and the living One; and I was dead, and behold, I am alive forevermore, and I have the keys of death and of Hades. ¹⁹"Therefore write the things which you have seen, and the things which are, and the things which will take place after these things. ²⁰"As for the mystery of the seven stars which you saw in My right hand, and the seven golden lampstands: the seven stars are the angels of the seven churches, and the seven lampstands are the seven churches. (Revelation 1:9–20)

As you now know, the menorah has immense symbolic meaning to the Hebrews, with vast import. It is not a random collection of candles on a common base. In this context the menorah represents seven congregations, and ultimately it represents mankind itself. The implication is that God desires to be surrounded by those He loves. It is also clearly implied that God is always in our midst.

Again, this is what we've called a shamash chapter – it's the introduction for what will soon follow and yet a story unto itself. The Creator has identified Himself as the Messiah and the Messiah has identified Himself as the Creator. He has also given us a picture of His throne, the place where He dwells. For those who are in covenant with Him, that is their destiny and His ultimate goal for each of us.

Keep in mind, also, that Revelation 1 is the first shamash chapter. Here, the apostle John is introducing information that will lead us into the first group of seven mini-menorah events. But more important, he's telling us more about God and His purpose. God is Elohim but He's also our Savior; He's our Messiah as well as *Yahweh*. He's the first and the last, the Creator of the universe.

As we come to additional shamash chapters, note how the various entities that are all part of the Wedding of the Lamb will be highlighted, one by one. This chapter introduces the Father of the Groom with whom "everything that is" has its beginning.

Interpreting the Seven Letters

The first mini-menorah (on the far right side of the master menorah) represents the seven congregations to which the seven letters were addressed. These congregations also represent mankind as a whole. Thus God is sending seven love letters of concern, correction, and encouragement, addressing seven different spiritual conditions to which man is prone. It is encouraging to note, however, that whatever condition these congregations were in, whether they were righteous or disobedient, God still loved them and still reached out to them with words of encouragement.

Please recall that, in Volume 1, we explained how the Scriptures should be interpreted according to ancient Hebraic understanding. The Scriptures are not Greek, and therefore Greek methods of exegesis are simply not adequate. The Hebrew itself operates on four levels simultaneously, while Greek does nothing of the sort.

Meanwhile, some modern interpretations have suggested that the conditions that characterize these congregations reflect the worldwide body of believers, from John's time until the modern day. So, in their view, the first letter, addressed to Ephesus, was describing the state of affairs among the first century believers, while the last letter, to Laodicea, would therefore be a letter addressed to the believers of today.

Other interpreters believe that each of these seven letters was written exclusively to congregations of the first century that literally existed then, and that nothing in any of them addresses the state of the believers throughout the next 2,000 years.

From a Hebrew perspective, both of these interpretations contain elements of truth. But, the Greek method demands that only one interpretation could be correct, while the Hebrew method allows for parts of both to be correct. And, the Hebrew method also allows for the possibility of further understandings as well.

The Seven Kinds of Covenant

In our Volume 1 discussion of covenant we identified four different types of relationships to which the Lord has called us. Each of the first three can be further broken up into two halves that reflect how each covenant comes about, for each must have (1) an initiator and (2) a responder. These relationships are represented by the seven Patriarchs of Covenant, starting with Adam, proceeding through David, and ending with Yeshua.

These seven letters in Revelation reflect each of those seven covenants, in terms of the responsibilities, obligations, and relationships that each one entails. The letters contain a number of obvious allusions to covenant-related instructions that bring righteousness to God's people, beginning with the concepts that define service and friendship covenants and extending through the inheritance and, finally, the marriage covenant.

Table 4-1: Covenants/Letters

Covenant	Type	Initiative	Patriarch	Color	Letter
Servanthood	Blood	Initiated by God	Adam	Red	Ephesus
Servanthood	Blood	Accepted by God	Noah	Orange	Smyrna
Friendship	Salt	Initiated by God	Abraham	Yellow	Pergamum
Friendship	Salt	Accepted by God	Jacob	Green	Thyatira
Inheritance	Sandal	Initiated by God	Moses	Blue	Sardis
Inheritance	Sandal	Accepted by God	David	Purple	Philadelphia
Bridal	All Three	Both, by God	Yeshua	White	Laodicea

Therefore, on one level these letters reflect God's plan to bring restoration to mankind throughout history, starting with Genesis and ending not in the Tanakh (Old Testament) but in the B'rit Hadashah (New Testament), with the book of Revelation. Yes, these are seven letters to seven real congregations. Therefore they function at both a surface and a deeper level, the latter level revealing the overall plan of restoration that God has ordained throughout time.

Going back to Volume 1 again, this is a perfect example of how the Hebrew Scriptures function at the *sod* (i.e., deepest) level.

A Small Geographic Focus

One final point before we begin to look at the letters individually. The seven congregations that received these seven letters were located in a small area in western Turkey. We sometimes think that John is writing to congregations interspersed throughout the known world, but actually they were all located in a specific, relatively small area. God must have recognized certain attributes and weaknesses within these seven congregations that would speak to most of the inherent strengths and weaknesses found throughout the body of believers as a whole.

4 - The Seven Letters

Where's the Syn in Synagogue?

Unfortunately, it's not hard to find parallels between ancient pagan words and rituals and some of the modern Christian words and rituals. For example, the Babylonian goddess, *Circe* (Seer-say), was believed to be associated with the moon. Thus the ancient pagan worshippers of Circe met for religious purposes while standing in a circle.

The Greek word from which we derive our word *church* is *ekklesia*. This word actually means "called out ones." The word *church* is not in the Bible; instead, it finds its root in the German word *Kirke* (Keer-kuh). In turn, this word comes from the Babylonian word, Circe, as mentioned above, which is also the root for the English word *circle*.

The actual Hebrew word used here is *kehilot*, which means "called out ones" or "congregation." This is the same Old Testament word that is used when God refers to the *congregation of Israel*. It speaks of a specially chosen people, and therefore, within this book we'll be using the term "congregation."

When Yeshua said "I will build My church [actually, "congregation" or "called out ones"]; and the gates of Hades will not overpower it" (Matthew 16:18) He was not starting something new. He was putting the finishing touches on the original plan that God began to implement way back when man fell out of his marriage relationship with the Creator God. The same plan was developed further when God called Israel out of Egypt, using the word *kehilot* (*called out ones*) to distinguish His people from the Egyptians.

The congregation in the B'rit Hadashah (New Testament) is also called by the same name (*called out ones*) because they are viewed as one and the same, and the original words referring to each are both the same word. The translators of our English Bibles use the word "church," but as we've already noted, that word is nowhere to be found in the Scriptures in either Hebrew or Greek. Sadly, though the Bible has its roots in God's mind it is constantly being interpreted by men to suit their own ways of thinking.

Thus, as Israel was called out of Egypt from slavery, so the so-called "church" of today is "called out" from evil. As always, God is being consistent whether we are or not. Starting with the people He called out from Egypt 3,500 years ago, Yeshua used exactly the same verbiage to refer to His people when He was walking on the earth.

Another Greek word that is sometimes translated as "church" in the New Testament is *synagôge*. But because the English interpreters didn't want their readers to recognize the Hebraic origins of Christianity they changed what should have been translated as *synagogue* to a pagan word, *church*, to hide the true Hebrew identity of the *called out ones*, whose meeting place was not a *church* at all but a *synagogue* hosting a *congregation*.

An excellent example would be James 2:2. In this chapter, James was warning his readers about showing undue partiality and used a classic illustration that involved two strangers entering into one of their meetings. As the half-brother of Yeshua Himself, James (*Ya'akov* in Hebrew, which would have been correctly translated as *Jacob*) was about as Hebrew as you can get and certainly would have used the word *synagogue*. Even the Greek manuscript of James 2:2 uses the Greek *synagôge*. Yet here are five popular renderings of the first portion of the same verse, followed by a sixth translation – this time of the complete verse – that just happens to be the only one that gets the first portion right:

- Suppose a man comes into your *assembly* . . . (NASB)
- Suppose a man comes into your *meeting* . . . (NIV)
- For if a person comes into your *congregation* . . . (AMP)
- For if there come unto your *assembly* . . . (KJV)
- For if a man wearing a gold ring and fine clothing comes into your *assembly* . . . (ESV)

- Suppose a man comes into your *synagogue* wearing gold rings and fancy clothes, and also a poor man comes in dressed in rags. (CJB)

The correct translation, of course, is the last one, the *Complete Jewish Bible*.

This way of understanding these passages also reveals a completely different view from what is understood to be *Dispensationalism*. The Lord never intended to be working with separate groups in different times. Rather, He started by choosing a group that He would "call out" from among the nations. He then intended to use them to minister to the rest of the world, to be a light to the whole world via an ongoing, constantly expanding plan.

The "Called Out" Ones of Revelation

In the book of Revelation the first mini-menorah on the right includes the seven letters to the seven congregations, the "called out" ones which, interestingly enough, are made up of Jews and Gentiles, most of whom were meeting in synagogues at the time. These seven are receiving seven "love letters" from their God, all of which include the same five components:

- **A description of Yeshua the Messiah.** God gives the recipients of each message a unique description of their Groom.

- **Congratulations.** The psyche of mankind is such that it receives correction much better if it is complimented first.

- **Rebuke.** With each one of these congregations (except for two) God brings some sort of correction.

- **Exhortation.** After each rebuke God then brings encouragement, by showing the members of the congregations what they can do to right their wrong.

- **Promise.** This amounts to a reward for those who overcome their weaknesses. As many parents know, rewards for responsible behavior amount to an especially effective way to encourage our children.

As we go through each of the letters individually, remember to look for these five components.

The Letter to Ephesus

Here is the complete text for the letter Yeshua instructed John to write to the congregation in Ephesus:

> ¹"To the angel of the church in Ephesus write: The One who holds the seven stars in His right hand, the One who walks among the seven golden lampstands, says this: ²'I know your deeds and your toil and perseverance, and that you cannot tolerate evil men, and you put to the test those who call themselves apostles, and they are not, and you found them to be false; ³and you have perseverance and have endured for My name's sake, and have not grown weary.
>
> ⁴'But I have this against you, that you have left your first love. ⁵'Therefore remember from where you have fallen, and repent and do the deeds you did at first; or else I am coming to you and will remove your lampstand out of its place – unless you repent. ⁶'Yet this you do have, that you hate the deeds of the Nicolaitans, which I also hate.
>
> ⁷'He who has an ear, let him hear what the Spirit says to the churches. To him who overcomes, I will grant to eat of the tree of life which is in the Paradise of God.' (Revelation 2:1–7)

As you may recall from Paul's first letter to Timothy, the latter was in charge of the congregation at Ephesus – although, in all of

4 - The Seven Letters

Revelation, Timothy is neither mentioned nor alluded to. Instead, in this letter the members of the Ephesus congregation are reminded of where they've fallen from. Basically, they're told that they've left their first love. This reminds us of God's relationship with Adam, who once walked perfectly before God in the Garden. But then, because of his disobedience, Adam fell away from that first love.

As Adam was then called to repentance after his failure, so too is this congregation. Recall that Adam was barred from the Tree of Life because of his sin. However, since the beginning, through covenant, all mankind has the opportunity to be granted access to the Tree of Life. Thus God is imploring mankind to return to the servanthood relationship that started it all, through the doorway called repentance.

The congregation at Ephesus is also complimented for their hatred of the Nicolaitans, whom Messiah says he hates as well. By way of background, the word *Nicolaitan* can be broken into two Greek roots: *nike*, which means "victory over" and is also a name for the Greek god of messengers (from which comes the name for a well-known athletic shoe), and *laitan,* from which we get our English word *laity,* meaning "the common people." The Nicolaitans were a group of pagan priests who wielded power over the laity, as represented by the "average person."

Even today, from the original Nicolaitan ideals we derive a certain disparity in authority within our own congregations. We often think that our pastors have greater power and authority and directly represent our intermediary. Certainly the Roman Catholic Church has promoted this concept, to a fault. Their own history includes dominance and control, even to the extreme of claiming that they were the only authorities who could correctly interpret Scripture.

This is not meant to imply that we believe God has no intention of creating and maintaining lines of authority within His congregations, both in the Tanakh and the B'rit Hadashah. Synagogues were almost always led by a *cohen* (a priest descended from the line of Aaron), and most or all teachers were Levites. God also saw fit to organize His congregations with authority structures that included other positions, such as elders and deacons. God is still a God of order.

First Timothy 2:5–6 could not say it more clearly: "For there is one God, and one mediator also between God and men, the man Christ Jesus [Yeshua, the Messiah], who gave Himself as a ransom for all, the testimony given at the proper time."

The reward Yeshua promises Ephesus is once more to have unlimited access to the Tree of Life. That is exactly what we also see as the foundational reward, salvation from death, for all faithful believers at the end of Revelation.

The Letter to Smyrna

Here is the complete text for the letter Yeshua instructed John to write to the church in Smyrna:

> 8"And to the angel of the church in Smyrna write: The first and the last, who was dead, and has come to life, says this: 9I know your tribulation and your poverty (but you are rich), and the blasphemy by those who say they are Jews and are not, but are a synagogue of Satan.
>
> [Notice the context in which the word "synagogue" is correctly translated in verse 9.]
>
> 10Do not fear what you are about to suffer. Behold, the devil is about to cast some of you into prison, so that you will be tested, and you will have tribulation for ten days. Be faithful until death, and I will give you the crown of life. 11He who has an ear, let him hear what the Spirit says to the churches. He who overcomes will not be

4 - The Seven Letters

Table 4-2: Comparing the Seven Letters

Church	Ephesus	Smyrna	Pergamos	Thyatira	Sardis	Philadelphia	Laodicea
How Yeshua is described	Holds seven stars in right hand. Walks among the seven golden menorahs.	The First and the Last, who was dead and has come to life.	The One who has the sharp two-edged sword.	The Son of God, who has eyes like a flame of fire and feet like burnished bronze.	He who has the seven Spirits of God and the seven stars	He who is holy and true, who holds the key of David, and who opens and shuts what no one else does	The Amen, the faithful and true Witness, the Beginning of the creation of God
Commendation	Good deeds, toil, perseverance, and unwillingness to tolerate evil men. You've endured for My name's sake and have not grown weary.	Despite tribulation and poverty you are rich. You endure blasphemy from those who say they are Jews but are not.	You dwell where Satan's throne is, yet you hold fast My name and did not deny My faith.	I know your deeds, and your love and faith and service and perseverance, and that your deeds of late are greater than at first.	A few of you have not soiled your garments and will be worthy to walk with Me in white.	You have a little power and have kept My word and have not denied My name. You have kept the word of My perseverance.	None
Rebuke	You have left your first love.	None	Some of you hold to the teaching of Balaam – to eat things sacrificed to idols and to commit acts of immorality. Some also hold to the teaching of the Nicolaitans.	You tolerate the woman Jezebel, who leads My bond-servants astray so that they commit immorality and eat things sacrificed to idols. I will throw you into great tribulation.	Your deeds are not complete. You have a reputation of being alive, but you are dead.	None	You are lukewarm – neither hot nor cold. I will spit you out. You say you are rich and need nothing, yet you are wretched, miserable, poor, blind, and naked.
Exhortation	Remember from where you have fallen. Repent, do the deeds you did at first.	Do not fear what you are about to suffer. You will have tribulation for ten days. Be faithful unto death.	Repent.	Hold fast until I come, and keep my deeds until the end.	Remember what you have received and heard, and keep it. Wake up. For I will come like a thief and you will not know when.	Hold fast to what you have. Let no one take your crown.	Buy from Me gold refined by fire, white garments to clothe yourself, and eye salve that you may see. I stand at your door and knock; hear My voice and open the door.
Reward for Overcoming	I will grant you to eat of the tree of life, which is in the paradise of God.	I will give you the crown of life. You will not be hurt by the second death.	I will give some of the hidden manna, and a white stone, with a new name written on it.	I will give you authority over the nations, and he shall rule them with a rod of iron.	I will clothe you in white garments, I will not erase your name from the Book of Life, and I will confess your name before My Father.	I will keep you from the hour of testing. I will make you a pillar in the temple of God, and I will write on you the name of My God, and the name of the city of My God, the new Jerusalem.	I will come in and dine with you and you with Me. I will grant you to sit with Me on My throne.

> The Smyrna congregation is promised a second life. In fact, in Revelation 2:11 they are told that the second death described in Revelation 20:14, following the Great White Throne Judgment at the end of the thousand-year reign, will have no power over them. Thus Yeshua encouraged this congregation not to fear suffering, just as Noah was encouraged as well. He endured the Flood but was protected in spite of it. And throughout everything he retained his hope and his faith that God would bring life from death.

In ancient Hebraic understanding, Noah's deliverance from the Flood was a type of baptism, which in Hebrew is called *tevilah*.[39] In any case, Noah was set apart (i.e., symbolically reborn) by passing through the waters that covered the earth. The same was understood when the Hebrews passed through the Red Sea – they were delivered from Egypt and born into a new nation.

The congregation of Smyrna is also warned of those who say they are Jews yet are really not, but are actually part of the "synagogue of Satan." This brings up the obvious question. Why do so many translators insert the name of a Jewish place of worship into an evil context, but when they encounter the word synagogue in a positive context it's translated as "church"?

Isn't that interesting? Is there an agenda at work here, by any chance?

In addition, many people use Revelation 2:9, as quoted above, to promote the idea that Jews were bringing division to these congregations through satanic influence. Nothing could be further from the truth. This text actually refers to philosophers, including Ageans, who were attempting to replace the Jews. "We philosophers who embrace this faith, gain the whole of truth, and enter into spiritual Israel. Thereby we become the true and perfect Israel."[40]

This type of second-century thinking is what started the false concept of Spiritual Israel and replacement theology, also known as British Israelism, the Ephraimite Movement, Armstrongism, and sometimes even the Church-at-Large.

The Smyrna congregation's reward will be like that of the Ephesians – but more so, for they are promised eternal life and the crown of life. These two congregations are a picture of God's promise of life after death and salvation. As we initiate the first covenant of servanthood, the promise we inherit includes eternal life and deliverance from evil.

The Letter to Pergamum

Here is the complete text for the letter Yeshua instructed John to write to the congregation in Pergamum:

> [12]"And to the angel of the church in Pergamum write: The One who has the sharp two-edged sword says this: [13]'I know where you dwell, where Satan's throne is; and you hold fast My name, and did not deny My faith even in the days of Antipas, My witness, My faithful one, who was killed among you, where Satan dwells. [14]'But I have a few things against you, because you have there some who hold the teaching of Balaam, who kept teaching Balak to put a stumbling block before the sons of Israel, to eat things sacrificed to idols and to commit acts of immorality.
>
> [15]'So you also have some who in the same way hold the teaching of the Nicolaitans. [16]'Therefore repent; or else I am coming to you quickly, and I will make war against them with the sword of My mouth.
>
> [17]'He who has an ear, let him hear what the Spirit says to the churches. To him who overcomes, to him I will give some of the hidden manna, and I will give him a

white stone, and a new name written on the stone which no one knows but he who receives it.' (Revelation 2:12–17)

The letter to Pergamum begins with the image of a sharp, double-edged sword coming out of Messiah's mouth, which will not be the last time we'll find that image in Revelation. The congregation at Pergamum is then encouraged because the members have been faithful even though they dwell where the enemy's throne also resides.

Likewise, the salt-covenant patriarch Abraham also dwelt where the enemy's throne was. He was a contemporary of Nimrod/Amraphel, who was a "mighty hunter before the LORD" (Genesis 10:9). However, the Hebrew of this passage from Genesis, explaining the meaning of Nimrod's name, would be more clearly interpreted as "a destroying tyrant in the face of God."

Abraham started out in Ur, near where Bosra is today, in eastern Iraq and next to the Persian Gulf. Ur was a pagan culture, practicing astrology, sorcery, and infanticide. In Hebrew the word Ur can also mean "light." One obvious connection is that Satan is always running around trying to convince people that he is an angel of light rather than an angel of darkness.

How interesting that God chose to pull Abraham out from this misnamed city, to be the source of the bloodline from which the ultimate Light of the World would be born. Meanwhile, Nimrod's attitude toward God was similar to that of Cain's, who was also a "destroyer in God's face." Nimrod was the king of Shinar, which is known today as the Mesopotamia Valley, which takes in part of Iraq and the surrounding region. This reference in Revelation points to Pergamum's situation at the time the text was written and parallels it with that of Abraham versus the ancient kingdom of Babylon.

In ancient writings, Nimrod was also known as a high sorcerer who led others to sacrifice to idols, and to commit gross sexual sins while living a lawless life. The righteous residents of Pergamum, like Abraham, are therefore instructed to leave the deeds of Satan behind even as God told Abraham to come out from Ur and away from the enemy. The righteous of Pergamum are instructed to spiritually leave behind all the vile temptations that would rob them of their godly reward.

Messiah again mentions the Nicolaitans and parallels them with Balaam and Balak. Balaam was a false prophet who came from Pethor, a small town near Babylon in the same Mesopotamia valley. Balaam and the Nicolaitans both promoted lawlessness (i.e., violation of Torah principles), idol worship, and sexual immorality. The congregation is told to turn from their sins and is promised hidden manna (i.e., bread), which is the symbol of salt/friendship covenant, the covenant of hospitality represented by Abraham.

They are also promised a white stone, which points to another ancient Hebrew custom. In a court of law, the judge would keep both a white stone and a black stone close at hand. If you were declared guilty of the offense you were accused of he would show the black stone. If you were innocent he would show the white stone. To further parallel the story of Abraham, their reward if they overcome is to be given a new name, as when "Abram" became "Abraham."

The Letter to Thyatira

Here is the complete text for the letter Yeshua instructed John to write to the congregation in Thyatira:

> [18]"And to the angel of the church in Thyatira write: The Son of God, who has eyes like a flame of fire, and His feet are like burnished bronze, says this: [19]'I know your deeds, and your love and faith and service and perseverance, and that your deeds of late are greater than at first. [20]But I have this against you, that you tolerate the woman Jezebel, who calls herself a proph-

etess, and she teaches and leads My bond-servants astray so that they commit acts of immorality and eat things sacrificed to idols.

[21]'I gave her time to repent, and she does not want to repent of her immorality. [22]'Behold, I will throw her on a bed of sickness, and those who commit adultery with her into great tribulation, unless they repent of her deeds. [23]'And I will kill her children with pestilence, and all the churches will know that I am He who searches the minds and hearts; and I will give to each one of you according to your deeds.

[24]'But I say to you, the rest who are in Thyatira, who do no hold this teaching, who have not known the deep things of Satan, as they call them – I place no other burden on you. [25]'Nevertheless what you have, hold fast until I come.

[26]'He who overcomes, and he who keeps My deeds until the end, TO HIM I WILL GIVE AUTHORITY OVER THE NATIONS; [27]AND HE SHALL RULE THEM WITH A ROD OF IRON, AS THE VESSELS OF THE POTTER ARE BROKEN TO PIECES, as I also have received authority from My Father; [28]and I will give him the morning star. [29]'He who has an ear, let him hear what the Spirit says to the churches.' (Revelation 2:18–29)

This letter parallels the covenant of Jacob (Ya'acov), although the connection is not immediately obvious. The reward for the overcomers in the Thyatira congregation is to rule nations with an iron scepter and to be given the morning star. This calls for a closer inspection of some similar but somewhat obscure promises to Jacob from Numbers 24:17:

> "I see him, but not now;
> I behold him, but not near;
> A star shall come forth from Jacob,
> A scepter shall rise from Israel,

And shall crush through the forehead of Moab,
And tear down all the sons of Sheth.

All Israel to Be Saved

The emphasis here is on the one who is the morning star, which parallels Yeshua as the Groom. This is the fourth letter, the shamash of this mini-menorah, which always tends to focus on Messiah. Here, Messiah is being identified as light, having the authority to rule his creation. Also, the emphasis on Jacob indicates that even though God Himself will be in the shamash position, sitting on His throne, He's going to share His authority with *Jacob*, who represents His Bride.

The concept of doing greater deeds later in life parallels Jacob's story. He was this kind of guy, who began by taking on the responsibilities of the firstborn in the absence of Esau's willingness to do so. Jacob then grew into manhood and took complete responsibility for the survival of his people. Thus his deeds were greater at the end of his life than they were at the beginning, which is why God eventually changed his name from *Jacob* to *Israel*.

In Numbers 24:17 Jacob is promised a rising star and a scepter. This verse (and those that follow it in the remainder of chapter 24) amounts to the final cap on a series of prophecies promising Israel that her enemies will be defeated and her people will be delivered. Later we are instructed to pray for the peace of Jerusalem in Psalm 122:6, and to intercede for the salvation of God's people.

Later on we are promised that all Israel will be saved, in Romans 11:26: "And so all Israel will be saved, as it is written: 'The deliverer will come from Zion; he will turn godlessness away from Jacob.'" (NIV)

Likewise we are promised that the rest of the nations will be blessed as well through the salvation of Israel. This is a clear call to love whom and what God loves, and to hate what God hates. In this case He uses the example of tolerating evil through Jezebel, whose very name means "Ba'al (i.e., a devil) flows in her veins." This pagan queen sought to pollute God's people and bring them down by convincing them to compromise with evil.

This letter (to Thayatira) is in the shamash position, which is the center light. Shamash is also the Hebrew word for "sun," the main source of light. In Revelation 2:28 we see that the reward is the Morning Star, which is what Yeshua is called. In Revelation 22:16 Yeshua rules with an iron sceptor, a "rod of iron" (Psalms 2:9).

Note also that Revelation 2:18 identifies Yeshua as "the Son of God, who has eyes like a flame of fire, and His feet are like burnished bronze." Thus He *is* a glowing, white hot light, a perfect description of a shamash.

The Letter to Sardis

Here is the complete text for the letter Yeshua instructed John to write to the congregation in Sardis:

> ¹ 'To the angel of the church in Sardis write: He who has the seven Spirits of God and the seven stars, says this: 'I know your deeds, that you have a name that you are alive, but you are dead. ²'Wake up, and strengthen the things that remain, which were about to die; for I have not found your deeds completed in the sight of My God.
>
> ³'So remember what you have received and heard; and keep it, and repent. Therefore if you do not wake up, I will come like a thief, and you will not know at what hour I will come to you. ⁴'But you have a few people in Sardis who have not soiled their garments; and they will walk with Me in white, for they are worthy.
>
> ⁵'He who overcomes will thus be clothed in white garments; and I will not erase his name from the

book of life, and I will confess his name before My Father and before His angels. ⁶He who has an ear, let him hear what the Spirit says to the churches.' (Revelation 3:1–6)

The letter to Sardis is unique, for the book of Revelation is the only place in the entire Bible in which Sardis is mentioned. That Sardis should be addressed while Rome is not should make us very curious about the underlying purpose of this important section of Scripture.

At the time Revelation was written, what is now called "the Church" was actually a sect of Judaism. The Romans themselves had declared that believers in Yeshua were converts to a form of the Jewish faith.[41] This would not be changed until AD 201, at the insistence of a group of Greek philosophers who had inherited headship of the faith. The warning to the congregation in Sardis now takes on particular importance, for they are warned to "strengthen that which remains" (Revelation 3:2).

Sardis had a few unique things about it, too. It was the place where *electrum* was produced. Electrum is a laminate of gold and silver and was thought to have very powerful mystical properties. Hence its use in divination. And, although Sardis was a small and sleepy community, it was noted for its wealth of commerce for it was also the city in which gold was gilded onto the statues for the pagan temples.

Apparently, most of the people of Sardis were like the Israelites during the forty days that Moses spent on Mount Sinai. When the restraints of slavery in Egypt were removed, the people of Israel reverted to a wanton, lawless lifestyle, fashioning for themselves an idol of gold. Notwithstanding all that, the principle contained in the letter to Sardis is that self-discipline is an expected attribute of the righteous, whose godly inheritance parallels the covenant of Moses.

A warning to repent is therefore given, which is followed by the admonition that there were very few in Sardis who had kept themselves undefiled and were worthy to "walk in white." God desires us to be good sons and daughters. He will accept us as servants, but that isn't His ultimate choice for us. The message of Sardis speaks to us yet today, for it is often easier to lose faith in the midst of plenty, with all the creature comforts of life on earth, than in the midst of adversity.

Also, it's worth noting that the reward gives us a hint as to what covenant the people being referenced are involved in. Based on our discussion of the patriarchs of covenant in Volume 1, and given their relationships to the different *types* of covenant, it seems clear that the Moses reference here is telling us that these people should be coming into the level of relationship called *inheritance* covenant, which started with Moses. In fact, verse 3 admonishes the readers to "remember what you have received and heard," which sounds exactly like what Moses told the people when they received the Torah at Mt. Sinai.

Also, note the reference in verse 5, which is what Moses said to God when he was interceding for the Israelites: "But now, if You will, forgive their sin—and if not, please blot me out from Your book which You have written!" (Exodus 32:32)

The Letter to Philadelphia

Here is the complete text for the letter Yeshua instructed John to write to the congregation in Philadelphia:

> [7]"And to the angel of the church in Philadelphia write: He who is holy, who is true, who has the key of David, who opens and no one will shut, and who shuts and no one opens, says this:
>
> [8]'I know your deeds. Behold, I have put before you an open door which no one can shut, because you have a

little power, and have kept My word, and have not denied My name. ⁹'Behold, I will cause those of the synagogue of Satan [Here we go again!], who say that they are Jews and are not, but lie – I will make them come and bow down at your feet, and make them know that I have loved you.

¹⁰Because you have kept the word of My perseverance, I also will keep you from the hour of testing, that hour which is about to come upon the whole world, to test those who dwell on the earth. ¹¹I am coming quickly; hold fast what you have, so that no one will take your crown.

¹²He who overcomes, I will make him a pillar in the temple of My God, and he will not go out from it anymore; and I will write on him the name of My God, and the name of the city of My God, the new Jerusalem, which comes down out of heaven from My God, and My new name. ¹³He who has an ear, let him hear what the Spirit says to the churches.' (Revelation 3:7–13)

The city of Philadelphia received letter number six, with a reference to David's covenant of inheritance appearing almost immediately in Revelation 3:7. In verse 8, God then acknowledges the "little power" of the people of Philadelphia. They do not have much strength, yet God honors them for their trust in His Word. He will therefore strengthen them so they may be overcomers.

This offers another parallel with David as well. David started out as a shepherd with very little authority and strength, but he was blessed by God and eventually became a powerful overcomer and a great king. He was even called the apple of God's eye, which is a very intimate designation similar to one by which a man might refer to his bride. Thus we see David squarely in the center of God's throne.

A further link to David is the promise of the temple in Jerusalem (Revelation 3:12), the city established by David as the capital of Israel. When John was writing Revelation, Philadelphia was a center of Greek philosophy and the main headquarters of training for Hellenized Jews. The heresy of replacement theology that had begun with Aegenus was already popular and well-established here in Philadelphia, as was the Gnostic school to which some Pharisees sent their rabbis to be trained.

As in the letter to Smyrna, through the words written down by John in Revelation 3:9 Yeshua refers once again to the "synagogue of Satan" as an entity to be overcome, although – as before – a more fair-and-balanced interpretation might be "assembly of those who worship Satan."

Despite all this, God still offers the Philadelphians a place in His presence in the temple, which is a very intimate position. He even offers His own name, which is very much a bridal/marriage kind of concept wherein the bride takes on the identity (the name) of the groom. Thus this letter represents the time period leading up to the coming of the Son of Man that will usher in His thousand-year reign with His Bride.

Ironically, many think that the letter to Laodicea was written to modern believers, but this is incorrect. This letter, to the Philadelphians, is the one directed to moderns. And what do we find in 2 Thessalonians, Matthew, and Revelation? Similar, repeated references to a coming perversion, as in "I am coming quickly; hold fast what you have so that no one can take your crown, your inheritance."

This congregation is one that God intends to protect, as specifically noted in verse 10:

> Because you have kept the word of My perseverance, I also will keep you from the hour of testing, that hour

which is about to come upon the whole world, to test those who dwell on the earth.

In contrast, as we'll see in a moment, the congregation of Laodicea is lukewarm and the most lukewarm congregations are those that come the closest to being essentially useless to God. Again, as we'll explain in detail momentarily, it's possible to be useful at either extreme but not in the middle.

The Letter to Laodicea

Here is the complete text for the letter Yeshua instructed John to write to the congregation in Laodicea:

> [14]"To the angel of the church in Laodicea write: The Amen, the faithful and true Witness, the Beginning of the creation of God, says this: [15]'I know your deeds, that you are neither cold nor hot; I wish that you were cold or hot. [16]'So because you are lukewarm, and neither hot nor cold, I will spit you out of My mouth.
>
> [17]'Because you say, "I am rich, and have become wealthy, and have need of nothing," and you do not know that you are wretched and miserable and poor and blind and naked, [18]I advise you to buy from Me gold refined by fire so that you may become rich, and white garments so that you may clothe yourself, and that the shame of your nakedness will not be revealed; and eye salve to anoint your eyes so that you may see.
>
> [19]'Those whom I love, I reprove and discipline; therefore be zealous and repent. [20]'Behold, I stand at the door and knock; if anyone hears My voice and opens the door, I will come in to him and will dine with him, and he with Me. [21]'He who overcomes, I will grant to him to sit down with Me on My throne, as I also overcame and sat down with My Father on His throne.

> [22]"He who has an ear, let him hear what the Spirit says to the churches.'" (Revelation 3:14–22)

The letter to Laodicea is not the longest of the seven (#4 to Thyatira and #6 to Philadelphia both contain more words), but given its parallel to the ultimate covenant of marriage it's undoubtedly packed with the most meaning, both for its original recipients and for us today.

Like the previous six, this letter opens by emphasizing a different aspect of the core description of Messiah that started the book of Revelation itself: "The Amen, the faithful and true Witness, the Beginning of the creation of God." The last few words are the most significant, for truly He *was* there at the creation.

Unfortunately, this letter has often been mistakenly interpreted as reflecting the condition of all believers just prior to Messiah's return. On the contrary, the congregation at Philadelphia is the one that more clearly parallels the condition of many end-times believers, and not the Laodiceans. Remember, Philadelphia is the only congregation of the seven that is not chastised in its letter.

The point here is not that these people have arrived at perfection, but that God has empathy for them because of the great tribulation and testing that they're going to go through. Thus His letter is one of great encouragement and support, and the message is: Keep your eye on the endgame – I'll do what I've promised and I'll protect you. So *hang in there!*

To repeat the basic message to the Philadelphians:

> [10]Because you have guarded and kept My word of patient endurance [have held fast the lesson of My patience with the expectant endurance that I give you], I also will keep you [safe] from the hour of trial (testing) which is coming on the whole world to try those who dwell upon the earth. [11]I am coming quickly; hold fast what

you have, so that no one may rob you and deprive you of your crown. (Revelation 3:10–11 AMP)

Thus the Philadelphians are promised protection through the tribulation that's coming upon the whole world. However, in contrast to the Philadelphians, the Laodiceans represent the time frame that includes the Messiah's return and extends through the end of the thousand-year reign. The Laodiceans are commanded to persevere; in verse 15 they are told that they are "neither cold nor hot. I wish you were cold or hot." God does not want them to be "lukewarm"; he would rather they be "hot" or "cold."

Neither Hot Nor Cold

To put all that in context, Laodicea was a city on the west coast of Turkey. In ancient times it was blessed with springs, some hot and some cold. All of these were rumored to have healing properties. However, the waters from both types of springs would eventually flow together, forming streams of lukewarm water into which each type of spring would then "give up" what had once made it distinctive, unique, and useful.

No one would bathe in the converged waters because they had lost their healing powers. Thus this congregation is being compared to waters that had lost their distinguishing temperatures and their healing properties as well. This is why verse 16 says that God would "spit them out of his mouth," which is a clear reference to being corrupt, defiled, and no good for consumption.

As Matthew 5:13 tells us:

> You are the salt of the earth; but if the salt has become tasteless, how can it be made salty again? It is no longer good for anything, except to be thrown out and trampled under foot by men.

God's people must not lose their saltiness, yet the Laodicean congregation had done exactly that.

Why is this so important? Well, as we shall learn in the chapters ahead, there will be people living on the earth during the thousand-year reign who are not in glorified bodies. Old Testament prophecies tell us that they (the "pure" humanity) will be marrying, dying, and sometimes even rebelling during this time. This is why we find warnings and threats of punishment in biblical prophecies that focus on the thousand-year reign. Humanity is then living in what *could* be a Messianic utopia, but some will be out of relationship with Messiah and therefore the overall conditions will not be quite perfect.

This is largely what the letter to Laodicea is all about. The Laodiceans think they are rich but they are actually poor, naked, and blind, all of which will become obvious when the Messiah actually dwells among them. In reality they are bankrupt, for they aren't in right relationship with God. And God's ultimate goal is not to co-exist peacefully; it's to be in covenant relationship at all times with all of humanity, which includes *you*.

In Hebraic terms, the description of nakedness also implies that one doesn't have clothing or "covering." This is a reference to Adam and Eve in Genesis. Remember how God offered to cover their nakedness? The concept of covenant involves being "covered" in relationship, which implies that those who are *not* covered are not in covenant with God. Laodicea is being chastised for not being in covenant relationship with Messiah, who will soon be on the earth and in their midst.

In addressing this congregation God is also emphasizing relationship as the key to life. "I stand at the door and knock" is a Hebrew idiom relating to marriage, the ultimate relationship. The potential groom would come to the home of the bride with his father and they would knock at the door. The bride (who knew exactly what was going on) had the choice to either open the door and accept his proposal or to simply do nothing. If she chose the latter response the groom would go away, disappointed and sorrowful. But if she opened the door the groom would enter and they would "sup together" as a prelude to working out a marriage agreement.

Messiah doesn't hate this congregation; rather he has great love for them. "Those whom I love, I reprove and discipline; therefore be zealous and repent" (Revelation 3:19).

It Isn't Always Easy

Sometimes doing the right thing requires very hard work; it requires fighting against both the enemy and our own evil inclinations. Sometimes this requires *extreme* effort. And one of the obstacles to righteous change is the mistaken belief that we don't have enough strength – mistaken because God does not allow us to face temptation or tribulation that He can't give us the strength to handle.

> Let no one say when he is tempted, "I am being tempted by God"; for God cannot be tempted by evil, and He Himself does not tempt anyone. (James 1:13)

> No temptation has overtaken you but such as is common to man; and God is faithful, who will not allow you to be tempted beyond what you are able, but with the temptation will provide the way of escape also, so that you will be able to endure it. (1 Corinthians 10:13)

The reward that this congregation is promised if they overcome temptation is the ultimate one. They will be allowed to sit beside Messiah on His throne, the same position of authority and responsibility that is reserved for the Bride. In that context, Zechariah 14, which is clearly a millennial prophecy, warns the inhabitants of the earth against violating God's ways:

> ¹⁶Then it will come about that any who are left of all the nations that went against Jerusalem will go up from year to year to worship the King, the LORD of hosts, and to celebrate the Feast of Booths. ¹⁷And it will be that whichever of the families of the earth does not go up to Jerusalem to worship the King, the LORD of hosts, there will be no rain on them. ¹⁸If the family of Egypt does not go up or enter, then no rain will fall on them; it will be the plague with which the LORD smites the nations who do not go up to celebrate the Feast of Booths. ¹⁹This will be the punishment of Egypt, and the punishment of all the nations who do not go up to celebrate the Feast of Booths. (Zechariah 14:16–19)

This text describes humanity in its mortal, unglorified bodies. And Isaiah also says the same thing in the passage below:

> ¹⁸But be glad and rejoice forever
> in what I will create,
> for I will create Jerusalem to be a delight
> and its people a joy.
>
> ¹⁹I will rejoice over Jerusalem
> and take delight in my people;
> the sound of weeping and of crying
> will be heard in it no more.
>
> ²⁰"Never again will there be in it
> an infant who lives but a few days,
> or an old man who does not live out his years;
> he who dies at a hundred
> will be thought a mere youth;
> he who fails to reach a hundred
> will be considered accursed. (Isaiah 65:18–20 NIV)

Bear in mind, however, that the Bible describes two separate bodies of humanity who will be present during the millennial reign. There *will* be a group of survivors who will *not* be in their glorified bodies. They will have offspring and will go through death. Meanwhile, another group has been resurrected and has received glorified bodies, never again to succumb to death. In other words, some have been glorified and others are still in their earthly bodies, as the apostle Paul indicates in the following verse:

> In a moment, in the twinkling of an eye, at the last trumpet; for the trumpet will sound, and *the dead will be raised imperishable*, and we will be changed. (1 Corinthians 15:52, italics added)

When you compare the people described in the passages from Zechariah and Isaiah with those described by the apostle Paul, it's easy to see the difference. These passages tell us that some of the people in the texts will be struggling with keeping God's principles. The result of their eventual rebellion is then prophesied also, as shown below:

> ⁷When the thousand years are over, Satan will be released from his prison ⁸and will go out to deceive the nations in the four corners of the earth—Gog and Magog—to gather them for battle. In number they are like the sand on the seashore. ⁹They marched across the breadth of the earth and surrounded the camp of God's people, the city he loves. But fire came down from heaven and devoured them. ¹⁰And the devil, who deceived them, was thrown into the lake of burning sulfur, where the beast and the false prophet had been thrown. They will be tormented day and night for ever and ever. (Revelation 20:7–10 NIV)

Toward Man's Final Chapter

The letter to the Laodiceans brings to a close the final chapter of man's earthly existence prior to the last Judgment Day – the Great White Throne Judgment. As such it describes the completion of His work to restore man back to Himself.

In Revelation 3:18 the Laodiceans are admonished to "buy from me gold refined by fire." Buying gold represents wisdom and the righteous deeds that come from it, but how does one "buy gold refined by fire?" The apostle Paul gives us the answer:

> [11]For no man can lay a foundation other than the one which is laid, which is Jesus Christ. [12]Now if any man builds on the foundation with gold, silver, precious stones, wood, hay, straw, [13]each man's work will become evident; for the day will show it because it is to be revealed with fire, and the fire itself will test the quality of each man's work.
>
> [14]If any man's work which he has built on it remains, he will receive a reward.
> [15]If any man's work is burned up, he will suffer loss; but he himself will be saved, yet so as through fire. [16]Do you not know that you are a temple of God and that the Spirit of God dwells in you? [17]If any man destroys the temple of God, God will destroy him, for the temple of God is holy, and that is what you are.
>
> [18]Let no man deceive himself. If any man among you thinks that he is wise in this age, he must become foolish, so that he may become wise. [19]For the wisdom of this world is foolishness before God. For it is written, "He is THE ONE WHO CATCHES THE WISE IN THEIR CRAFTINESS"; [20]and again, "THE LORD KNOWS THE REASONINGS of the wise, THAT THEY ARE USELESS." (First Corinthians 3:11–20)

Scripture frequently refers to following God's precepts as *wisdom*, and to wisdom as *gold* (e.g., Proverbs 3:14). So, to follow God's commands through covenant is the same as "buying gold." Thus Yeshua is telling them to pursue knowledge of Him so they will know how to "walk out" God's ways. Yet even so, some people during the millennial reign are choosing to ignore God's ways and are choosing their own ways instead, which equates to sin.

Can you imagine that? Even with Yeshua the Messiah dwelling in their midst, with Satan locked in the abyss and not bringing them temptation, humanity will still struggle with obedience, commitment, and adoration for their Creator. This seems almost incomprehensible, yet we know it will happen. Some people will have the audacity to suppose that there must be another way to bring light and hope into their life, by spurning the one who sacrificed Himself for them. And, even though He is the one who has demonstrated beyond all doubt that He loves them, some will still question that and will try to "do their own thing."

Even without Satan and his relentless temptations, man will still be able to make dangerous choices. Though they are told that "He who overcomes, I will grant to him to sit down with Me on My throne, as I also overcame and sat down with My Father on His throne" (Revelation 3:21), in effect some people will still spurn the offer.

Remember that during the thousand-year reign, at the beginning, Satan is locked away but will be released again. So humanity is choosing to sin *without* Satan's influence, which makes it especially hard to claim that "The devil made me do it."

They will literally turn down the ultimate reward for walking out a covenant relationship with Yeshua and overcoming their own sins.

It's unbelievable but true.

In Closing . . .

The seven letters form the first of seven groups of sevens mentioned in the book of Revelation. Within these letters God reveals His instructions to His congregation.

Unfortunately, some believe that these admonitions were meant to be applied to believers throughout the last two thousand years.

They see parallels in the general condition of believers through time, with His comments about the lukewarm congregation of Laodicea describing believers today. But a broader understanding – especially one that recognizes the obvious parallels to ancient biblical covenant – reveals that these letters contain messages God has given to His people ever since His creation of mankind.

Since the time of the fall, God has been re-establishing covenant with us. Throughout human history He has been offering restoration and relationship with Himself. These letters refer to the covenants that God has offered to man. And, because God instituted covenant directly after the fall, the letters reflect God's messages to His people throughout the entire 6,000 years that have elapsed since then.

Therefore, the book of Revelation begins with a brief history of the Creator's guidance and instruction to mankind throughout time, starting with those who lived before the Flood and ending with those who will live during the time of Yeshua's Second Coming, including the 1,000-year reign.

Finally, let us reiterate once again that all we have said so far represents just one level of understanding. An individual, modern-day believer could be reflected in *any* of these letters. If you therefore see yourself mirrored in one or more of the seven, please take that as an indication of what you need to work on to improve your personal relationship with God.

5

Shamash to the Seven Seals

IT'S FAIRLY COMMON FOR LOVERS OF CLASSICAL MUSIC to speak in terms of "signatures" that identify various composers. These might be no more obvious than the repetition of a particular kind of phrase that only Mozart might write; a certain sequence of notes or a characteristic embellishment that only Handel might use; a particular use of harmonies (or *dis*harmonies) that only Richard Strauss might employ; a specific "feel" or "pattern of movement" that only Bach brought to the keyboard.

We do the same with art. Experts can identify Van Gogh by his brushstrokes; they know Vermeer by the way he painted a wall; they recognize Miro in the way he worked with shapes and spaces; they see Monet in the gauzy look that gives us brilliant impressions without the boring detail of a photograph.

We do the same thing in a number of other fields of expression as well, both popular and classical, whether written on paper, painted on canvas, carved in stone, played on instruments, or conveyed to our senses in some other provocative way. Likewise with performers – it's nothing for connoisseurs of the human voice to identify the vocal signatures of various singers in three notes or less.

What makes all the above especially ironic is that – when we come to a true example of signatures that really are exactly what the name implies, in the world's most widely printed and distributed book – we call them something else and thereby think of them in entirely different terms. Such is the case with the seven seals of the book of Revelation, with which every reader of the Bible has some level of awareness but which almost no one seems to identify for what they really represent.

Let's take a moment to fill in some blanks.

What They Are NOT

Here's the text:

> I saw in the right hand of Him who sat on the throne a book written inside and on the back, sealed up with seven seals. (Revelation 5:1)

First of all, the "book" referred to here is not a Roman document with seven little drops of clay (or wax) positioned as "seals" on it. What's been taught to the church for decades (or even centuries) is also not true, to the effect that each of these "seals" represents a Roman practice of separating sections of a scroll and then impressing each section with a seal of authority. In such a scenario, each section could only be opened by someone with the authority to break that particular seal, as with different levels of security clearance in the modern age.

On the contrary, as with the rest of the Bible – which is neither a Roman nor a Greek book – this particular scroll is as Hebraic as it could possibly be.

5 - Shamash to the Seven Seals

Into the Throne Room of God

Our previous chapter, on the seven letters, completes the first mini-menorah. Within that first menorah we see the sweeping panorama of God's interaction with man throughout time. On the most basic level the seven letters deal with specific problems within specific congregations that existed in the first century AD. But on a deeper level they deal with the seven basic forms of biblical covenant, and on a deeper level still they reflect God's overall plan for restoring mankind to Himself, as detailed in Genesis through Revelation.

When we have finished lighting the seventh light on the first mini-menorah, by reading the seventh letter, we are then introduced to two shamash chapters that lead us into the chapters dealing directly with the next menorah, the one devoted to the seals. However, those two shamash chapters (Revelation 4 and 5) give us information that is absolutely critical for us to understand, from God's perspective, before we study the next group of events that unfold in chapters 6 and 8.

Most important of all, the shamash chapters introduce us to primary participants in the Wedding of the Lamb in a logical sequence that begins right here. Chapters 4 and 5 take us to God's throne room in heaven, with several other celestial beings gathered around the throne. John the Apostle then witnesses a peculiar situation. There is much weeping in heaven because no one seems able to open a certain scroll, or "book" as it is identified in some translations (see Revelation 5:4). We are not told what this scroll represents (at least, not in so many words), nor why opening it up should be so important, but all these things become obvious rather quickly.

Fortunately, someone is finally found who is worthy to do the job. In the process he "opens" the seven seals, one at a time, which leads to a series of seven events that begin in chapter 6. Taken together, all seven of these events fit metaphorically onto the next mini-menorah, effectively "lighting" each of its seven lamps. And, as you should expect by now, the opening of the seventh seal (Revelation 8:1) also leads directly into the next mini-menorah that groups together the next seven events, the seven trumpets.

But first, a word of explanation about what's really going on in these shamash chapters. Most everyone knows about the Wedding of the Lamb that takes place near the end of Revelation. With that in mind, notice who we are introduced to in the first two shamash sections. In the first shamash (Revelation 1) we're introduced to the Father of the Groom. In the second shamash (Revelation 4 and 5) we again see the Father sitting on His throne, but we are also introduced to His Son who turns out to be the Groom Himself.

Remember our discussion of flashbacks and cutaways back in chapter 2 of this volume? We might be tempted to think of those storytelling devices as fairly modern, but clearly this is not the case. Most of what's in the shamash chapters of Revelation is part of a clear pattern that will soon take on a recognizable shape. The trick is to know who the players are in an ancient Hebrew wedding (see Volume 1 in this series), so you'll be able to recognize them as they begin showing up a few chapters down the road.

The Rapture That Does Not Happen

Chapter 4 opens with a passage that is all too often misunderstood:

> ¹After these things I looked, and behold, a door standing open in heaven, and the first voice [Yeshua] which I had heard, like the sound of a trumpet speaking with me, said, "Come up here, and I will show you what must take place after these things." ²Immediately I was in the Spirit; and behold, a throne was standing in heaven, and One sitting on the throne. (Revelation 4:1–2)

These first two verses describe the apostle John's experience in being taken up to heaven. Some commentators suggest that this passage represents the so-called "Rapture" that many end-times prognosticators have been espousing since the Rapture theory first surfaced in 1830. It postulates an extra but invisible coming of Christ to "rapture" believers off to heaven prior to his visible Second Coming.

According to our research,[42] this whole theory originated with a preacher named Edward Irving, in Scotland, in the early part of the nineteenth century. It was then "envisioned" (and thus completely ratified, according to Irving) by an otherwise unknown lady named Margaret MacDonald, also of Scotland, and was then amplified by John Darby and made respectable by Cyrus Scofield (who gave us the Scofield Bible) and many others in the years since. Adherents of the theory now tend to use the above two verses, Revelation 4:1–2, as a proof text for their hypothesis.

However, without going into the exhaustive arguments that use Scripture alone to discount the Rapture theory, if we simply recognize that the book of Revelation is the most specific, detailed, and comprehensive source of information that we have, leading up to the second coming of Messiah, doesn't it seem logical that we should expect to find a clear, detailed description of the Rapture if that's really what's in view here? In later chapters of Revelation we will encounter more detail about a "Harvest," dealing with its timing and a number of other details, but none of that is found here in chapter 4.

In other words, we believe that the study of this particular passage gives no evidence of any Rapture at all. We have found none. On the contrary, this passage is extremely simple and direct in terms of what it tells us. In Revelation 4:1–2, the apostle John is the *only one* taken up to heaven so that God can reveal specific information *to him* (and ultimately to us) about the future.

The Rainbow

Revelation 4 then continues:

> ³And He who was sitting [i.e. on the throne of the preceding verse] was like a jasper stone and a sardius in appearance; and there was a rainbow around the throne, like an emerald in appearance. ⁴Around the throne were twenty-four thrones; and upon the thrones I saw twenty-four elders sitting, clothed in white garments, and golden crowns on their heads.
>
> ⁵Out from the throne come flashes of lightning and sounds and peals of thunder. And there were seven lamps of fire [menorahs] burning before the throne, which are the seven Spirits of God; ⁶and before the throne there was something like a sea of glass, like crystal; and in the center and around the throne, four living creatures full of eyes front and behind.
>
> ⁷The first creature was like a lion, and the second creature like a calf, and the third creature had a face like that of a man, and the fourth creature was like a flying eagle. ⁸And the four living creatures, each one of them having six wings, are full of eyes around and within; and day and night they do not cease to say, "HOLY, HOLY, HOLY IS THE LORD GOD, THE ALMIGHTY, WHO WAS AND WHO IS AND WHO IS TO COME." ⁹And when the living creatures give glory and honor and thanks to Him who sits on the throne, to Him who lives forever and ever . . . (Revelation 4:3–9)

John then beholds the throne, with God sitting on it and a rainbow surrounding it.

In fact, some of the details mirror God's manifestation on Mt. Sinai (e.g., lightning, voices, and thundering). Other aspects of this characterization are mirrored in multiple places in the Old Testament. For example, the rainbow surrounding God's throne, which John tells us is "like an emerald in appearance," certainly bears some resemblance to the rainbow with which God sealed His covenant with Noah in Genesis 9:11–17.

Recall what we explained in Volume 1 about the colors of covenant that make up the rainbow. The rainbow is not just green like an emerald;[43] if it were surrounding God's throne it could also be shaped like one, and green would be one of its colors. More important, the rainbow is a sign of God's ultimate covenant with mankind and with all the earth. What John saw would then be a symbolic insight into how to draw near to Him, directly to His throne.

Beyond all that, there's an even more important comparison/conclusion we might make concerning the extended vision that Ezekiel describes in the first chapter of his own book. To understand where we're coming from, let's pause for a moment and broaden the picture.

The Throne Itself

Have you ever seen someone run with a Fourth of July sparkler? Whatever their age, most people will run back and forth – or wave it in a circle – to create a trail of light that hangs in the air just long enough to register with whoever's watching. That usually includes the proud parents, which is a good thing because even sparklers can create fires!

However, to the kids' dismay, sparklers never last very long. By their very nature they're designed to burn out in a minute or so. But suppose they never burned out, and suppose you could attach one to something that would spin it in a circle, around and around, forever. What would it look like if you could do that?

Hold that thought because it'll make sense in a moment.

Through the years of our study and research we have come to the conclusion that the master menorah is actually an image of God's throne. However, the pictures that we include in this volume are all one-dimensional. In actuality the master menorah should be depicted as three-dimensional, with the branches spinning around the center shamash.

There are even ancient pictures that show a three-dimensional menorah. And, if you were to look at one of these three-dimensional menorahs from above it would have six sides. We believe that God has used this model of a central light source, with other bodies or beings that revolve around it, as His creative model for His entire universe, beginning with the atomic structure and extending all the way to the solar and galactic structures.

Thus Ezekiel sees spinning wheels. However, Ezekiel's vision (Ezekiel 1:15–21) and John's vision here in Revelation are one and the same, each describing God's throne but from different perspectives. Ezekiel was seeing God's throne from *below*, while John was seeing it from *above*. In both cases it appeared to be a spinning, master menorah.

This additional passage from Daniel, chapter 7, further illustrates our point:

> [9]"I kept looking until thrones were set up, and the Ancient of Days took His seat; his vesture was like white snow and the hair of His head like pure wool. His throne was ablaze with flames, its wheels were a burning fire. [10]"A river of fire was flowing and coming out from before Him; thousands upon thousands were attending Him, and myriads upon myriads were standing before Him; the court sat, and the books were opened. (Daniel 7:9–10)

The Only Logical Conclusion

The only logical conclusion is to recognize that God has built his universe and his relationships to emulate His throne. His throne thus becomes a picture of the kind of relationship He desires to have with all of His creation, with Him at the center and everything else revolving around Him. In a very real sense, God is "on the throne" of every single atom that makes up the universe.

Is God therefore hinting to us, just as Paul suggested in Romans 1:20, that no one will have a legitimate reason to doubt His magnificence because God's majesty is absolutely self-evident to anyone who will examine the evidence of his own five senses? From the sub-atomic to the galactic level, God continually speaks to us via the structure and the value system of His kingdom.

Also, to come back to John's own vision, if we could get the earth out of the way we'd see that rainbows are circular, which becomes obvious from a high-enough vantage point. Thus the rainbow that he saw completely encircled God, just like that spinning sparkler can form a circle of light around one of your kids.

Was it made up of master menorah-like structures, colored as we've suggested in Appendix A and both rotating and revolving around God, just as the earth rotates and revolves around the sun? Certainly all this is a distinct possibility.

The Twenty-Four Elders

Next John sees twenty-four elders, wearing white (the color of marriage), crowned with gold and seated on twenty-four thrones. Who are these elders? Are they ancient rabbis?

Let's begin with the following quote of Yeshua addressing His disciples:

> And Jesus said to them, "Truly I say to you, that you who have followed Me, in the regeneration when the Son of Man will sit on His glorious throne, you also shall sit upon twelve thrones, judging the twelve tribes of Israel. (Matthew 19:28)

This passage strongly suggests that half of the twenty-four elders will be his twelve disciples. Ancient rabbinic writings suggest that the other twelve could well be the twelve tribal leaders of Israel, which certainly makes sense.

In contrast, modern Christianity seems to believe that the twenty-four elders are angelic beings with unknown qualifications. This understanding has its roots in *De Coelesti Hierarchia, Pseudo-Denys*, by Dionysius the Areopagite, going back to the 5th century AD.[44] But here again, the church is deriving its interpretations from people, however well-meaning, who are nonetheless Greek or Latin, rather than from Hebraic scholars using Hebraic models of analysis.

The Four Living Creatures

Next, with respect to the four living creatures that John saw in Revelation 4:6, we are inserting below a short passage from Volume 1, chapter 4 of this series. The original passage was much longer and describes the three types of angels. If you haven't read it recently we highly recommend doing so at this point.

> This is an abbreviated version of the portion that discusses the cherubim, of which the four that we specifically name (paragraph six in the following quotation) are almost certainly the four that John saw surrounding God's throne. He saw each of them from one of four different *perspectives*, which thereby revealed one of the four different faces that each one had:

> > As we know, God created all things. But even before God created all the life forms on earth He also created a huge

5 - Shamash to the Seven Seals

host of heavenly beings, commonly called *angels*. They were dedicated to eternal service to Him. In a sense, from their moment of creation they have been God's hands and feet, for they are the ones who carry out many of His missions throughout His creation.

But not all angels are equal, for Scripture tells us that God created three separate "orders," each one having a unique form, function, and purpose. In the Hebrew singular their titles were *teraph, seraph,* and *cherub.* The Hebrew plural forms are as follows.

The c*herubim*,[45] also called *archangels*, are angels of the highest and the most powerful order. They literally surround the throne of God. Cherubim have six wings, four faces, and are quite large. The four faces (Revelation 4:7, Ezekiel 1:10) are a man's face, a lion's face, a bull's face, and an eagle's face. They are also covered with eyes.

We are introduced in the Bible to four cherubim. The most commonly known are the Archangel Michael (the Prince of Israel), the Archangel Gabriel, and the two who fell, one called *Lucifer* in the King James Version of Isaiah 14:12 . . . and one called *Abaddon*, now the angel of Death (see below). The other two, *Uriel* and *Raphael*, are referred to in extra-biblical writings – the Talmud, Mishnah, and apocryphal books.

Here are the meanings of the names of the four cherubim/archangels who did not rebel and thereby kept their positions around the throne of God:

- **Michael**   Warrior (Prince) of God
- **Gabriel**   Redeemer of God
- **Raphael**   Healer of God; Bringer of God's Healing
- **Uriel**   Light of God; Bringer of God's Light

All these names end with "el," which is a Hebrew word (or suffix) meaning *God*. Each of these four angels represents some attribute, characteristic, or service that originates with God.

Two of the original cherubim (one-third of the original six) rebelled against God. The four named above remained true to God, while the one we (probably mistakenly) call Lucifer (again, the one who often claims to be a Cherub of Light) and Abaddon (originally the Cherub of Life, who was once the foundation of the throne and is now the Cherub of Death) both fell. Lucifer's downfall is indelibly recorded in Ezekiel 28:13–19.

The four living creatures are these four cherubim – Michael, Gabriel, Raphael, and Uriel.

An Awesome and Inspiring Scene

Next John describes a scene in heaven that is at once both awesome and inspiring.

> ¹I saw in the right hand of Him who sat on the throne a book written inside and on the back, sealed up with seven seals. ²And I saw a strong angel proclaiming with a loud voice, "Who is worthy to open the book and to break its seals?" ³And no one in heaven or on the earth or under the earth was able to open the book or to look into it. ⁴Then I began to weep greatly because no one was found worthy to open the book or to look into it; ⁵and one of the elders said to me, "Stop weeping; behold, the Lion that is from the tribe of Judah, the Root of David, has overcome so as to open the book and its seven seals." (Revelation 5:1–5)

God is sitting on His throne, and in his hand he holds a scroll (Hebrew *sefer*, meaning *book* or *scroll*) written on both sides, which is about to be opened. Some people think that this is the Book of Life containing the names of all the saints of God. However, this theory isn't correct. There is a Book of Life but it won't be opened until the end of time, as detailed in Revelation 20:12, at the Great White Throne Judgment when God judges the righteous and the wicked.

5 - Shamash to the Seven Seals

On the contrary, this book/scroll is actually something else entirely. Most ancient scrolls were written on only one side. However, there is one particular book/scroll in the Bible that is written on both sides, as described in the following passage from Exodus:

> Then Moses turned and went down from the mountain with the two tablets of the testimony in his hand, tablets which were written on both sides; they were written on one side and the other. (Exodus 32:15)

As we explained in Volume 1, chapter 3 of this series, the Torah (i.e., the first five books of the Bible, as described in the passage above), is written as a ketubah, an ancient Hebrew marriage contract. Thus the five books in the Torah correlate to the five sections in a ketubah. This book in God's hand is obviously a marriage contract; i.e., the Torah.

Next, John tells us that no one is found worthy to open the Torah/ketubah in all of heaven, either *on* the earth or *under* the earth. What's intriguing is John's emotional reaction to this dilemma. He must realize the supreme importance of this book. In Hebrew culture, the marriage contract was signed by seven individuals, including the bride and the groom. At the wedding ceremony that typically came many months after the ketubah was written, the groom is the only individual who is permitted to open (and thereby to read from) the scroll. Only then does the groom proclaim his bride worthy and pure and ready for marriage.

Indeed, we have retained a residual custom in our own culture. It comes up during our own wedding ceremonies when the minister asks those in attendance, "Does anyone have cause that these two should not be wed?"

Now let's come back to the Torah. To reveal who the Bride of Messiah was, the scroll really needed to be opened. In it was critical information about her identity, her lineage, and her authority.

Another reference to this scroll could be the following passage from Zechariah. Here we see a flying scroll and some details about it, including its dimensions. It's interesting to note that the dimensions just happen to correlate precisely with the dimensions of the Holy of Holies, which is where the future wedding will take place.

> ¹Then I lifted up my eyes again and looked, and behold, there was a flying scroll.
> ²And he said to me, "What do you see?" And I answered, "I see a flying scroll; its length is twenty cubits and its width ten cubits." ³Then he said to me, "This is the curse that is going forth over the face of the whole land; surely everyone who steals will be purged away according to the writing on one side, and everyone who swears will be purged away according to the writing on the other side.
>
> ⁴"I will make it go forth," declares the LORD of hosts, "and it will enter the house of the thief and the house of the one who swears falsely by My name; and it will spend the night within that house and consume it with its timber and stones." ⁵Then the angel who was speaking with me went out and said to me, "Lift up now your eyes and see what this is going forth." (Zechariah 5:1–5)

The Groom's act of opening the scroll and proclaiming his Bride faithful and ready for marriage (as explained in further detail in the following pages) requires us to come in line with His proclamation. At the same time, in the ancient Hebrew culture, the groom could open the ketubah and proclaim his bride's purity even if she *wasn't* pure, but *only if he himself had already paid the price for her sin.*

In the passage above we see Yeshua taking the scroll and then hearing the following words proclaimed:

> And they sang a new song, saying, "Worthy are You to take the book and to break its seals; for You were slain, and purchased for God with your blood men from every tribe and tongue and people and nation. (Revelation 5:9)

The word "purchased" does not actually mean "purchase" but "to redeem," also meaning to "pay their debt." Thus the people in question were in bondage to sin, but He has paid their price by His death on the cross and thus He can now redeem them – not "purchase" them.

And this, of course, is exactly what took place. Yeshua died on the cross and paid the price for our sin. Therefore, John's tears were wiped away when Yeshua, the Lamb of God and the Root of David, was found worthy to open the scroll (Revelation 5:5).

And thus we are formally introduced – in this shamash chapter – to the primary participant in the Wedding of the Lamb, the Groom Himself.

When a Seal Is NOT a Seal

In the process of opening the scroll, Yeshua at last encounters the seven seals and deals with them directly. However, contrary to the sense of what so many biblical expositors teach, this was not an ancient Greek or Roman document. Therefore it was not sealed up with a series of wax impressions bearing the unique marks of signet rings worn by seven different individuals. Had they existed, such "seals" would prove that the document itself had not been tampered with, because they would automatically be destroyed when it was opened up.

On the contrary, this was an ancient Hebrew scroll, and the seven seals were the signatures of the seven individuals who would have signed this particular document – without doubt the most important ketubah ever created. In Volume 1 of this series we explained who we thought those seven individuals might be. In Table 5-1 we provide a little more detail, including the names of the patriarchs whom we believe signed, their formal status as signatories, the seal number corresponding to their signatures, and the separate judgments on mankind that corresponded to each of the seven. The actual Hebrew verbiage in the text itself[46] means, He "uttered the words" or He "spoke open" the first seal. Thus they're not "broken" open, they're "spoken" open instead.

Also, the Greek-to-English translation of Revelation 5:5 says that "the Lion that is from the tribe of Judah, the Root of David, has overcome so as to open the book and its seven seals." The correct Hebraic understanding of that passage, literally, would be "The lion that is from the tribe of Judah, the Root of David, has overcome so as to open the book and speak forth the seals/oaths." Likewise with opening the first of the seven seals in Revelation 6:1. These "oaths" signify the levels of covenant involved with each of the signatures.

Finally, let's take a closer look at Revelation 5:9:

> And they sang a new song, saying, "Worthy are You to take the book and to break its seals; for You were slain, and purchased for God with Your blood men from every tribe and tongue and people and nation."

First, understand that the reference to a "new song" (really, in Hebrew it is a "renewed song") is also a reference to Revelation 20:4–6, in which we are promised that those who constitute His Bride will be made priests (Hebrew: *cohenim*) and will rule over all the earth during the thousand-year millennial kingdom, prior to the final Judgment Day. Also, as we noted earlier, the correct translation of the word "purchased" should really be "redeemed," as in what happens when a kinsman redeemer (which is precisely what Yeshua is, having paid the price for all of us) redeems someone within his own family, as Boaz did in Ruth 4:1–12.

5 - Shamash to the Seven Seals

Table 5-1: The Ketubah in Revelation 5-8

Patriarch	Status as Signatory	Seal Number (description)	Judgment for Violating Ketubah
Adam	Witness	Seal #1: White horse rider	Spiritual deception
Noah	Witness	Seal #2: Red horse rider with sword; power to take peace away from earth	Peace removed from the earth; war
Abraham	Father of Groom	Seal #3: Black horse rider with scales, weighing obedience or disobedience, and judgment that comes from each	Famine, economic upheaval
Jacob/Israel	Father of Bride	Seal #4: Death riding decaying, putrefied pale horse	Death given authority to kill one-fourth of the world's population by sword, famine, plague, and wild beasts
Moses	Scribe	Seal #5: Altar in heaven, souls who have been killed for their faith told to wait a bit longer	Promise of further judgment for those still rejecting God; promise of further care and protection for those in relationship with God (Revelation 12)
David	Bride	Seal #6: Great earthquake; sky turns black; moon becomes blood red; stars fall from heaven to earth; mankind fears God but does not repent	Consequences for rejection of ketubah, Torah, and God's principles
Yeshua	Groom	Seal #7: Silence in heaven for 1/2 hour; prayers of saints offered up in heaven; Yom Kippur; Day of Judgment	Coming of the King whether we are ready or not

In Closing . . .

- Chapter 4 of Revelation does not refer to any kind of a "Rapture" (or "Harvest"), despite hundreds of conjectures about this very subject.

- The throne of God, as observed by Ezekiel, could very well have been structured like the master menorah by which we diagram the book of Revelation. However, it would not have been one-dimensional like our printed versions; it would have had to exist in three (or more!) dimensions, in living color.

- Although the Bible does not specify who the twenty-four elders surrounding the throne of God are, Yeshua's twelve disciples and the twelve tribal leaders of Israel are undoubtedly the best possibilities.

- The angelic beings surrounding His throne are most likely cherubim – Michael, Gabriel, Raphael, and Uriel.

- The only one who could legally open the "little book" was Yeshua Himself, as the official Bridegroom whose impending marriage to His Bride was the sole concern of that little book – his marriage contract.

- The seven seals were definitely not seven globs of wax, melted in place, by which ancient documents were sealed shut. They were seven signatures as required on every ancient ketubah.

6

The Seven Seals

LET'S TAKE A QUICK LOOK AT where we have come so far, to help us keep things straight as more and more events unfold. As we explained in chapter 4 of this volume, the seven letters have given us an overview of God's dealings with man from creation to the end of the millennial reign, a period of time lasting approximately 7,000 years. The sixth letter amounts to a message to God's people in the days just before the second coming of the Messiah, which occurs at the dawning of the seventh letter. The seventh letter then describes the ending of the 6,000-year rule of mankind and the setting up of the Messiah's kingdom at the beginning of the thousand-year millennial reign, which will then complete this 7,000-year period.

The seventh letter is represented by the left light on the letters mini-menorah on the farthest right side of the master menorah. This light leads directly to and literally *becomes* the shamash – the middle light – of the second mini-menorah as we move from the outer right toward the center. The shamash of this second mini-menorah is then used to light the first light of the seal mini-menorah.

The seal events that we will describe in a moment then follow immediately, which brings us to the perfect moment for correcting a common misunderstanding. Many people believe that, starting with the first seal event, there will then be only seven years left before the start of the millennial reign. We shall see that this is not correct. Many also believe that only a few events – or even none at all – are left to take place before all prophecy is fulfilled, which will allow the Second Coming to occur. We shall see that this also is not true.

On the contrary, the seal events represent the *beginning* of the end and *not the end itself*. There are, in fact, many more than just seven years left to unfold between the first seal and the Second Coming. Indeed, many events have yet to occur before we shall even see the promised *signs* of the Second Coming.

To see this from another perspective, consider how many times Yeshua said, as in Matthew 24 but in other places as well, that these are just the beginning of birth pangs. They start off slow and are not very strong, but as time progresses each individual pang lasts longer and becomes more intense. Then, they gradually begin to get closer and closer together as the whole process picks up speed, until He arrives and delivers us.

Also, it's important to note that, from here on, the book of Revelation will develop an Old Testament (Torah) concept in which we will see three groups of judgments coming upon the people on the earth. These amount to three specific groups of seven judgments each, to be visited upon those who choose to reject God and continue to rebel. Each group of seven judgments will be worse than the previous group. So, as we work through the first of the three groups of seven (see illustrations in chapter 4 of this book), we will point out numerous judgment parallels in Revelation that represent the fulfillment of judgments first given by God back in Deuteronomy, chapters 30–32.

6 - The Seven Seals

Now let's talk about the seals, which are actually arranged into *two* sections. The first four events occur one after the other, in linear fashion. The first four are also commonly known as the famous "Four Horsemen of the Apocalypse," for obvious reasons, for each of the four riders sits on a horse of a different color.

Seal/Signature #1 – The Rider on the White Horse (Deception)

The first horseman rides on a white horse, as described in Revelation 6:1–2:

> [1]Then I saw when the Lamb broke one of the seven seals, and I heard one of the four living creatures saying as with a voice of thunder, "Come." [2]I looked, and behold, a white horse, and he who sat on it had a bow; and a crown was given to him, and he went out conquering and to conquer.

Some commentators believe that this rider represents what they call the "Rapture" (rather than the taking of John up to Heaven), based on the understanding that Yeshua Himself will be coming back on a white horse for His Bride. And here He is, right there at the very beginning of all the troubles on earth, coming to snatch His Bride and take her away so that no true believer will have to suffer a single inconvenience from that moment on.

The problem with this theory is that this is not the Messiah. Nor is there any text describing how this rider will be coming to take anyone away. On the contrary, this rider is clearly a Messianic wannabe who carries a bow and wears a crown, for which the redacted-back Hebrew equivalent is actually not a word that means "crown" exclusively at all, in the commonly accepted meaning of that word.

On the contrary, it's the Hebrew word *atarah*, which can mean "crown" in a looser sense but, strictly speaking, just as often refers to the portion of the tallit, or prayer shawl, that covers the wearer's head when the tallit is pulled up into a "prayer closet (see "A True Prayer Closet" below). More specifically, it's the word for the tallit *neckband*, or *collar*, which is often highly decorated and typically features a series of Hebrew letters woven into the fabric, spelling out a blessing directed toward God the Father. "Blessed are you, Lord our God, King of the universe, who sanctifies us by your commandments and commands us to wear tzit-tzit" is one such blessing.

In other words, this particular wearer is not quite willing to wear a complete tallit, which is also a symbol of authority. But he does wear the small portion of one that he believes represents glory – falsely, in his case.

A True Prayer Closet

As you will recall from Volume 1 of this series, the tallit (or *tallis*) was the outer garment that all devout Hebrew men wore during Yeshua's time, and in modern times as well. And contrary to what modern Christianity often teaches, when such a devout Jew went into his "prayer closet" he would not go into a private room in a building. Instead, he would pull the collar of his tallit up over his head and thereby create his own closet, with the collar draped over his head like a crown. In this way the whole tallit acted as a covering of protection. At the same time, the wearer wrapped the tzit-tzit (i.e., the knotted strings hanging from the four corners) around his fingers, each of which embodied the name of God (YHWH) within the numerical sequence of its knots.

This white horse rider has no desire for any kind of "prayer covering" at all. Plain and simple, he's interested only in the glory and the splendor of power. And, the Hebrew word translated as "conquer" in Hebrew is *gabar*, which means "to be strong, to prevail, to be proud and insolent with respect to one's own identity and agenda."⁴⁷

Also, every time Messiah Himself comes into the picture in Revelation we see a dramatic contrast in the way the text changes. Most times it gives us something that evokes either pictures or characteristics of Him and His godliness. For example, when Yeshua shows up we often get a dramatic description of Him or His throne, as in chapters 1, 2, 4, 5, 7, 10, 11, 19, and 22. Most often He appears on His throne. And, if we don't get those connections we get a description, such as "His face was like the sun shining in its strength (1:16), or "his face was like the sun" (10:1).

We believe that this horse rider is a deceiver (or, "deception") – someone who wants to make us believe that he's the Messiah. Indeed, the Hebrew word for "bow," *keshet*, can also mean "deceptive archer," one who has a deceitful intention for the arrow's flight. In fact, we should keep in mind that one of the meanings of the Hebrew word Torah is to "hit the mark." This particular archer is not trying to hit the mark (Torah) at all; he's trying to mislead people instead. His real aim is to hit something else entirely.

Plus, the same Hebrew concept behind the word *gabar* can be used as a Hebrew metaphor indicating "strength is increasing," which doesn't fit Messiah. Messiah's strength is constant, but at the end of time God *will* allow *Satan's* strength to increase. This is partly how he will eventually have such strong influence, as foretold in Paul's second letter to Thessalonica:

> ⁹That is, the one whose coming is in accord with the activity of Satan, with all power and signs and false wonders, ¹⁰and with all the deception of wickedness for those who perish, because they did not receive the love of the truth so as to be saved. ¹¹For this reason God will send upon them a deluding influence so that they will believe what is false, ¹²in order that they all

> may be judged who did not believe the truth, but took pleasure in wickedness. (2 Thessalonians 2:9–12)

As you might also recall, in Elijah's day God didn't allow the prophets of Ba'al to call fire down from heaven. But in the end times God will allow Satan to do exactly that. Thus his power will be increasing by God's allowance, but not by his own ability.

Finally, let us tie in something else here, once again, that has somehow been accepted by millions of people as an end-times truism. A giant end-times revival is simply not prophesied anywhere in the Bible. On the other hand, perhaps this horse rider is coming to fulfill numerous prophecies about the great "falling away" that will occur in the end times, as spoken of by Paul (who also references the book of Daniel) in the following passage:

> [3]Let no one in any way deceive you, for it will not come unless the apostasy comes first, and the man of lawlessness is revealed, the son of destruction, [4]who opposes and exalts himself above every so-called god or object of worship, so that he takes his seat in the temple of God, displaying himself as being God. (2 Thessalonians 2:3–4)

On the whole it seems quite clear that this particular rider, from a Hebraic perspective, will initiate the whole chronology of catastrophic, cascading events that we're about to encounter in the remainder of Revelation. He's not Messiah; he's the deceiver himself, coming on a white horse – the color of purity – to suggest that he's something he's not. This is exactly what we should expect from the Antichrist/False Messiah, who will pretend to be pure and righteous but who will love pomp and false authority, as indicated by the "crown" that he wears. However, we are not proposing that the False Messiah will be revealed to mankind at this point.

As we'll soon see, all the horse riders embody a particular destructive characteristic, and this horse rider is deception itself. At the same time, as we've learned in the B'rit Hadashah, all those passages that talk about the lawless one actually mean that he is the "Torah-less" one. So, despite his pomp, apparent authority, and perceived righteousness, and especially in spite of the miracles he's able to perform, we'll still be able to identify him because he will have a major conflict with God's laws.

Beyond all that, the Bible mentions the fiery arrows and fiery darts of the enemy more than once. But Yeshua is not an archer; neither does He have any need whatsoever to "hit the mark." He *is* the mark.

Seal/Signature #2 – The Rider on the Red Horse (War)

The rider on the red horse is introduced to us in Revelation 6:3–4:

> ³When He broke the second seal, I heard the second living creature saying, "Come." ⁴And another, a red horse, went out; and to him who sat on it, it was granted to take peace from the earth, and that men would slay one another; and a great sword was given to him.

As is so typical of all of us in our "human selves," once people begin to buy into deception, even at the most basic and unthreatening level, more deception is immediately born. For example, because we are told that the red horse rider comes "to take peace from the earth" many commentators are deceived into thinking that he's coming to bring about the famous Battle of Armageddon.

However, what they often seem to forget is that the book of Revelation actually describes four separate and distinct wars, none of which have occurred yet. As of the writing of this book, with Iran about to possess its own nuclear weapons, we might be coming closer and closer to the beginning of the first of those four wars.

But, as described in the Revelation passage above, the second seal war is certainly not Armageddon. Consider some of the reasons:

- Armageddon ends in victory for the armies of God, yet no armies of God win here. Nor are they even described.

- Armageddon ends with God coming and setting up His reign, which does not happen here, either.

- A few verses later, in Revelation 6:11, God tells His martyrs to wait. But why would He do that if He's come to set up His kingdom?

- The temple needs to be rebuilt but that process has not even started yet.

- In Revelation 19:14–21, where we encounter the *real* Battle of Armageddon, Messiah eliminates his foes via the sword (not a bow) that comes out of His mouth, which equates to the Word of God. Here in the seals, many people will be killed by men, wild beasts, famine, and plague, but not by the Word of God. There's also no mention of blood coming up to the bridles of horses (Revelation 14:20), a well-known feature in the Battle of Armageddon.

Clearly, the description of the second seal war is not a duplicate description of any other war that occurs in Revelation. Some also claim that the color of the horse (red) represents Russia and/or China, which brings up another false notion that sometimes seems to get a lot of play within both Christendom and the secular world. But despite what so many have been taught, the Arabs are not the descendants of Abraham's son, Ishmael, by his concubine, Hagar.

On the contrary, the Bible is a Hebrew book and red is the primary symbol of Jacob's brother, Esau. According to the Scriptures (and most anthropologists), the Arabs are actually Esau's descendents, the *Edomites*. In fact, the very word "Arab" has its origin in the valley in which Esau and his descendants dwelt, which was known as the *Arabah Valley*.

As further confirmation, it's interesting to note that several prophecies from the Old Testament refer to the Edomites who attack and bring on a huge war with Israel in the last days. These prophecies also give us considerable detail about the events that will precede this war, how it actually takes place, and its eventual outcome.

Thus we believe that the war in seal #2 of Revelation is a war between Israel and the Arabs (the Edomites – the word *Edom*, incidentally, is spelled exactly the same as the Hebrew word for *red* when the vowel points are left out, as they were in the original Hebrew text of the Bible) as we will learn if we follow the chronology of events in the book of Ezekiel. There, we encounter certain prophecies, starting with chapter 34 and continuing through Ezekiel 48, that clearly parallel the order of events in Revelation.

In the three examples below we have included highly relevant prophetic passages from Ezekiel 36, Psalm 83, and Isaiah 34. In addition, we would highly recommend Ezekiel 34 (the entire chapter), plus Ezekiel 35:10–15.

1) Therefore thus says the Lord GOD, "Surely in the fire of My jealousy I have spoken against the rest of the nations, and against all Edom, who appropriated My land for themselves as a possession with wholehearted joy and with scorn of soul, to drive it out for a prey." (Ezekiel 36:5)

2) ²For behold, Your enemies make an uproar,
And those who hate You have exalted themselves.
³They make shrewd plans against Your people,
And conspire together against Your treasured ones.
⁴They have said, "Come, and let us wipe them out as a nation,

That the name of Israel be remembered no more."
⁵For they have conspired together with one mind;
Against You they make a covenant:
⁶The tents of Edom and the Ishmaelites,
Moab and the Hagrites;
⁷Gebal and Ammon and Amalek,
Philistia with the inhabitants of Tyre;
⁸Assyria also has joined with them;
They have become a help to the children of Lot. Selah.
¹²Who said, "Let us possess for ourselves the pastures of God."
(Psalm 83:2–8; 12)

3) ⁵For My sword is satiated in heaven,
Behold it shall descend for judgment upon Edom
And upon the people whom I have devoted to destruction.
⁶The sword of the LORD is filled with blood,
It is sated with fat, with the blood of lambs and goats,
With the fat of the kidneys of rams.
For the LORD has a sacrifice in Bozrah
And a great slaughter in the land of Edom.
⁷Wild oxen will also fall with them
And young bulls with strong ones;
Thus their land will be soaked with blood,
And their dust become greasy with fat.
⁸For the LORD has a day of vengeance,
A year of recompense for the cause of Zion.
⁹Its streams will be turned into pitch,
And its loose earth into brimstone,
And its land will become burning pitch.
¹⁰It will not be quenched night or day;
Its smoke will go up forever
From generation to generation it will be desolate;
None will pass through it forever and ever.
(Isaiah 34:5–10)

6 - The Seven Seals

Among other things, these passages are telling us quite clearly that the irrational hatred of God's people, which started with Esau and perhaps was best exemplified by the anti-Israelite actions of the Amalekites (who were *also* descendants of Esau) in the wilderness, has really never ended or even diminished. For example, both Haman and Herod were descendents of Esau, and both were examples of illogical, unreasonable hatred of God's people.

Thus a very definite end-times war is prophesied, between the Arabs and the nation of Israel, which also sounds like it will be worldwide. The obvious reason would be God's punishment for the Arabs' lusting after the land God promised to the Israelites so many centuries earlier. Plus, of course, the Arab world's hatred of the Jews, which we just mentioned above. It's no secret that the Arabs have been scheming for decades, behind the back of the rest of the world, to find ways to destroy the nation of Israel once and for all – literally, to wipe God's people off the face of the earth.

Beyond all that, both ancient and modern history are replete with graphic illustrations of the same hatred, boiling over again and again. For example:

- During the Babylonian invasion of 600 BC, the Edomites were invited inside Jerusalem to help protect it from warring hordes, but once they got inside they turned their back on their "brothers" and started attacking from within, thus benefiting the Babylonian attackers. The Jewish historian Josephus tells us that 20,000 "helpers" were allowed in. But once inside they pillaged the city, raping and killing and not sparing even the priests.

- In the Six-Day War of 1967, which the Arabs (Edomites) expected to win handily, they were soundly defeated by the Israelis, who wound up gaining quite a bit of breathing room.

- Also, please consider what we are told in the book of Obadiah, which essentially chronicles the second-seal war.

The red horse rider heralds strife and conflict on the earth. We believe that the prophecy about the Edomites going to war against Israel is the lynchpin for that war. This text and the accompanying Old Testament prophecies talk about a war in the Mideast. We believe it's very likely, however, that such a war could extend well beyond the Mideast. China, North Korea, and other nations could easily take advantage of an opportune moment to accomplish things they've wanted to do for a long time – for example, taking on Taiwan and finishing the Korean War.

Understand what's being conveyed here. The basic "massive deception" starts first, followed by war. But that same deception continues all the way through, and additional deceptions are layered in on top of that. Eventually the original deception will lead to armed conflict, then to disruption of the world economy. Certainly all of its currencies, trade patterns, and production of goods and services will be massively affected. And, as usually happens during and after most wars, food production will plummet and that will cause additional famine, disease, and death.

Meanwhile, let's see what happens with the next rider.

Seal #3 – The Rider on the Black Horse (Famine)

These are the verses that tell us about the rider on the black horse:

> [5]When He broke the third seal, I heard the third living creature saying, "Come." I looked, and behold, a black horse; and he who sat on it had a pair of scales in his hand. [6]And I heard something like a voice in the center of the four living creatures saying, "A quart of wheat for a denarius [a day's wage], and three quarts of barley for a denarius; and do not damage the oil and the wine." (Revelation 6:5–6)

This rider is commonly known as "famine." He's carrying a pair of scales and apparently weighing grain. The voice then tells us how much wheat and barley can be bought for a denarius,[48] which at one time was a standard measurement for a day's work.

The symbology of the scales, balanced against the amounts of grain that are being measured out for a day's work, strongly implies that food has become very expensive. This implies (1) rampant inflation, so that one has to work an entire day to earn enough money to buy a loaf of bread, and/or (2) that there will be a global famine so extensive that, no matter how much a person works and earns, most people will have to spend significant amounts of their money to get something that is in very short supply.[49]

Thus the book of Revelation is following the judgments of God in logical order. As we have already noted, history teaches us that it's typical after a major war to find many productive resources destroyed, so that goods and services become scarce. Prices then soar to the sky, and people can't find the things they need even if they could afford them. Likewise, many homes are destroyed and countless people become destitute. What then follows is a major famine, symbolized in this case by a black horse pointing toward a bleak future.

Many times in secular history, echoing the history recorded in the Old Testament, we find these same judgments being poured out on a civilization, especially one that has rejected God's principles (as suggested by the white horse rider) and has chosen to follow its own path. It's a well-known fact that before the fall of these empires the primary principles of socialism (gimme something for nothing), and the lack of a strong work ethic, were prominently displayed in their laws and their society. The great Roman and Greek civilizations of ancient times are prime historic examples, not to mention what's happened in more recent times in France, England (once the "Ruler of the Seas" on whom "the sun never set"), and the Arab countries that once hosted great Muslim civilizations.

Which begs the question: Is America walking down the same path?

These are not random successions or sequences of events that happen to some people who have obviously fallen away from God. These judgments are the fulfillment of what God warned about back in Torah; the Bible is developing a theme from the beginning to the end. That's why, here at the end of the book, we have Leviticus 26 being fulfilled. We have the blessing side first, which correlates with the parallel story in Revelation being told in the shamash chapters. Then Leviticus 26 closes with a rundown of the seal judgments, which will occur before the Second Coming. These judgments, fulfilling the curses that we are told in Torah will come upon mankind, are described in the mini-menorah text in Revelation.

Here's the passage from Leviticus 26:

> [14]"But if you do not obey Me and do not carry out all these commandments, [15]if, instead, you reject My statutes, and if your soul abhors My ordinances so as not to carry out all My commandments, and so break My covenant, [16]I, in turn, will do this to you: I will appoint over you a sudden terror, consumption and fever that will waste away the eyes and cause the soul to pine away; also, you will sow your seed uselessly, for your enemies will eat it up.
>
> [17]I will set My face against you so that you will be struck down before your enemies; and those who hate you will rule over you, and you will flee when no one is pursuing you. [18]If also after these things you do not obey Me, then I will punish you seven times more for your sins. [19]"I will also break down your pride of power; I will also make your sky like iron and your earth like bronze.

²⁰'Your strength will be spent uselessly, for your land will not yield its produce and the trees of the land will not yield their fruit. ²¹'If then, you act with hostility against Me and are unwilling to obey Me, I will increase the plague on you seven times according to your sins. ²²'I will let loose among you the beasts of the field, which will bereave you of your children and destroy your cattle and reduce your number so that your roads lie deserted.

²³'And if by these things you are not turned to Me, but act with hostility against Me, ²⁴then I will act with hostility against you; and I, even I, will strike you seven times for your sins. ²⁵'I will also bring upon you a sword which will execute vengeance for the covenant; and when you gather together into your cities, I will send pestilence among you, so that you shall be delivered into enemy hands. ²⁶'When I break your staff of bread, ten women will bake your bread in one oven, and they will bring back your bread in rationed amounts, so that you will eat and not be satisfied.

²⁷'Yet if in spite of this you do not obey Me, but act with hostility against Me,
²⁸then I will act with wrathful hostility against you, and I, even I, will punish you seven times for your sins. ²⁹'Further, you will eat the flesh of your sons and the flesh of your daughters you will eat. ³⁰'I then will destroy your high places, and cut down your incense altars, and heap your remains on the remains of your idols, for My soul shall abhor you. ³¹'I will lay waste your cities as well and will make your sanctuaries desolate, and I will not smell your soothing aromas.
³²'I will make the land desolate so that your enemies who settle in it will be appalled over it.

³³'You, however, I will scatter among the nations and will draw out a sword after you, as your land becomes desolate and your cities become waste. ³⁴'Then the land will enjoy its Sabbaths all the days of the desolation,

while you are in your enemies' land; then the land will rest and enjoy its sabbaths. ³⁵'All the days of its desolation it will observe the rest which it did not observe on your sabbaths, while you were living on it.

³⁶'As for those of you who may be left, I will also bring weakness into their hearts in the lands of their enemies. And the sound of a driven leaf will chase them, and even when no one is pursuing they will flee as though from the sword, and they will fall. ³⁷'They will therefore stumble over each other as if running from the sword, although no one is pursuing; and you will have no strength to stand up before your enemies. ³⁸'But you will perish among the nations, and your enemies' land will consume you. ³⁹'So those of you who may be left will rot away because of their iniquity in the lands of your enemies; and also because of the iniquities of their forefathers they will rot away with them.

⁴⁰'If they confess their iniquity and the iniquity of their forefathers, in their unfaithfulness which they committed against Me, and also in their acting with hostility against Me – ⁴¹'I also was acting with hostility against them, to bring them into the land of their enemies – or if their uncircumcised heart becomes humbled so that they then make amends for their iniquity, ⁴²'then I will remember My covenant with Jacob, and I will remember also My covenant with Isaac, and My covenant with Abraham as well, and I will remember the land.

⁴³'For the land will be abandoned by them, and will make up for its sabbaths while it is made desolate without them. They, meanwhile, will be making amends for their iniquity, because they rejected My ordinances and their soul abhorred My statutes. ⁴⁴'Yet in spite of this, when they are in the land of their enemies, I will not reject them, nor will I so abhor them as to destroy them, breaking My covenant with them; for I am the LORD their God. ⁴⁵'But I will remember for them the

> covenant with their ancestors, whom I brought out of the land of Egypt in the sight of the nations, that I might be their God. I am the LORD.'"
>
> ⁴⁶These are the statutes and ordinances and laws which the LORD established between Himself and the sons of Israel through Moses at Mount Sinai. (Leviticus 26:14–46)

The black horse rider is prophesying tremendous economic disruption during or after the war heralded by the preceding rider on the red horse. People will be displaced, homes will be lost, the normal rhythms of life will be disrupted, and the world will be unable to feed its own population. Ultimately, hundreds of thousands (and perhaps millions) of people will be weakened and displaced, a natural outcome of which will then be widespread sickness and increased vulnerability to new diseases. And all of that will be preparation for the fourth rider on the pale horse, who will soon be on his way.

Seal #4 – the Rider on the Pale Horse (Death)

Revelation describes the fourth rider like this:

> ⁷When the Lamb broke the fourth seal, I heard the voice of the fourth living creature saying, "Come." ⁸I looked, and behold, an ashen horse; and he who sat on it had the name Death; and Hades was following with him. Authority was given to them over a fourth of the earth, to kill with sword and with famine and with pestilence and by the wild beasts of the earth. (Revelation 6:7–8)

The Hebrew word used here, commonly translated as *pale*, actually means *sickly*, *putrid*, and *decaying* – or *rotting*. In fact, this horse will actually be a mottled black-and-blue-and-green, putrid, zombie horse. The pale horse rider is given the authority to bring death to one-fourth of the earth's population, which is what follows a famine when people are not getting enough to eat. The tools he will use will include "the sword" (meaning any kind of weapon, which could refer to everything up to and including hunting rifles and machine guns), famine, plagues, and wild beasts. The word for "wild beasts" certainly means lions and tigers, but it could also include microbes and all sorts of diseases that are carried by microbial "beasts" – death-and-misery causing agents unidentified in biblical times.

Given that God has chosen to identify the fourth seal event by using a rider on a putrefied horse, it's clear that, with regard to this war and its aftermath, death is a *persona* with a definite identity. It's also interesting to note that, with respect to the two additional wars to follow, in each case we are told specifically how people will die. In the next war they will be killed by fire, smoke, and sulfur – and death will apprehend not one-fourth but *one-third* of the remaining population. Finally, in the actual war of Armageddon, which occurs near the end of Revelation, they will be killed in a completely different manner altogether.

Seal #5 –Martyrs

These are the verses that tell us about the fifth seal:

> [9]When the Lamb broke the fifth seal, I saw underneath the altar the souls of those who had been slain because of the word of God, and because of the testimony which they had maintained; [10]and they cried out with a loud voice, saying, "How long, O Lord, holy and true, will You refrain from judging and avenging our blood on those who dwell on the earth?" [11]And there was given to each of them a white robe; and they were told that they should rest for a little while longer, until the number of their fellow servants and their brethren who were to be killed even as they had been, would be completed also. (Revelation 6:9–11)

Here we find the first example of the four/three pattern that we'll talk about in considerable detail in upcoming chapters. This mini-menorah outlines seven events, arranged in a four/three grouping. The four horsemen of the apocalypse came first, leaving the final seals as a grouping of three. Also, even as the first four seals focused our attention on events that were occurring on earth, the next three seals will split our attention between heaven and earth.

Obviously this passage occurs in the original temple in heaven. The altar it refers to is not the golden altar in the inner court, but the bronze altar in the outer court. Most experts agree that this particular altar, in ancient times in the earthly temple, was somewhere between 180 and 220 feet high. In other words, contrary to what we so often seem to assume, it was huge. It cannot even begin to be compared to the two-foot-high "kneeling altar" we might see at the front of the auditorium in a modern church. This is the bronze altar that stood in the outer court of the temple, where the Levites and the other worshippers would offer up their sacrifices and prayers to God during certain portions of the morning and evening service.

Perhaps more important, the word "beneath" in this context does not mean "underneath" in a purely physical sense, as a cat might go underneath a car. It means "at the base of" even as we might stand at the base of (and thus "beneath") a modern office building. To make the point a little more clearly, please understand also that these people are not some kind of mystical, see-through "souls" who are underneath a piece of furniture in the outer court of the temple.

To Be Absent from the Body

In fact, this passage also provides indisputable evidence that we should "prefer rather to be absent from the body and to be at home with the Lord" (2 Corinthians 5:8). We see up in heaven the souls of people who have died but have not yet received their perfected bodies. They're still in their soul form and we see them interacting with God in worship.

This scene is set in one of the morning or evening services that have been observed every day in the temple in heaven since God first set the universe in motion. Eventually the same services will be conducted once again on earth after the earthly temple has been rebuilt. Remember, Scripture points out that the temple of Solomon's time was only a shadow of what's in heaven, and worship was conducted in the same way even as it will be again. The souls beneath the altar, in this particular case, are those who were slain for their relationships with God.

Perhaps most important of all, as we will explain at the beginning of chapter 8 in this volume, as Revelation proceeds it will describe for us a typical daily service occurring at the temple in heaven, to which many of the key events in Revelation will be inextricably linked. The first time we encounter this scene we see God on His throne, with His angels. Now we're moving out from the throne room to the outer court, seeing the beginning of the daily temple service, which itself was common practice on earth when there *was* a temple.

These souls have been "slain because of the word of God" (Revelation 6:9), undoubtedly meaning that they were martyred because they refused to stop testifying about their relationship with God the Father and His Son, Yeshua. Also, it's worth noting that the specific word for "slain" in this passage contains the meaning of "being murdered." As we look back over the history of the world it's not hard to find millions of people who would fit into this category, starting with Abel.

They are given white robes, which indicates that they will be part of the Bride of Yeshua, or were at least invited to the wedding. We have no way of knowing for sure, either way. But this passage does remind us of the parable in the first fourteen verses of Matthew 22, which makes it clear that everyone in the wedding wears white, from the guests all the way to the Bride. Here we see preparations for the wedding. Someone is being given their garments and told to wait a little while, because things aren't quite ready yet.

As a matter of fact, when the people "underneath" the altar ask, "How long before you judge the people on the earth and avenge our blood?" the answer is, "Wait a little while until your friends and brothers, like those who have already been poured out like a sacrifice [as you have been], are 'full.'" In other words, "full" meaning that "all those who will be slain for His sake have met their fate."

At the same time, to be a warrior for Messiah is to wear His bridal garments. Indeed, the very Hebrew definition of the white robes in this passage involves preparation for warfare, which further involves the warriors' assumption of power and authority that God has promised them. In essence, then, this becomes a prophecy-within-a-prophecy, a prophetic allusion foretelling some of the events that will occur later in Revelation 19. These people will be given the honor of becoming part of the army of Messiah. Likewise, in the 24th chapter of Matthew, after He talks about deception, war, and famine, Yeshua tells his disciples that they will also be persecuted (Matthew 24:9–14).

Thus God gives us more than one insight into the persecution that has both already come and will be coming yet, during the days ahead. That the people are asking God when He will avenge their blood and sit in judgment on their persecutors implies that some time has already elapsed; people are becoming impatient and wanting to know when the promised judgment will come. At the same time they are still being given white robes and told to be patient a little while longer. In the end, this whole scenario simply reinforces the idea that more suffering and martyrdom will follow.

In addition, as we have already explained, the basic language of this scene places it "at the foot of the altar," meaning the altar of bronze, which is considered a place of honor. The people are also praying, which is what is done in that location. And, the smoke of the incense from the golden altar represents the prayers of the saints that are worshipping and praying by (i.e., "under" or "at the foot of") the bronze altar in the outer court. Just as coals from the bronze altar are taken to the golden altar, the incense representing the prayers of those at the bronze altar is burned on the coals on the golden altar.

Seal #6 – Terror

Perhaps our understanding of the sixth seal can best be enhanced by looking at it from two different vantage points.

- **First,** let's talk about the actual events.

- **Second,** let's talk about a series of overlays from Matthew 24, in which Yeshua prophesies the same events and gives us quite a bit more insight.

- **Third,** before we move on to the seventh seal at the beginning of the next chapter in this volume, although we mentioned only two vantage points above, let's bring together all that we've talked about so far, from an *entirely different* vantage point, by examining the fascinating yet *decidedly perverse correspondence* between the events of *all* the seals and the events of counter-covenant, as discussed in Volume 1 of this series.

So . . . when we encounter the sixth seal, which we call "terror," we find ourselves dealing once again with the future. Unlike the fifth seal, which focuses on the past, the present, and the future, this one focuses solely on what will be going on in the years ahead. Here's how Revelation lays it out:

6 - The Seven Seals

> ¹²I looked when He broke the sixth seal, and there was a great earthquake; and the sun became black as sackcloth made of hair, and the whole moon became like blood; ¹³and the stars of the sky fell to the earth, as a fig tree casts its unripe figs when shaken by a great wind. ¹⁴The sky was split apart like a scroll when it is rolled up, and every mountain and island were moved out of their places. ¹⁵Then the kings of the earth and the great men and the commanders and the rich and the strong and every slave and free man hid themselves in the caves and among the rocks of the mountains; ¹⁶and they said to the mountains and to the rocks, "Fall on us and hide us from the presence of Him who sits on the throne, and from the wrath of the Lamb; ¹⁷for the great day of their wrath has come, and who is able to stand?" (Revelation 6:12–17)

Clearly, by bringing about a whole series of cataclysmic astronomical and geological events, God is trying very hard to get man's attention one more time, to see if He can convince more of mankind to turn back to Himself. By the time the world reaches this point it could look like a *Mad Max* movie. But sadly, most of God's efforts will be ignored, as shown by the way the "kings of the earth . . . the great men . . . the commanders of the rich and the strong . . . and every slave and free man" all hide in caves and among the rocks in the mountains, begging the mountains to fall on them to hide them from God.

If this isn't running from God – literally – we don't know what is. Instead of repenting, which is what God so strongly wishes they would do, people are so overcome by terror, based on their total lack of a covenant relationship with the same God who is now beginning to bring judgment upon them, that they do the exact opposite and try desperately to run away.

In the Tanakh, God often called the Jews stiff-necked. Now it looks like *every*body is stiff-necked. Thus they also make the same huge mistake King Saul made so many centuries earlier. Saul ran from God and embraced witchcraft rather than trusting the only one in the universe who actually could have helped him. There is no obvious reference to witchcraft in the above verses, but God clearly intends to demonstrate that He alone controls the earth, the sky, the sun, the moon, the planets, the stars, and the winds, all of which are elements common to various kinds of witchcraft and sorcery, including astrology, tarot cards, necromancy, and various other futile attempts to tap into false-idol power over things that God alone commands.

Even more sad from God's perspective, in the lives of so many people God has already tried numerous warm-fuzzy-with-arms-around attempts to draw us to Himself, giving us multiple opportunities to make a decision and start protecting ourselves by integrating His principals into our lives. So now He finally begins to turn up the heat, not because He's a mean ogre but because His divine standards of justice and love demand that He bring upon them the curses they chose themselves.

This same pattern of behavior, on the part of mankind, will be seen again and again as it was in Torah throughout Israel's history. As just one example, it should remind us of the confrontation between God and Pharaoh back in Exodus. Beginning by turning the waters to blood and ending by killing all the firstborn of the people and their beasts, God used the very things that the Egyptians worshipped to judge them.

All of this also amounts to a very strong allusion to the judgments in Torah, for ignoring God. The lesson is clear – mankind has violated Torah, in multiple ways, and now come the curses as promised in Deuteronomy 28 and Leviticus 26.

The only controversy we sometimes encounter in discussions of these verses involves the false notion that, because the stars fell to the earth and the sky was split apart and rolled up like a scroll, these must be signs of the Second Coming. In actuality, the Second

6 - The Seven Seals

Coming is quite a ways away yet. These verses are simply telling us that the very sky itself has been wounded by the centuries and centuries of apostasy in which mankind has indulged.

Even so, many people may still cling to the notion that the principles in Torah apply only to the Jews. And yet, throughout the book of Deuteronomy we see that the principles God gave to Moses, to give to the Jews, were *also to be given to the rest of the nations* (Deuteronomy 4). Thus we now see, right here in Isaiah, that various other nations are being judged by the very same principles. We have included the introductory verses below, but to get the complete picture you need to read the whole 66th chapter of Isaiah:

> ¹Thus says the LORD,
> "Heaven is My throne and the earth is My footstool
> Where then is a house you could build for Me?
> And where is a place that I may rest?
> ²"For My hand made all these things,
> Thus all these things came into being," declares the LORD.
> "But to this one I will look,
> To him who is humble and contrite of spirit, and who trembles at My word.
> ³"But he who kills an ox is like one who slays a man;
> He who sacrifices a lamb is like the one who breaks a dog's neck;
> He who offers a grain offering is like one who offers swine's blood;
> He who burns incense is like the one who blesses an idol
> As they have chosen their own ways,
> And their soul delights in their abominations,
> ⁴So I will choose their punishments
> And will bring on them what they dread
> Because I called, but no one answered;
> I spoke, but they did not listen
> And they did evil in My sight
> And chose that in which I did not delight."
> (Isaiah 66:1–4)

Overlays in Matthew 24

Most believers in Yeshua are familiar with the 24th chapter of the book of Matthew, in which He answers the question below, from His disciples:

> "Tell us, when will these things happen, and what will be the sign of Your coming, and of the end of the age?" (Matthew 24:3)

This particular chapter is one of the most fascinating in all of Scripture and contains a whole series of very definite, very specific clues to the end times, some of which are completely missed and/or misunderstood by Western/Greek-oriented commentators. Some of these "failures to apprehend" we will discuss later, but right here we want to point out something that we find especially interesting.

When Yeshua responded to His disciples He spoke in a very ordered, very linear way about what was coming in the end times. In fact, in terms of their order of presentation, His own comments correspond exactly to the sequence of the seven seals. For example:

- Matthew 24:4–5 talks about being careful and letting no one mislead you, even those who come in His name and claim to be the Messiah, for they will lead many astray. All of this, incidentally, reminds us of what Paul said in his second letter to the believers at Thessalonica:

> ¹BUT RELATIVE to the coming of our Lord Jesus Christ (the Messiah) and our gathering together to [meet] Him, we beg you, brethren, ²Not to allow your minds to be quickly unsettled or disturbed or kept excited or alarmed, whether it be by some [pretended] revelation of [the] Spirit or by word or by letter [alleged to be] from us, to the effect that the day of the Lord has [already] arrived and is here. ³Let no one deceive or beguile you in any way, for that day will not come except the apostasy comes first [unless the predicted great falling away

of those who have professed to be Christians has come], and the man of lawlessness (sin) is revealed, who is the son of doom (of perdition), ⁴Who opposes and exalts himself so proudly and insolently against and over all that is called God or that is worshiped, [even to his actually] taking his seat in the temple of God, proclaiming that he himself is God. (2 Thessalonians 2:1–4 AMP)

Thus we have Yeshua's prophecy about many who come and falsely claim to be the Messiah, thereby causing much deception and leading people into error. All of this precisely corresponds to what the first rider on the white horse is all about.

- In Matthew 24:6, Yeshua talks about wars and rumors of wars. These refer to the second horse rider, who comes to take peace from the earth.

- Matthew 24:7 says that "nation will rise against nation, and kingdom against kingdom, and . . . there will be famines and earthquakes," which overlays the third horse rider.

- Matthew 24:8 reminds us that the death and disease brought by the fourth horse rider are "merely the beginning of birth pangs."

- Matthew 24:9 talks about tribulation, hatred, and death for God's people, which correspond to the fifth seal.

- Matthew 24:10–16 speaks of increasing lawlessness, false prophets, and the Abomination of Desolation prophesied in the book of Daniel, all of which relate to the 6th and 7th seals, and to some prophtic material in the trumpets.

Thus the confrontations we see in the seals, and in Matthew 24 (which embellishes that material), indicate that this is just the beginning of end-times difficulties. God is not through offering salvation yet, but the road is going to get tougher.

The Seal Events Versus the Counter-Covenants

One eternal truth that we have tried to reinforce over and over again is the amazing correspondence and remarkable consistency between various elements of biblical covenant, which have unfolded so dramatically over the centuries. Nowhere is this more true than in the book of Revelation, in which all those elements come together for one last time, in glorious fulfillment for those who have chosen to be in never-ending covenant with God. Unfortunately, Revelation tells us that same fulfillment will strike absolute terror into the hearts of those who have consistently disdained covenant with God, in a manner that will be both awe-inspiring and heartbreaking to behold.

Then we have another "expression" of covenant (if we can call it that), the pathetic copycat attempts by Satan to establish what we've chosen to call "counter-covenant" with himself (see Volume 1 of this series), which also comes to final fruition in Revelation. But it's not a happy-camper convention, as Table 5-1 in this volume will show. Truly, counter-covenant with the devil leads one down the path of total destruction, for what we have in the seals is judgment being poured out on those who don't identify with the authorities/signatories on the ketubah. Everyone is supposed to look like the Bride, but they don't. As the seals are spoken God compares what you look like to see if you fit the right profile, and you either get the blessings or the curses. Your life should identify with the authorities in Torah, as represented by those signatures.

By this point it's very apparent that life on earth has changed substantially. It's very desolate, and more and more we'll see our modern lifestyles degraded back to 19th-century, third-world standards. Millions of people will be massively stressed, especially those who lived luxurious lives before all this began. Even so, as with all wars, some areas will remain unscathed.

In Closing . . .

These are the main points to remember with respect to the first six seals:

- During the first six seals we will see vast increases in spiritual deception, leading to a great falling away from God's principles. This is occurring, with increasing intensity, even as we write this book.

- These events will also usher in a time of increasing warfare and terror, which will involve more and more people throughout the world. We will see increasing economic instability, famine, diseases of all kinds, and lots of death. And, of course, God's people can expect increased persecution during this time.

- Finally, when we get to the sixth seal we will see a great deal of geological and astronomical instability. All this will precipitate extreme fear in the minds of many people, who will eventually do almost anything to escape God's judgment except to repent. In fact, by refusing to accept the truth many will usher in even harsher judgments on themselves.

- We have also seen how the seal events described to John and recorded by him in the book of Revelation parallel the events that Yeshua spoke about to John and the rest of His disciples when they asked Him to reveal the signs of His coming again, as recorded in Matthew 24. Unfortunately for everyone on earth, when these events eventually come to pass, He said that they would represent just the beginning of the time of trouble, not the end.

- As is further confirmed in the book of Revelation, many more signs and troubles will come upon the earth after the sixth seal. These will take much longer than seven years to unfold – in fact, we are still many events away from the last seven years. *None of the events we have discussed up to this point will be included in the last seven years.*

- However, we do believe that the events of the first seal – in particular the perverse spiritual deception that will encompass the entire world – have already begun. Indeed, it has been with us since the Garden of Eden but it has certainly intensified since the death and resurrection of Yeshua. It has especially accelerated during the latter half of the twentieth century and continues doing so to the present day. Over the last few decades we've seen signs that the second horse rider has begun his ride.

- We believe that the fallout from these two riders will multiply in the years immediately ahead, leading to increased immorality and much greater levels of terror and warfare worldwide. All of this will then lead to the events described in the rest of the seals.

7

Shamash to the Seven Trumpets

WE COME NOW TO THE SEVENTH CHAPTER of Revelation, which is the third shamash chapter and is interposed between the sixth and seventh seals. The seventh seal is not due to be introduced until we get to Revelation 8, so we'll never have a better time to pause for a moment, review what we've already learned from previous shamash chapters, and see how this next batch of "dual-layer, parallel-scenes information" fits into the overall scenario.

In this chapter we see a major shift away from the main focus of the shamash chapters, from background scenes in heaven to background scenes on earth. We see four angels given power and authority to do certain things throughout the earth – but not before a special group of people, dwelling on earth, is singled out and marked for a specific purpose.

But before we consider all that, let's review what we've been told in the previous two shamash chapters and the mini-menorah chapters between them.

- Chapter 1 of Revelation, the first shamash chapter, introduced us to God the Father as Yeshua the Messiah, who made a very clear and distinct claim to be the One and only God, the aleph and the tav, both the creator of the universe and the One who would renew it in the latter days. The message He then gave to John included a vision of Himself, surrounded by seven menorahs representing the seven congregations to which He instructed John to write. This scene then introduced the seven letters that occupy chapters 2 and 3. These chapters covered the first mini-menorah.

- In turn, the seven letters revealed the heart, purpose, and plan of God from the creation all the way through His Second Coming to the end of the 1,000-year reign. Clearly, it was His intention to highlight – from Adam through David to Yeshua – certain things for His followers to be aware of and guard against. Knowing their temptations and weaknesses He was giving them alerts, and He was further motivating them by encouraging and applauding whatever they had accomplished. He also gave them something to reach for by giving them various promises – you do this/I will do this – as any good father would do.

- Chapters 4 and 5, the next shamash chapters, took us back to heaven and gave us a more detailed look at what was going on there. God the Father was now seated on His throne with the four cherubim standing guard on all four sides. We also saw the 24 elders, wearing white garments and seated on thrones of their own that surrounded the throne of God. Clearly, God used this scenario to put Himself in the center of the picture, to give us a broader sense of the power and majesty of His kingdom and to further establish His authority.

From the information given to us so far, in these chapters, it becomes very clear that we're being introduced, one-by-one, to the major participants in the Wedding of the Lamb, beginning with the Groom and His Father.

- We then witnessed the first actual heaven-based event of the shamash chapters. It was introduced by manifold weeping because no one could be found who could open up what most translations of the Bible call either a "scroll" or a "book" – although "scroll" is unquestionably more accurate within Revelation's Hebraic/historic context. And then John saw the Lamb, "standing as if slain," who took the scroll and opened it, *exactly as only the bridegroom was legally empowered to do with his own ketubah at an ancient Hebrew wedding.*

As we move along, the basic flow of the narrative that underlies all this should become clearer and clearer. First an individual is introduced. Then we see what he or she does either *in* or *during* the wedding. Then we see the corresponding action played out and amplified by the corresponding mini-menorah that follows each shamash chapter. Keep all that in mind as we move forward.

Chapter 6 of Revelation explains and describes the events that occur at the "opening" of each of the seals. In contrast to the events that are being played out in the shamash chapters, these events involve catastrophes on the earth, the theme of which is death and destruction. Meanwhile, in the shamash chapters, as in the familiar sheep and goats metaphor (Matthew 25:31–33), the sheep are being prepped for the wedding and the goats are being judged. The only real difference here in Revelation is that the goats are being given one last opportunity to be invited.

The Two Major Players

In the shamash chapters up to this point we have met two of the major players in the much-anticipated Wedding of the Lamb. Everyone who has ever read Revelation knows this wedding will occur; it celebrates the victory and re-establishment of all of God's authority over his entire creation, especially the earth. And He shares that authority with His Bride.

But to make sure that we're all on the same page, let's clarify just one more time. Those two players – both of whom are absolutely essential to everything that happens next – are the Father of the Groom (Elohim) and the Groom Himself (Yeshua). In the context of the ancient Hebraic betrothal tradition, as described at length in Volume 1, chapter 3 in this series, the introductions that the book of Revelation have now given us correspond to the coming of the prospective groom and his father to the door of the prospective bride's home, where they would knock for admittance as in the following verse:

> Behold, I stand at the door and knock; if anyone hears My voice and opens the door, I will come in to him and will dine with him, and he with Me. (Revelation 3:20)

However, by chapter 7 we've progressed beyond that point. Therefore, these two shamash chapters do not reflect the writing of the contract itself; they now reflect the purpose and the responsibilities that were written into the contract.

The next three paragraphs come from Volume 1 in this series and shed considerable light on Revelation 3:20:

> Think . . . in terms of the four types of covenant. Remember that they are progressive in nature, meaning that you must enter into the first three covenants, *in order*, before you can enter into number four. Remember also the names and the implications of each one, for you're about to see how the servant, friendship, and inheritance covenants are woven into covenant number four. Each one helps to establish, to support, and to reinforce the ancient Hebrew betrothal contract. In turn, the progression of commitments about to take place during the betrothal process, beginning on the evening when the groom comes and knocks, mirrors the sequence of commitments in the four covenants.

In His capacity as the Ultimate Master of Symbolism, God established four cups of wine as milestones, or "markers," to signify exactly where the betrothal parties were in their negotiations. Each cup corresponded to a covenant, but it also represented something that all the participants had to physically grasp, to physically consume and make part of themselves. It goes without saying that each person would also have to participate mentally and spiritually at each step of the way, or the process would break down.

Now, refer back to the reference to "sup with him" from Revelation 3:20, for it has to do with what traditionally happened next. Once the prospective groom and his father were inside the prospective bride's home, as they worked out all the details of the wedding they would eat dinner together with the prospective bride's family. In this instance, the visiting father and son represented their entire family.

In that same context, by his very presence the Father has shown his approval of what His Son is about to do, and the bride's father will show *his* approval by opening the door. Likewise, the prospective Bridegroom has proven Himself worthy by doing what only the bridegroom was allowed to do within the ancient Hebraic wedding tradition. He has proven his identity and His authority by opening the *ketubah,* which is the marriage contract.

So what comes next? Well, obviously we should expect to meet the next player – or group of players – in the upcoming Marriage of the Lamb. But first, let's consider what the apostle John saw, according to Revelation 7, before those next players are introduced:

> [1]After this I saw four angels standing at the four corners of the earth, holding back the four winds of the earth, so that no wind would blow on the earth or on the sea or on any tree. [2]And I saw another angel ascending from the rising of the sun, having the seal of the living God; and he cried out with a loud voice to

the four angels to whom it was granted to harm the earth and the sea, ³saying, "Do not harm the earth or the sea or the trees until we have sealed the bondservants of our God on their foreheads." ⁴And I heard the number of those who were sealed, one hundred and forty-four thousand sealed from every tribe of the sons of Israel. (Revelation 7:1–4)

When you look at this passage from a Hebraic perspective you get a meaning that's much deeper than what is commonly put forth here. Yes, there are four angels standing at the four corners of the earth. And yes, these four angels have authority over all the earth. And yes, they've been given that authority by God.

But from a broader perspective, throughout all the ages God has maintained a wall of protection around mankind – to bless us, to keep us safe, and to spur us on to do better and greater things. But in this passage, on several layers at once He's pulling back His protection from us. As we've discussed earlier, what's being described here is the initial fulfillment of the blessings and curses of Deuteronomy.

When man totally and willfully rejects God, God begins to withdraw His protection. In fact, the word used for "wind" here is "ruach," which relates to *ruach ha kodesh*, which means *Holy Spirit*. Thus God is withdrawing the protection of His Spirit, to get our attention so we'll come back to him. Thus we also saw His punishment falling upon mankind in Revelation 6, coming exactly as God promised it would to men and women who have literally disdained a close relationship with Him. In this context, in these four verses we should also note the following implications:

- Holding back the wind is a Hebrew idiom meaning that God is holding back His blessings from the earth. Basically, it means that God is withholding His blessing on the harvest, as in Deuteronomy 28 and 29.

- In short, we can see multiple layers of symbology in this chapter. On the simple level there actually are four angels standing on the four corners, holding back the wind. However, the word used for those four corners is *kanaf*, which is also used as a reference to the four corners of the tallit (i.e., the prayer shawl), where God's authority resides.

This introduces the symbolic representation of a tallit, and the authority it embodies is clearly implied here. We all know that the earth is not flat and does not have four corners, but God is using an ancient Hebrew garment to symbolize where his power and authority reside. A tallit is a covering, which equates to covenant. Thus the Father is waiting for His covenant with mankind to be fulfilled. And the Son is the one who made this covenant possible.

As we explained earlier about a tallit, when a Hebrew man holds the tzit-tzit the name of God would be, literally, "in his hands." This is an unmistakable reference to where the ultimate authority of the entire universe lies – within God Himself. He's the one we're talking about when we so often say that safety, healing, and comfort are "in His wings," as demonstrated so dramatically in Psalms 17:8, 36:7, 57:1, 61:4, 63:7, 68:13, and 91:4, to mention just some of the Old Testament references. And "wings," of course, is the English equivalent of the Hebrew word *kanaf*, which brings us back to the four corners of the tallit and the four corners of the earth – i.e., the "wings."

Probably the two most dramatic references to tzit-tzit and "wings" in the B'rit Hadashah would involve Yeshua's own words when he came to Jerusalem for the last time and spoke of His desire to draw His people under the protective covering of His "wings" (Matthew 23:37) even as a hen shelters her chicks. As we explained in Volume 1 in this series, this was a clear, deeper-level reference to His desire to bring us all under the protection of His wings in a marriage relationship.

The second reference would be to the woman with the issue of blood, who touched His tzit-tzit and was instantly healed. Of course, this is not to say that those inanimate pieces of string healed her by themselves; she was healed because of her powerful faith in the One who wore that tallit, who knew instantly what she'd done.

What Does All This Mean?

Let us return, now, to the current passage in Revelation. When the ancient Hebrew people prayed they drew their tallits ("prayer closets") over their heads and grabbed their tzit-tzit, to acknowledge that the only true authority resides in God Himself. And they were also reminding themselves of what they were responsible to do.

Now, add to all this the language of Revelation. Recall that the word for the winds that would not blow "on the earth or on the sea or on any tree" (v. 1) is *ruach*, or *spirit*. In other words, we have here a Hebrew idiom that signifies "holding back a blessing" or "holding back God's spirit," which normally would bring the rains that led to a regular harvest.

However, understand that this reference does *not* mean that God will hold back the blessings of His Spirit from all of mankind. He is *only* drawing back the blessings that would otherwise protect those (including whole nations) who have rejected his "covering" of protection.

In other words, He's pulling back His blessings only from those who have rejected Him. And to be even more specific, He's pulling back the kind of protection that, down through history, has often covered even those who disdained having a righteous relationship with Him. Through the centuries many people have been "covered" by God's blessings despite themselves, via their close associations with those who *did* have such relationships.

Many times God brings a covering over a family, a nation, or a people because of a few who hold strong to their faith in Him. The 18th chapter of Genesis, in which God agreed to spare Sodom and Gomorrah if as few as ten righteous men could be found there, is a perfect illustration of this principle – and also, of course, of the principle that God Himself is unchanging throughout time.

> **Ten Righteous People**
>
> When Abraham bartered with God in Genesis 18, to spare Sodom and Gomorrah if enough righteous people could be found there, he started at 50 and worked his way down to 10. Some people wonder why Abraham stopped at 10 and have even accused him of not being persistent enough, suggesting that God might have been willing to go down to 5, or 3, or even 2.
>
> In our society we embrace the concept of a quorum of 10, which reflects the Hebrew concept of what the number 10 means. Ten, in Hebrew, is the symbol for righteous government. Abraham knew that 10 righteous people could provide a righteous covering/government over a city or a nation. Conversely, he would have known equally well that if he didn't have 10 righteous people (i.e., a righteous government) there simply would not be any hope for that city.

This also parallels what happened in Egypt a few centuries after the Sodom and Gomorrah debacle. God pulled back his blessings, which had previously covered the Egyptians since the days of Joseph because of the presence of His people in their midst. Yet He continued to protect the Israelites. Why? Because He wanted both to *teach Egypt* and to *win as many as possible to Himself*, via the contrast between what happened to His people and what happened to those who refused to believe in Him and would not join His people.

The same thing is happening here in Revelation 7:1–4. This passage is basically saying that He will no longer "cover" anyone by proxy. Everyone will now get what they have earned. Thus, in this scene God is allowing us to see that He will withhold from the earth the *blessings* promised in His Word and will instead allow the *curses* promised in His Word, as found in several places in the Tanakh but especially in the 28th chapter of Deuteronomy and the 26th chapter of Leviticus.

Ironically, given the general conduct of mankind down through the centuries, these same curses have been hanging over our heads for thousands of years, and many of us have richly deserved them. But God has been holding them off. The book of Job is like an extended metaphor illustrating the same point. Evil constantly does its best to destroy everyone even as God constantly protects those who reside under His wings. What happened to Job graphically illustrates what Ha Satan might do to any of us if God withdrew His protection, even temporarily, although even in that case God prevented Ha Satan from doing what he really wanted to.

This whole understanding also answers the question that others have asked so many times, and was once even the title of a popular book: "Why does God allow bad things to happen to good people?" In truth He's not allowing them in the sense that He's promoting or causing them. Most of the time, in millions and millions of situations over the years, He's preventing them.

But now, when the ultimate accounting finally begins, those who have rejected Him and become Satan's bride instead will get exactly what their master wants for them. It's probably no coincidence that, on a human level and in the preponderance of cases (at least in Western countries), it's the bride herself who ultimately chooses who will be her groom.

Now, here in Revelation, just before the events of chapter 8 begin to unfold, we see the very same curses that were promised in

Deuteronomy, which involve God's withholding of the rains (i.e., the blessings of God on the earth) that literally keep all the earth's natural systems functioning properly. All this ties in directly to the concept of withholding the covering of the tallit – "If you're not among my people you don't get my covering of protection." To put it even more simply, it's not a matter of God "adding" or "allowing" curses; it's simply a matter of His withholding His own blessings.

Whenever God's presence resides somewhere, blessings are automatic. But when He withdraws, His blessings go with Him. Here He is finally saying, "All right already! I've jumped up and down and done everything possible to show you that your way is not my way, but you won't see it!" And thus the day finally comes when God gives us completely over to our own choices.

However, right here in this shamash chapter, before we get to the events that result from mankind's God-defying choices, God wants to introduce to us the next players in the bridal party.

The Mysterious 144,000

Because of the "withholding" dynamic explained above, there will be problems with the harvest because God is about to bring some major judgments on the earth. In the next few chapters we will learn what these judgments are. However, before this will happen, He literally seals, or claims, a special group of people to Himself, as detailed in the following verses:

> ⁴And I heard the number of those who were sealed, one hundred and forty-four thousand sealed from every tribe of the sons of Israel: ⁵from the tribe of Judah, twelve thousand were sealed, from the tribe of Reuben twelve thousand, from the tribe of Gad twelve thousand, ⁶from the tribe of Asher twelve thousand, from the tribe of Naphtali twelve thousand, from the tribe of Manasseh twelve thousand, ⁷from the tribe of Simeon twelve thousand, from the tribe of Levi twelve thousand, from the

tribe of Issachar twelve thousand, ⁸from the tribe of Zebulun twelve thousand, from the tribe of Joseph twelve thousand, from the tribe of Benjamin, twelve thousand were sealed. (Revelation 7:4–8)

He's putting a wall of protection around this group, to preserve them intact in spite of all the judgments that will soon come, because they have a very special purpose and calling. Thus we are told in verse 3 that no harming of any kind can begin until His own angel has sealed the 144,000 "bondservants of our God" on their foreheads.

Now. Hundreds of thousands of well-meaning words have been written, over the centuries, about these mysterious 144,000 people, speculating on everything from who they are to why they've been chosen and what they've been chosen for. Along with a lot of other things they've been called "Jewish witnesses for Christ" who will somehow spark a gigantic end-times revival, and they've also been falsely identified as the only people to be extracted from the entire history of mankind who will spend eternity in heaven with God.

On the other hand, nowhere in this passage are the 144,000 described as the *only* witnesses, the *only* ones taken to heaven, or even that their primary job will be to witness. On the contrary, none of the end-times prognostications that turn these people into a huge throng of last-minute witnesses for Him are even remotely biblical. In fact, we see just the opposite of what these people would achieve if many of the popular interpretations were correct – a massive end-times falling away.

A Secret That's Not Really a Secret

On the other hand, to understand who the 144,000 are, all we need to do is examine the Scriptures themselves in their Hebrew context. This instantly provides us with plenty of clues. First, we are told that the 144,000 must be sealed on their foreheads by an angel assigned to that particular task, using a signet ring to do the job. The word for "sealed" symbolizes "choosing"; it also means to "lock up and protect." These guys are being chosen for protection by being "sealed up."

This word for seal has nothing to do with the Hebrew word for "seals" in Revelation 6.

Throughout the Scriptures the signet ring has been used as a symbol of covenant, or two-way commitment. For example:

- Then Pharaoh took off his *signet ring* from his hand and put it on Joseph's hand, and clothed him in garments of fine linen and put the gold necklace around his neck. (Genesis 41:42)

- The king took off his *signet ring* which he had taken away from Haman, and gave it to Mordecai. And Esther set Mordecai over the house of Haman. (Esther 8:2)

- "As I live," declares the LORD, "even though Coniah the son of Jehoiakim king of Judah were a *signet ring* on My right hand, yet I would pull you off." (Jeremiah 22:24)

- A stone was brought and laid over the mouth of the den; and the king sealed it with his own *signet ring* and with the signet rings of his nobles, so that nothing would be changed in regard to Daniel. (Daniel 6:17)

- 'On that day,' declares the LORD of hosts, 'I will take you, Zerubbabel, son of Shealtiel, My servant,' declares the LORD, 'and I will make you like a *signet ring*, for I have chosen you,'" declares the LORD of hosts. (Haggai 2:23)

Each of these six passages (in which we have italicized the words "signet ring" to make them more easily noticed) illustrates the role of the ancient signet ring as a symbol of authority in establishing a covenant and making a commitment. In each of these cases the authority vested in the person wielding the signet ring was absolute, as was the integrity of any subsequent contracts or agreements they might have established. No one else could argue; that person's word was *law*.

But more important, each use of the signet ring in the above references involves a *transference of someone's authority* to someone else, who is then authorized to act on behalf of the first person. The closest modern concept would be giving a power of attorney, which authorizes almost exactly the same kind of "you speak for me" relationship.

In Ezekiel 9:4, 9, and 10 we see a remarkably similar passage, clearly a prophetic "look ahead" to this particular end-times event:

> ⁴The LORD said to him, "Go through the midst of the city, even through the midst of Jerusalem, and put a mark on the foreheads of the men who sigh and groan over all the abominations which are being committed in its midst."
> ⁹Then He said to me, "The iniquity of the house of Israel and Judah is very, very great, and the land is filled with blood and the city is full of perversion; for they say, 'The LORD has forsaken the land, and the LORD does not see!'
> ¹⁰"But as for Me, My eye will have no pity nor will I spare, but I will bring their conduct upon their heads."
> In the Ezekiel passage above, the original Hebrew word for the "mark" on the forehead means "to attach a covenant." That word, as used in this case, is spelled tav-vav, which can also mean "to attach the sign of the covenant." What was the sign of the covenant? The ancient Hebrew tav was a cross, the very one that God told the Israelites in Egypt to put on their doorposts. (Exodus 12:7)

In the Revelation passage, the word that is used for "seal" can also mean the impression left by a signet ring. God is making a covenant with a group of Jewish individuals for His own private reasons. He is picking them out specifically, and it's as though He is writing His name – *or impressing His seal* – on their foreheads.

Thus these 144,000 persons have clearly been marked and given authority for a special purpose, which is yet to be made clear. Obviously, God wants to draw attention to them at this point, quite possibly to make sure we realize that they *will* be protected from any additional judgments that fall upon the earth. They are *not* going to be hurt by anything that might happen next.

Note also that these 144,000 come from the twelve tribes of Israel. Thus they are not symbolic or figurative representatives of Gentiles – the text goes out of its way to talk about the specific Israelite tribes they come from. Plus, in Hebrew the number 12 means *perfected righteous government*; thus 12 times 12 makes it clear that God has determined that *this will not change*. In other words, this part of His plan is firmly established and will not be altered for any reason whatsoever. From a Hebrew perspective this is truly profound.

What's Really Going on Here?

Given all the above, to figure out what's going on here we need to go back to the shamash chapter concept we've already talked about so extensively, to see what comes next in the Marriage of the Lamb sequence.

- The first shamash chapter introduces us to the Father.

- The second shamash introduces us to the Groom.

What comes next? Well, now that He has been recognized as the Groom, Yeshua takes the next logical step and picks out His *groomsmen*, as was done in an ancient Hebrew betrothal sequence. As the prospective groom went away to prepare a place for his bride, he would also "mark out" his groomsmen, giving them authority to act on his behalf. This is what groomsmen do; they serve at the feet of the groom.

Meanwhile, the groomsmen have some very specific markers that should help us identify them as such:

- Ancient Hebrew grooms always picked out *unmarried virgin men*.

- These men always came directly from the groom's own people.

- The groomsmen could also be called *watchmen* or *bond-servants* who generally followed and served the groom, helping him prepare for his wedding with great dedication.

Their Primary Job

Now – at this point in the text of Revelation, these 144,000 young men have still not been specifically identified as what we in the modern age would call *groomsmen*. In truth they won't be, for "groomsmen" is very much a modern term. Even so, to verify that our understanding is correct we need to look at what they do and compare that to the traditional role of those entrusted with groomsman responsibilities, both in the preparations for an ancient Hebrew wedding and during the ceremony itself. Chapter 7 of Revelation does not provide much of this information, but the shamash portion of chapter 14, which talks about the 144,000 in more detail, certainly does. And, of course, you'll find even more information in Ezekiel 9.

However, given the space limitations in this volume – and our even more compelling decision to deal with the chapters of Revelation *in the sequence in which they occur* – we'll quote those chapter

14 verses and expound on them quite a bit more in Volume 3. For the present, let us simply note that these men appear to be groomsmen because:

- They are all from the groom's family. Indeed, they are literal blood descendants of Abraham, Isaac, and Jacob with very specific responsibilities. Yes they are Jews, but they are not last-minute survivors of anything. And they most definitely are not chosen by default because they suddenly opened their eyes in 144,000 end-times "salvation epiphanies" that all just happened to occur at the same propitious moment.

- Everything they are instructed to do in the entire book of Revelation correlates precisely to the traditional role of a groomsman in an ancient Hebrew wedding, as mentioned above. The evidence is overwhelming, which becomes especially self-evident when you read Volume 1 of this series and concentrate on the details of a Hebraic wedding. Even so, as promised above, we will deal with this whole issue in considerably more detail in Volume 3.

About Those Judgments

The mini-menorah of the seals contains events that occur as the proper authorities and promises are addressed by the Groom. The basic principle corresponds to what happened in Deuteronomy, where God told the children of Israel that if they did certain things He would bless them, and if they did not they would rain down curses on themselves.

All mini-menorah judgments are God's judgments for disobedience. These are layered judgments that start out small and end up big, until we will eventually be told that everything is complete and that's it. Like so much else in the Scriptures, all of this corresponds to covenant – the deeper the level the more extensive the consequences for not maintaining the covenant relationship.

No Witnesses in Sight

Perhaps most significant of all, in view of the many misconceptions that have grown up around these 144,000 men, there is absolutely no evidence at all, anywhere in the Scriptures, to support the notion that these are "end-times Jews" who have somehow been assigned to "witness" to others. We don't see any witnessing going on at all, nor are these men the only ones involved in any of these scenes.

Neither are they figurative or symbolic figures representing another people group, organization, or denomination. They are identified as literal blood descendants of Abraham, Isaac, and Jacob, and are not referred to metaphorically in any other way whatsoever.

Likewise, there has been no mention of any "Rapture" yet, and certainly you'd think there'd be some reference to it by now if these men were truly supposed to be "left behind" so they could witness. Indeed, *none of what they are assigned to do includes "missionary work" of any kind whatsoever.* They have completely different assignments, to do exactly what ancient Hebrew groomsmen did at ancient Hebrew weddings – and still do.

Also, nothing that they are assigned to do brings on any end-times revival. Plus, no great end-times revival is prophesied anywhere in the Bible – what's prophesied instead is a great falling away. Even the argument that these men will be witnesses because they couldn't possibly be anything else simply does not wash. This one brings up its own instant, built-in repudiation, for God doesn't do anything by default.

Finally, if these people are supposed to be end-times witnesses and revivalists, since almost no one repents they would be obvious failures. But God doesn't make bad choices; surely, if leading a revival were their assignment they would be far more successful than the rest of Revelation indicates.

An Erroneous Interpretation

This might be an excellent spot in which to add a little note on how to interpret the Hebrew Scriptures. We touched on this subject in numerous places in Volume 1 in this series. In this volume we'd like to refer you to Appendix B, at the back of the book, which explains in far greater detail how to interpret the Scriptures from a proper Hebraic perspective. The material in this appendix has come to be known as the "Seven Rules of Hillel," although the rules were not original with him. They predated Hillel (who died when Yeshua was still a boy) by hundreds of years, and it's even possible that they were written down by others before he came along. However, Hillel was the first one to write them down in a form that has survived to the present day and has long since become the established standard.

Beyond all that we need to be especially careful about making assumptions and teaching ideas that are not found in the text. When we interpret God's Word we need to be super-careful not to impart undue importance to prophecies and predictions that are extra-biblical, including all words and all agendas that support our own pet theories but are not an intrinsic part of the Scriptures we're studying.

Some of the mainstream misinterpretations of Revelation that have come about in this way are very comforting and reassuring to those who believe in them. Chief among these might be the common assumption that the 144,000 are "Jewish witnesses" to those who remain after the Rapture. After all, who wants to go through all the troubles detailed in the pages of Revelation? However, we have not been introduced to a Second Coming yet, and the 144,000 we've discussed briefly above, as much as we might like them to witness to the unfortunate people "left behind" after we "saved" folks have been lifted out, are not called to do that at all.

Neither do we believe that we "saved" ones will be off to heaven by this point, but that's another matter.

Before the Chuppah

The text of Revelation 7 reveals two separate scenes. The first one, involving the angels on the four corners of the earth and the marking of the 144,000, we've already discussed. The second one is a completely different scene, although it includes some of the folks we've already met. These scenes are chronological but they don't follow each other immediately.

However, scene one gives us information we need to have. Thus the second half of chapter 7 introduces us to a huge group of people who are assembled before the throne of God, clothed in white robes and carrying palm branches in their hands. Let us look at the text:

> [9]After these things I looked, and behold, a great multitude which no one could count, from every nation and all tribes and peoples and tongues, standing before the throne and before the Lamb, clothed in white robes, and palm branches were in their hands; [10]and they cry out with a loud voice, saying, "Salvation to our God who sits on the throne, and to the Lamb."
>
> [11]And all the angels were standing around the throne and around the elders and the four living creatures; and they fell on their faces before the throne and worshiped God, [12]saying, "Amen, blessing and glory and wisdom and thanksgiving and honor and power and might, be to our God forever and ever. Amen."
>
> [13]Then one of the elders answered, saying to me, "These who are clothed in the white robes, who are

7 - Shamash to the Seven Trumpets

> they, and where have they come from?" ¹⁴I said to him, "My lord, you know." And he said to me, "These are the ones who come out of the great tribulation, and they have washed their robes and made them white in the blood of the Lamb.
>
> ¹⁵"For this reason, they are before the throne of God; and they serve Him day and night in His temple; and He who sits on the throne will spread His tabernacle over them. ¹⁶"They will hunger no longer, nor thirst anymore; nor will the sun beat down on them, nor any heat; ¹⁷for the Lamb in the center of the throne will be their shepherd, and will guide them to springs of the water of life; and God will wipe every tear from their eyes." (Revelation 7:9–17)

These people have often been described as "the Bride of Christ" and "the Church," but that would be an incomplete and incorrect understanding. If we mean that they are among those who have repented of their sins and accepted Yeshua as their personal Savior, that much would be accurate. But they are certainly in no position – literally – to be mistaken for His Bride.

To explain what we mean we need to back up for a moment. Anyone who has ever witnessed a traditional Hebrew wedding, even here in the modern age, will know instantly what we're talking about when we say the word "chuppah" – pronounced *hoop´-ah* with the accent on the first syllable.

The chuppah is that dome-shaped covering which every traditional Hebrew bride and groom for centuries has stood under during the actual marriage ceremony itself. In modern times the chuppah is often a fairly solid, awning-like covering supported by four wooden or metal poles. But perhaps just as often it can be somewhat of a makeshift-looking affair – perhaps a tallit or two, draped over a framework that serves the same purpose as a more enduring structure. More than once an acceptable chuppah has even consisted of nothing more complicated than the groom's tallit, held over his and his bride's head by his groomsmen.

More Than a Physical Covering

At the same time, in a much larger symbolic sense, the chuppah actually represents quite a bit more. The word chuppah means "a covering," a "protecting," or "a veil," and is connected to the word *kafar*, or *kippur*, which essentially means "to cover" and/or "to make atonement."[50] This is the same word that is used to describe the sixth Hebrew feast that God commanded His people to celebrate, known as *Yom Kippur* (Leviticus 23:26–32), honoring the day on which God closes the Book of Life. It's a celebration of all those who have had their sins "covered" or "forgiven" for that year.

Unfortunately, most modern Christian believers generally know almost nothing about what *Yom Kippur* really represents. So, rather than re-inventing the wheel we have taken the following quote from Volume 1, chapter 8 of this series:

> Ten days after Rosh HaShanah comes Yom Kippur, the Day of Atonement. "On exactly the tenth day of this seventh month is the day of atonement; it shall be a holy convocation for you, and you shall humble your souls and present an offering by fire to the LORD." (Leviticus 23:27)
>
> Yom Kippur is the holiest day on the Hebrew calendar, but it is an odd mixture. It is a day of fasting and mourning for sin, yet a day of rejoicing in God's provision of a covering. The Jewish custom of wearing the kippah further represents this concept. We dress entirely in white, not black. Kippur, or "covering," is the word for the mercy seat on the ark of the covenant, where the Shekinah presence of God rested. Those who are humble in spirit, and truly repentant, shall find grace as a covering. Those who are not repentant

will find judgment. So it is that we wear white, trusting in God to forgive our sins and to complete the work of purity in us.

The last two feasts work together. Hebrew tradition maintains that we are to examine ourselves for thirty days prior to the Feast of Trumpets. God then inscribes our names in the Book of Life on the Feast of Trumpets. After that we have a "final call" of ten more days in which to ask for forgiveness and make restitution. Whether we heed or ignore the trumpet call, what is written in the Book of Life is sealed on Yom Kippur.

Meanwhile, we know what we are made of yet we trust our Lord to be merciful. He is, after all, not only Master of all creation, He is our friend and extends to us a hand of adoption on the Day of Atonement.

Another related word, *kaforat*, is the one for the covering over the Holy of Holies. The Holy of Holies, of course, is where the ark of the covenant was kept, which itself was also "covered" by the wings of the angelic cherubim. This was also where only the high priest could go in, and then only once a year on Yom Kippur. At that moment – wearing only white linen – he was acting as the Bride, coming in to commune with the Groom in the world's most special place. This act was also a symbolic prophecy of what God's future plan would be, which was to reunite with mankind in marriage.

Another familiar extraction from the same root word would be the word *kippah*, which refers to the small round "cap" that most Jewish congregants wear in their synagogues (especially males, although many women wear them too – and sometimes men wear them elsewhere as well), to honor God's injunction in Exodus 28:4:

> These are the garments which they shall make: a breastpiece and an ephod and a robe and a tunic of checkered work, a turban

and a sash, and they shall make holy garments for Aaron your brother and his sons, that he may minister as priest to Me.

Granted, this reference to "turban" actually applied only to the High Priest, but countless generations of Jewish men have extrapolated this into a God-given injunction to wear a head covering (no matter how small) at all times, out of respect for God. Indeed, it has long been part of the Code of Jewish Law,[51] which says: "It is forbidden to walk four cubits without a head covering."

> **To Cover or to Uncover the Head**
>
> Ironically, for hundreds of years Christianity has done precisely the opposite of what the Jews do and has insisted that men remove all head coverings when they came into a church. Supposedly they do so out of respect for God, although nothing in the Bible suggests such a thing, including the 11th chapter of 1 Corinthians. This particular passage refers to the veils that prostitutes wore in Paul's day to show their availability. Prostitutes in Greek society were soliciting relationships with their own gods, and were actually coming into synagogue services trying to win converts.
>
> Nowadays, of course, the Christian custom of uncovering the head has largely disappeared. In many modern churches you can find young men wearing baseball caps, skull-tight scarves, and even fedoras, which indicates either that (1) uncovering the head really must not have been "biblical" in the first place; or, that (2) most Christians just don't care anymore, which means either that it never really mattered to God or that all who do so now are courting His disapproval.
>
> Nonetheless, the origin of the custom of uncovering the head, in the Christian church, came about because of Roman persecution of the Gentilic portion of the Sect of the Nazarenes. The early congregations were composed of both Jews and Gentiles. When the Romans outlawed Judaism, which then included Gentile believers,

> the Gentiles chose to do everything they could to stop looking like Jews. Thus they switched their wedding rings from the right to the left hand (even though the right hand has always been the honored hand), stopped celebrating the Old Testament feasts, switched the Sabbath from Saturday to Sunday, and took their kippahs off. Eventually, all these newer things (and others as well) became "honored customs" even as they replaced the original practices of which they were now complete opposites.
>
> In contrast, the opposite Jewish custom of always covering the head, based on the Bible, the Talmud, and archeological evidence, still prevails within both traditional and Messianic Judaism.

Thus the modern chuppah – and the one in Revelation as well – is related linguistically to (1) Yom Kippur, the Day of Atonement; (2) the Holy of Holies, which had a cloud covering it; (3) the angelic (cherubim) "covering" over the mercy seat on the ark of the covenant.

All of this must be taken into consideration when we read chapter 7 of Revelation. In typical Hebraic thought, the reference to the four angels who are standing at the four corners (i.e., the "points of authority") of a "covering" encompasses all these interrelated meanings. It involves the Holy of Holies, God's desire for marriage "under the chuppah" with His Bride, and especially in this case, the literal removal of God's protection from "over the top" of much of mankind.

Where Do the Bride and Groom Stand?

Let's now consider one more point that the second half of chapter 7 of Revelation makes clear. The proper, traditional position of the bride and groom is always *under* the chuppah. And the proper, traditional position of all the guests at the wedding is always *in front of* the chuppah. And that's precisely what's going on with that vast multitude in Revelation 7:9 who were "standing before the throne [i.e., the Holy of Holies] and before the Lamb, clothed in white robes, and palm branches were in their hands." This multitude is the wedding guests, not the Bride. And yes, the Wedding of the Lamb will occur in the temple of God.

This brings up two more details about this vast throng, besides its placement, that immediately identify these people as guests and not as the Bride. First, guests at ancient Hebrew weddings were always given white robes to wear before the wedding started. They were not permitted to be there if they were not clothed in white, just as the bride and groom were, and by tradition such coverings were always provided at the door. The idea was that everyone in attendance should represent and support the concept of purity in marriage as ordained by God.

In a further example of oft-missed biblical symbolism, the "purity" of the guests, as represented by their single "covering," goes back to the first layer of covenant. Blood (or service) covenant is one layer only; here (i.e., in both Revelation 7 and Matthew 22, as explained momentarily) that one layer would represent the guests' *only* layer of covenant with respect to the marriage happening in front of them.

Thus the reference to the white garments worn by the guests is also a metaphor that should serve to remind us of the first time the single-layer covenant (servanthood) was mentioned in the Bible. It should remind us of how that first covering came about when God "covered" Adam and Eve, and how the Lamb Himself fulfilled the promise of that first covering for His guests. In contrast, the bride wore four layers of covering to represent all four layers of covenant.

All of this information helps to explain why the king in Yeshua's parable, in the 22nd chapter of Matthew, was so angry. One of the wedding guests was pretending to have the authority to be at the wedding without having any appropriate covering, as follows:

> ⁸Then he said to his servants, 'The wedding feast is ready, but those invited were not worthy. ⁹Go therefore to the main roads and invite to the wedding feast as many as you find.' ¹⁰And those servants went out into the roads and gathered all whom they found, both bad and good. So the wedding hall was filled with guests. ¹¹"But when the king came in to look at the guests, he saw there a man who had no wedding garment. ¹²And he said to him, 'Friend, how did you get in here without a wedding garment?' And he was speechless. ¹³Then the king said to the attendants, 'Bind him hand and foot and cast him into the outer darkness. In that place there will be weeping and gnashing of teeth.' ¹⁴For many are called, but few are chosen." (Matthew 22:8–14 ESV)

The word from which we get "friend" in verse 12, above, can be interpreted as either enemy *or* friend.[52] You had the choice to be either one. This passage is also a prime example of what will eventually happen to people who try to gain salvation – or to deal with God in other ways – on their own terms. The great Creator of the Universe, who retains all knowledge and all authority, is not about to let us be in charge of anything as important as the basis on which we will enjoy eternal fellowship with Him. Simply put, we don't make the rules any more than the waiters and the busboys decide how the Hilton Hotels will run their business.

Second, the guests in front of the throne are all holding palm branches, which by ancient tradition they would throw down in front of the bride and groom at a wedding, or in front of Passover lambs as they were led in for slaughter. Indeed, they would do the same at the inauguration of a new king, thereby to convey a sense of honor and praise. Likewise, the multitude did this for Yeshua when he entered Jerusalem for the last time, thus recognizing and even worshipping Him as their King.

Also, all ancient brides and grooms were recognized as kings and queens when they were first married, especially during their first week together. And that's how they were treated for their initial week of married life, with palm branches thrown in their paths. This is exactly what the guests before the throne are prepared to do.

One final point. In the portion of Revelation that we've covered so far we've been introduced to the Father of the Groom, the Groom Himself, and the groomsmen. Now we're starting to catch a glimpse of the preparations at the site where the wedding will occur.

The Hebraic verbiage implies both a present and a future tense at the same time. In other words, it's happening and WILL be happening. Thus, the participants are already beginning to congregate at the site of the future wedding.

In Closing . . .

- Revelation 7 is the third shamash of the mini-menorahs. It has given us a description of what's going on in heaven and on the earth, and gives us further information to introduce us to the next seven events that will be unfolding very soon.

- Here in chapter 7 of Revelation God makes it clear that the time has come for Him to render certain judgments on earth.

- The first of these judgments (and the only one fully detailed in this chapter) involves His decision to remove his "covering of protection" from the earth, meaning that those who are not in personal covenant with Him will no longer be protected from "coming events."

- However, before we learn more about those events we are introduced to the next group of participants in the Wedding of the Lamb, the 144,000. Contrary to what many commentators have told us, these men will function as Yeshua's groomsmen and *not* as "Jewish witnesses for Christ" during the end times.

- We see a great throng of people before the throne (i.e., the "chuppah" under which the Groom and His Bride will be married), rather than under the chuppah with the Groom Himself.

- This last distinction, coupled with the white robes the people in front of the throne are wearing, clearly identifies them as guests at the wedding and not as part of the Bride.

- The second half of Revelation 7 is also a picture of what is taking place, arranged in chronological order. We've seen all the players being identified, and now the people are beginning to assemble where the wedding ceremony is about to take place. However, please note that no Bride or Groom is present yet.

- Now that these participants in the wedding have all been identified we can look forward to the blowing of the shofars – the "trumpets" – that will signal the coming of the Groom for His Bride.

8

The First Trumpets

IT WOULDN'T BE THE SLIGHTEST EXAGGERATION to say that our decades-long studies of Revelation have brought us a lot of delightful discoveries. Some of those might even qualify as "Aha!" moments, during which we might be equally inclined – like Archimedes – to holler "Eureka!" except that we don't want to encourage any more Greek associations.

There's too much of that going around already, which is probably why many biblical scholars don't seem to "get" the ancient Hebraic context of the trumpet chapters, Revelation 8, 9, and 11. There's nothing even remotely Greek about them, but certainly there are a lot of built-in Hebraic connections. One of the biggest and grandest is introduced to us at the very beginning of chapter 8:

> [1]When the Lamb broke the seventh seal, there was silence in heaven for about half an hour. [2]And I saw the seven angels who stand before God, and seven trumpets were given to them. [3]Another angel came and stood at the altar, holding a golden censer; and much incense was given to him, so that he might add it to the prayers of all the saints on the golden altar which was before the throne. [4]And the smoke of the incense, with the prayers of the saints, went up before God out of the angel's hand.

⁵Then the angel took the censer and filled it with the fire of the altar, and threw it to the earth; and there followed peals of thunder and sounds and flashes of lightning and an earthquake. ⁶And the seven angels who had the seven trumpets prepared themselves to sound them. (Revelation 8:1–6)

As other references and events in this chapter indicate, that "silence in heaven for about half an hour" in verse 1 is a clear reference to the thirty minutes of silent prayer that always accompanied a major portion of each of the ancient temple services that occurred twice each day. Via what God allowed him to see, the apostle John is giving us one more fascinating glimpse into the events in heaven that lead directly up to the Marriage of the Lamb.

The trumpet chapters of Revelation detail an ancient temple service. The only difference is that it's not a temple service on earth; it's a temple service in heaven on which the earthly services were based – and will be again someday. Except that it's not just one service; it's actually a picture of what begins on Friday morning and concludes on Friday evening with the Erev Shabbat ("Evening of the Sabbath") service. In fact, this particular Erev Shabbat is a very *specific* Erev Shabbat that occurs only once a year, on the eve of Shavuot, last of the seven God-ordained Hebrew feasts, which we will discuss in greater detail in chapter 10 of this volume.

In a sense we're back to that three-legged chair we mentioned way back in chapter 2, whereby we repeatedly discover distinct linkages between ancient Hebraic rituals and what's happening in the book of Revelation. And such connections are fascinating, direct, and absolute, for they tell us things we could otherwise only wonder about.

Daily Repetition

Given all the above, before we can understand Revelation's explanation of the seven trumpets – especially those details that are more or less "in the background" – we need to have a clear conception of what took place during the ancient temple services that occurred on a regular basis in Jerusalem. Again and again, throughout Revelation we will see short flashes, or "visions," of these services. So please bear with us momentarily while we provide more information, at which point we'll come back to the main subject of this chapter.

In ancient times, each temple day would start at the rising of the sun with the opening of the temple gates. The day would then be broken up into two main parts: the morning service and the evening service. Sacrifices would be brought to the priests at both services, and incense would be taken inside the inner court and put on the hot coals on the golden altar. These coals had originally come from the bronze altar out in the outer court. The incense would then burn up and produce thick smoke that would fill the area with a wonderful aroma.

No Need for Perfume

In fact, it was often said that women did not need to wear perfume in Jerusalem because the aroma from the burning incense on the golden altar filled the air all the way to Jericho about eighteen miles away. To bring that reference into modern times, one of our good friends is a Levite currently on duty in Jerusalem, working on researching and restoring some of the ancient Israelite temple implements and customs.[53] He and his co-researchers now know the exact formula for the incense that was once offered on the golden altar, based on extensive research that included analyzing small samples that have survived to the present day. And, even though they're about 2,000 years old, when those samples are burned in very small amounts they still produce an incredible odor that almost certainly could be smelled several miles away, if it were burned in quantities roughly equal to what was once offered twice every day on the golden altar.

At the same time, while the smoke from the incense wound its way upward from the inner court, in the outer court of the temple the Levites ceased their musical praise to God and all the worshippers fell on their faces in silent prayer.[54] The qualities of this incense, especially its ability to saturate the air to such an amazing extent, is a clear reflection of how God sees our prayers and our communications with Him, both as something very sweet but also as something that "saturates the air" and moves Him to pay attention and respond.

Olfactory Excellence

The formula for the ancient incense that God provided His priests – and which He required them to guard carefully since it was intended for use only in the temple – has truly amazing properties that function on at least two major levels at once. First, given the large numbers of animals that were slaughtered as offerings every day, it would be perfectly logical to expect to encounter some horrendous smells. Even modern meatpacking plants, using modern refrigeration, advanced ventilation systems, and featuring the very best in additional odor-control procedures, do not very often provide pleasant olfactory experiences. But when the incense produced by the God-given formula is burned it has the amazing ability to almost completely "knock down" and mask any unpleasant smells that might otherwise rule the daily air.

More amazing still, all the flies and other insects that would normally be attracted in overwhelming numbers were completely held at bay. Those flies don't hunt at all! The result is another of God's magnificent "hedges of protection" that sheltered His people when they did what He prescribed in the way that He prescribed it.

In other words, the incense doubled as God's fumigation system.

Thus the smoke from the burning incense symbolized the prayers of the Israelites, going up before God. This period of prayer would then end when the priest of the day, chosen previously by lot to enter the inner court and burn the incense on the golden altar, would re-emerge from the inner court after completing his obligation for that service. With his hands at shoulder height, each one held in a way that resembled a *shin* (which is a Hebrew letter that is basically shorthand for *El Shaddai*, meaning "God Almighty"), he would then pronounce the Aaronic blessing[55] over the worshippers, symbolizing that their prayers had been accepted by God.

Most important to our understanding, the time period during which the incense burned, the smoke "went up," and the worshippers prayed silently, lasted approximately half an hour. And all of this corresponds precisely to what's happening in these two verses from the eighth chapter of Revelation:

> [1]When the Lamb broke the seventh seal, there was silence in heaven for about half an hour.
>
> [4]And the smoke of the incense, with the prayers of the saints, went up before God out of the angel's hand. (Revelation 8:1, 4)

Sideways for a Moment

Now let's go sideways a little more for just a moment and talk about something else we mentioned earlier. In the previous shamash chapter we saw a huge congregation of people (Revelation 7:9), standing before the throne. These were obviously the worshippers who assembled twice a day, every day, during the morning and evening services. In the two verses above, these people were offering up their personal prayers simultaneously with what the priests were doing as they poured the incense onto the coals on the altar.

The silence in heaven amounted to reverence before God. The Hebrew word used here is *demamah*, meaning *"Be still before God."*

In other words, be calm; be astonished (reverent); be silent so you can hear.

The temple services were conducted twice a day to provide various offerings, including sin offerings, thanksgiving offerings, and burnt offerings, all of which are described in detail in several places in the Bible – but especially in the book of Leviticus. These offerings were brought by anyone seeking forgiveness and cleansing, and by those wanting to offer praise and worship to God. The familiar passage from the 4th chapter of Ephesians about not letting "the sun go down on your anger" is a reference to getting yourself right with God and with others before the evening service ended.

> [26]Be angry and do not sin; do not let the sun go down on your anger, [27]and give no opportunity to the devil. (Ephesians 4:26–27 ESV)

The Daily Trumpet Blasts

During the course of the day, seven separate trumpet blasts were deployed at the temple as follows:

- One trumpet blast occurred in the morning when the gates of the temple were opened.

- Three more trumpet blasts occurred during the morning service.

- Three additional trumpet blasts occurred during the evening service.

Thus there were four trumpet blasts in the morning and three more in the evening, for a total of seven trumpet blasts throughout the day. However, these trumpets themselves were not hand-hammered silver trumpets; they were ram's horn *shofars*. To make a shofar you remove all the soft material from the inside of a ram's horn, dry out the inside surface and smooth it down, bore a hole in the tip (i.e., the small end) that fits into your mouth, and blow through the mouthpiece you've now created.

However, if you've ever blown a shofar you know that doing so is not quite as simple as putting it to your lips and blowing. It takes a lot of practice to develop good technique. But, even though it's really not possible to play Haydn's trumpet concerto on a shofar, a truly accomplished shofar blower can create a surprising mix of rhythms and sounds. As you might expect, the smaller, single-twist horns tend to be higher pitched while the longer ones tend to produce lower tones.

Probably the most surprising quality of a good shofar is the incredible volume of sound it can produce – literally sufficient to be heard for miles in the open air. This is undoubtedly why the shofar was used in warfare to communicate with the troops. The ancient Israelites blew four main shofar patterns, each for specific purposes. Each of these four "blast-patterns" was used in the temple services, as follows:

- **Tekiah** – a single blast used as a call to gather or assemble

- **Shevarim** – three short blasts, used to call to repentance and also to signify mourning

- **Teruah** – nine staccato blasts; this is the call to war

- **Tekiah Gadolah** – the long, *great* blast, which is the call of Messiah

The Trumpets Begin

Now that we understand a little more of the background for what's coming up, let us continue. In chapter 8 of Revelation we are introduced to the seventh seal. The sixth seal finished at the end of chapter 6, and as we have seen, chapter 7 was a shamash chapter that provided us with introductory information and a foundation for understanding the next seven events. These are what we will call the "trumpet" events, corresponding to the trumpet mini-menorah on our diagram in chapter 3 of this volume.

Now we see seven angels before Him about to blow their trumpets. Another angel is then given the responsibility to take coals from the golden altar and throw them upon the face of the earth. Not surprisingly, in the Old Testament, throwing coals from the altar represented God's judging of the earth, as exemplified in Ezekiel 10.

As each one of the angels blows his trumpet, that "scattering over the city" (Ezekiel 10:2) is exactly what is about to happen on the earth. Seven disasters will then befall the earth and its inhabitants, as introduced by the individual trumpet blasts that – as we explained above – are arranged in two separate groups, four in the morning and three in the evening, exactly as they were in the daily temple services on earth. Four of the resulting disasters affect the earth, the atmosphere, and the seas and springs of water, while the last three are called the "woes" and are very different from the first four, as we shall see.

These trumpet events unfold in a definite sequence, as though God is offering to each of us, both individually and corporately, a series of final opportunities to come on our own initiative and offer ourselves, through repentance, to Him. Like Paul, who died daily to his own sinful desires, so God asks us to abandon our own ways and replace them with His ways. We have the choice to willingly submit our lives to conform to His plan, to lay our lives down willingly for God. Or, He will take our lives through judgment. The coals can either bring purity through humility or death through our own rebellion. We get to choose.

Thus the coals represent an outpouring of the judgment of God, and signify cleansing. And the earth, His creation, will be cleansed either by our own initiation, individually, or through *His* initiation via judgment. The time for prevarication has now passed; in a word, it's over.

First Trumpet: The Earth Is Struck

As we have explained, the seven trumpet calls can be separated into two groups. The first group, comprising trumpets one through four, describes various catastrophic disasters that destroy at least one-third of specific portions of the earth. Many of these disasters are brought on by stars, mountains, or fire mingled with blood falling from the sky upon the earth.

Revelation 8:7 tells us:

> The first sounded, and there came hail and fire, mixed with blood, and they were thrown to the earth; and a third of the earth was burned up, and a third of the trees were burned up, and all the green grass was burned up.

The word used here for "burned" is *seraph*, which means "to burn, to consume," especially via the burning of dead bodies. In contrast, other words are often used for "burn," including *esh*, *ba'ar*, *barad*, and *kharar*, none of which carry the same connotation as *seraph*.

As explained in Volume 1 of this series, a seraph is also a *flaming angel*, full of fire and covered with eyes. The word *seraph* implies heavenly fire, which is exactly what a seraph (i.e., a burning angel) both *is* and *does*. Therefore, this judgment is coming at the hands of angelic beings, functioning at the Lord's behest, causing fire. In symbolic terms, this judgment results indirectly from the influence of angels who have been sent to earth to bring such judgments on earth's inhabitants.

Also, the word seraph comes from the root word, *sar*, which means *prince*. Thus the word seraph also means "prince of heaven," even – for example – as Nebuchadnezzar means "prince of the god Nebo." A prince is a servant of a king, which communicates a whole new dimension here.

Sar is also the word from which we get our English word "sir." Thus may all the "misters" and "sirs" out there serve God as well as these angels do!

Vegetation Struck

Now, what would happen if you took away a third of all the trees and the grass? Certainly you would introduce a great deal of instability into the earth's atmosphere, causing significant change. We're talking about a massive amount of smoke and soot being released into the atmosphere, preventing normal solar heating and nighttime cooling. The eventual results could include volatile temperatures and other extreme weather changes resulting from different atmospheric gas ratios. This could cause changes in the ozone layer, which would then allow significant increases in how much of the sun's radiation reached the earth, which could cause far more serious sunburns and skin cancers than what we might usually experience.

Under normal conditions, when we experience a huge disaster in one area of the globe, the earth has the ability to compensate and adjust. But given this kind of catastrophic event, it is quite possible that the earth's moderating ability would be lost or severely reduced. In that case, the eventual results could easily be more catastrophic than the immediate results themselves.

Some prognosticators speculate that the fire could be from an atom bomb and thus would be manmade. Others suggest that it could come from an extra-terrestrial source, such as a catastrophic collision with an asteroid or even a mega-volt electrical zinger from the good folks on Venus.

Others believe that it would derive from nothing any more unusual than God's own hand of divine judgment, finally acting to bring about the curses He promised rebellious mankind so long ago. Overall, the text itself is very general so we can only speculate and arrive at rough conclusions about what will actually happen. But, at the very least, the literal implications would be destruction – or serious impairment – of the earth's ability to sustain life by providing food and shelter.

Second Trumpet: The Seas Are Struck

Revelation 8:8–9 tells us:

> [8]The second angel sounded, and something like a great mountain burning with fire was thrown into the sea; and a third of the sea became blood, [9]and a third of the creatures which were in the sea and had life, died; and a third of the ships were destroyed.

The mountain in these verses is probably just what the text says, crashing into the sea and causing some kind of ocean-wide catastrophe. However, any such "mountain" could also be an asteroid, a comet, a meteorite, or some other cosmic entity landing in the sea, flooding our seashores and causing tidal waves big enough to swamp our largest ships. By necessity, something of that type would have to be far bigger than any sort of "ecological disaster" brought about by countries or corporations, for ships to perish instantly.

Mountains also represent nations, so possibly one-third of the nations of earth will be affected. Plus, it's worth remembering that mountains in the Bible often symbolize "high places" which, in historic terms, were places of false worship, especially of Ba'al and

Ashteroth. So, God could well be saying here that He is going to "throw down on you the very gods you worship, so you can see once-and-for-all who they really are and how much real influence they actually have."

In modern terms, such high-place-worshipped gods could be many things amounting to modern-day equivalents of Ba'al himself – money, status, and other forms of earthly power to name just a few. And any or all of these could be involved, if only symbolically or in a more causative role, as in the casting of a mountain into the sea. This whole business could also be reminiscent of the judgments God brought upon the Egyptians, during Moses' time. He literally used their gods (and/or symbols of their gods) against them, to demonstrate His own vast superiority.

In verse 9, in the "third of the sea became blood" passage, the word for blood is *dahm*, also meaning *red*. But from a Hebrew perspective the connotation is the "guiltiness that comes from shedding" blood. The sea also represents mankind; taken together, this passage strongly suggests that *man's* blood will be required. Indeed – in Hebrew thought – when blood is spilled via murder the only thing that purifies the land on which the blood was spilled is the blood of the murderer. At this point mankind is guilty of many murders (including "abortions") about which God is certainly going to have a few things to say at some point.

What could this do to the ecology of the earth? The literal implications are that something such as a meteorite or comet is colliding with the earth, by falling into the ocean. This would have cataclysmic repercussions, certainly for the oceans but also for those who live along the edge. Tidal wave, anyone?

Also, all the resources that the oceans provide man will be vastly diminished.

8 - The First Trumpets

Third Trumpet: The Waters Are Struck

Revelation 8:10–11 tells us:

> ¹⁰The third angel sounded, and a great star fell from heaven, burning like a torch, and it fell on a third of the rivers and on the springs of waters. ¹¹The name of the star is called Wormwood; and a third of the waters became wormwood, and many men died from the waters, because they were made bitter.

In biblical times the plant called *wormwood* was well known for the poisonous extracts that came from its flowers and leaves. In more modern times wormwood became the source of an alcoholic drink called *absinthe*, one of the more potent liquors (and not a liqueur, incidentally) that achieved quite a bit of popularity in the late 19th and early 20th centuries, especially among the so-called European intelligentsia, particularly in France. Absinthe made somewhat of a comeback in the 1990s; however, it has to be sweetened with sugar and diluted with water at up to a 5-to-1 ratio before most people can drink it.

What has all this to do with the passage above, from Revelation? To answer that question we have inserted two additional passages below, from the books of Deuteronomy and Proverbs, in which the references to wormwood are clear and unambiguous. In the first case, wormwood is connected to poison and death. In the second case, wormwood is equated to the bitterness and emptiness that comes from sexual immorality, which is a devastating sin against God and which we also know for certain will be (indeed, already *is*) one of the main hallmarks of the end of days.

> So that there will not be among you a man or woman, or family or tribe, whose heart turns away today from the LORD our God, to go and serve the gods of those nations; that there will not be among you a root bearing poisonous fruit and wormwood. (Deuteronomy 29:18)

> ¹My son, give attention to my wisdom, incline your ear to my understanding;
> ²That you may observe discretion and your lips may reserve knowledge.
> ³For the lips of an adulteress drip honey and smoother than oil is her speech;
> ⁴But in the end she is bitter as wormwood, sharp as a two-edged sword.
> (Proverbs 5:1–4)

Conversely, the "springs of waters" spoken of in the passages from Revelation are symbols of the source of life, which could also refer to women who – in Hebraic thinking – are considered exactly that. Likewise, as we indicated above, the sea represents mankind. Thus man's life is literally being obliterated even as all primary life-producing mechanisms on the earth have been damaged, including springs of water.

Thus God seems to be making it clear that the time during which He allowed us to choose idol worship is over. The time for judgment has come at last, and any of those who persist in defying Him will receive the judgments predicted back in Deuteronomy, 3,500 years ago. He is no longer holding back the price for disobedience. Even though the pagans (and many well-educated but "enlightened" people as well) worship stars, trees, and rivers, the inability of all such lowercase gods to accomplish anything except what God Himself ordains is now about to be revealed.

Incidentally, the word translated as "star" literally does mean "star," so perhaps we'll have a flaming rock – or something of that type, such as a meteorite – falling to earth and causing death and destruction. When this star (or meteorite) falls on the earth it will affect fresh water all over the globe, which will further degrade the food supply and make it even more difficult for life as we know it to exist.

8 - The First Trumpets

Fourth Trumpet: The Heavens Are Struck

The fourth trumpet on the trumpet mini-menorah is in the shamash position. Given how central and prominent that position is, we really ought to be paying attention. Revelation 8:12 tells us:

> The fourth angel sounded, and a third of the sun and a third of the moon and a third of the stars were struck, so that a third of them would be darkened and the day would not shine for a third of it, and the night in the same way.

At one time or another, all celestial bodies have been considered gods. Even today, through our various deceptions (especially including astrology), in many ways we still bow down to the same things. In the end, God will make it clear to us that they are all powerless on their own. They are all subject to His governance, based on His regulations. Thus the judgments of God will be poured out, as they were in Egypt, against the very things that man has worshipped down through the centuries.

Also, the language of this passage parallels the kind of language that was used in ancient days to allude to celestial phenomena such as lunar and solar eclipses. Thus this very language could well be fulfilled in that way.

In terms of immediate repercussions, remember that the sun was created on the fourth day, even as it now sits in the fourth (i.e., *shamash*, the Hebrew word for "sun") position. On our planet the sun also represents the beginning of the food chain, via photosynthesis. Obviously, with a third less sunlight the plants of the earth will produce less oxygen. And so the spiraling cycle, which began with the first three trumpets, will continue.

In Hebrew thinking the sun also represents God, the source of life. As we learned in Revelation 7, where the *ruach* was being withheld, this is a perfect example of what happens when God withholds Himself – His relationships, His warmth, His wisdom, and His direction. An obvious parallel comes in Genesis when God turned away from Cain, meaning that He turned His face away and removed His identity from this one man in particular.

In Hebrew thinking, the moon metaphorically represents mankind and is a reflection of life and God. God is revealing here that He will take away His identity from some people because of their rejection of Him. Their lives and their identities will be dimmed and eventually will be darkened because of their lack of trust and reliance on Him.

The precise cause of what's foretold in verse 12 is unknown. It could be something major – a comet, volcanic activity, an asteroid – or something less dramatic but equally harmful. We simply do not know, but we can be sure that the environmental repercussions will be huge.

However, on the bright side, for at least a third of the time, global warming will not be a problem.

Much Delusion and Little Repentance

This whole discussion of the first four trumpets brings to mind the following passage from Isaiah:

> ⁶Wail, for the day of the LORD is near!
> It will come as destruction from the Almighty.
> ⁷Therefore all hands will fall limp,
> And every man's heart will melt.
> ⁸They will be terrified,
> Pains and anguish will take hold of them;
> They will writhe like a woman in labor,
> They will look at one another in astonishment,
> Their faces aflame.

8 - The First Trumpets

> ⁹Behold, the day of the LORD is coming,
> Cruel, with fury and burning anger,
> To make the land a desolation;
> And He will exterminate its sinners from it.
> ¹⁰For the stars of heaven and their constellations
> Will not flash forth their light;
> The sun will be dark when it rises
> And the moon will not shed its light.
> ¹¹Thus I will punish the world for its evil
> And the wicked for their iniquity;
> I will also put an end to the arrogance of the proud
> And abase the haughtiness of the ruthless.
> ¹²I will make mortal man scarcer than pure gold
> And mankind than the gold of Ophir. (Isaiah 13:6–12)

One of the most striking, revelatory episodes in the entire Bible occurs in the 24th chapter of Matthew, when Yeshua's disciples asked him, "Tell us, when will these things happen, and what will be the sign of Your coming, and of the end of the age?" (Matthew 24:3). We have already discussed this chapter in some detail, and it's certainly true that "of that day and hour no one knows, not even the angels of heaven, nor the Son, but the Father alone" (Matthew 24:36), but there is another set of parallels embedded within this chapter that seldom seem to be recognized for what they are.

Let's begin with another short passage from Volume 1, chapter 8 in this series:

> In Hebrew, this festival [i.e., Rosh HaShanah] was called *Yom Teruah* or "Day of the Trumpet Blast." While it occupied just one day on the calendar, it occupied a twenty-four-hour time slot within a forty-eight-hour period. No one knew exactly which hour or on which of the two days the trumpet blast, literally the "alarm" trumpet blast (the call to war) called *Yom Teruah*, would sound. In Yeshua's time, Rosh HaShanah was known as "The Day and the Hour Which No Man Knows." It is the first of the three fall feasts which,

grouped together as a unity, another *echad*, are called "The Days of Awe."

In the larger scheme, God is literally "calling the nations" by using these trumpet judgments to do what He has always called His people to do on Rosh HaShanah, which is commonly known in English as the *Feast of Trumpets*. Rosh HaShanah is preceded by a thirty-day period of introspection and repentance, to allow us to make sure that our relationships are right with God and our fellow man. More important, by bringing our worthiness up-to-speed we prepare ourselves to be part of the army of God. A major focus of Rosh Hashanah is *preparation*, making ourselves ready for what will happen when God comes.

At the same time, to put things in a slightly broader perspective, Rosh HaShanah is the culmination of a thirty-day period as described above, which then ushers in an additional ten-day period of self-examination and repentance during which His people are expected to act on what they've discovered about themselves. This is what "making ourselves ready" truly involves. The goal is to prepare for God's review, to make ourselves "right with Him" prior to Yom Kippur. At one extreme, this clearly equates to the curses in the book of Deuteronomy and the final Day of Judgment. At the other extreme it equates to what the righteous will inherit.

Sadly, the Scriptures make it clear that many people – perhaps even millions of temporary survivors – will still not be willing to repent. Even as they are today, and perhaps even more so in the days ahead, many people will be so incredibly deceived that, rather than responding to God's near-final attempts to get their attention and call them to repentance by demonstrating over and over the absolute accuracy of His repeated warnings, they will curse Him instead.

The more trouble they go through the more they will curse God, even as so many people are doing today as we write these words.

8 - The First Trumpets

The Rapture Delusion

The Western church of today has been set up for a massive delusion via the widespread belief that all its members will be swept up to safety in what's commonly called the end-times "Rapture," the origin of which is discussed more fully in chapter 5 of this volume. Unfortunately, the events of the letters, seals, and trumpets in Revelation make no mention of any such Rapture.

Nonetheless, the Rapture theory teaches that God's people will not experience any of the tribulations found in Revelation. Yet nothing could be farther from the truth. In fact, God has given us a parable that predicts how people will respond to the coming of tribulation. Matthew 24:45–51 tells us the following story about a servant of God:

"Who then is the faithful and sensible slave whom his master put in charge of his household to give them their food at the proper time? Blessed is that slave whom his master finds so doing when he comes. Truly I say to you that he will put him in charge of all his possessions. But if that evil slave says in his heart, 'My master is not coming for a long time,' and begins to beat his fellow slaves and eat and drink with drunkards; the master of that slave will come on a day when he does not expect him and at an hour which he does not know, and will cut him in pieces and assign him a place with the hypocrites; in that place there will be weeping and gnashing of teeth."

As end-time events unfold, this servant reacts by rejecting his Master, thinking that his Master had delayed His coming. People who are invested in a non-biblical theory that assures protection from end-times troubles could be set up to respond in the same way. As various catastrophes begin to occur, the faith of believers could also waver as they realize that Yeshua is not returning in the manner and the time frame they expected. Scripture predicts that commitment to God will grow cold among many believers (Mat-

> thew. 24:12; I Timothy 4:1). This would be especially true in an atmosphere in which belief in Messiah would not be fashionable. Persecution, temptation, and deception have their greatest impact when faith and belief in God's Word are most weak, and especially when that Word has been misinterpreted.

The Three Woes

Revelation 8:13 introduces trumpets five, six, and seven by referring to them three times as "woes." These final trumpets are terrible indeed, bringing unsurpassed afflictions as a precursor to God's final wrath upon mankind.

However, before we consider the last three woes individually, notice the parallels between the construction of each of these mini-menorahs. Recall how the seven seals included the *four* horsemen of the Apocalypse and the *three* seals that followed. Here we have *four* trumpets afflicting nature and then we have the last *three* afflicting mankind, separated from the first four by a slightly different designation – the *three woes*. Obviously, it's a four/three pattern paralleling several aspects of the temple services that we've already identified.

The Fifth Trumpet (First Woe)

Revelation 9:1–12 tells us:

> ¹Then the fifth angel sounded, and I saw a star from heaven which had fallen to the earth; and the key of the bottomless pit was given to him. ²He opened the bottomless pit, and smoke went up out of the pit, like the smoke of a great furnace; and the sun and the air were darkened by the smoke of the pit.
>
> ³Then out of the smoke came locusts upon the earth, and power was given them, as the scorpions of the

earth have power. ⁴They were told not to hurt the grass of the earth, nor any green thing, nor any tree, but only the men who do not have the seal of God on their foreheads. ⁵And they were not permitted to kill anyone, but to torment for five months; and their torment was like the torment of a scorpion when it stings a man.

⁶And in those days men will seek death and will not find it; they will long to die, and death flees from them. ⁷The appearance of the locusts was like horses prepared for battle; and on their heads appeared to be crowns like gold, and their faces were like the faces of men. ⁸They had hair like the hair of women, and their teeth were like the teeth of lions. ⁹They had breastplates like breastplates of iron; and the sound of their wings was like the sound of chariots, of many horses rushing to battle.

¹⁰They have tails like scorpions, and stings; and in their tails is their power to hurt men for five months. ¹¹They have as king over them, the angel of the abyss; his name in Hebrew is Abaddon, and in the Greek he has the name Apollyon. ¹²The first woe is past; behold, two woes are still coming after these things.

The fifth trumpet (and the first woe) involves a falling star (i.e., a fallen angel) identified as *Abaddon* in Revelation 9:11. Abaddon has fallen from heaven and has been given the key to the shaft of the abyss. In Hebrew this star is called *kokhav Nephal*, which means a "fallen star" but can also imply a "devil-Nephal."

This introduces a whole catalog of important facts that we need to understand, which we have taken the liberty of listing below, under bullet points:

- **Verse 1:** Where does this key come from and who was it given to? To answer that, let's review a little bit of history.

First of all, when did this angel/star actually fall? Note that verse 1 says that John *saw* a star that *had* fallen. This verse was written around 92 AD; meanwhile, about sixty years prior, Yeshua died on the cross and then went down with the key to Gehenna (hell) to free those of His who were locked up there. Until that moment, Abaddon had held the key.

How did he get it? Well, before man chose to sin against God back in the third chapter of Genesis, two cherubim rebelled and brought about the fall of man. Abaddon took with him the key to the shaft of the abyss, and thus he's known as the Angel of Death. And, he has the power to lock people away after they die, because of their sin. Remember, the Angel of Death was the one who passed over Egypt, "passing over" the Israelites who put the blood on their doorposts but taking the firstborn of all other families.

But as soon as Yeshua died without sin He won back the authority to own that key. Therefore, the first thing He did after His resurrection was to go down into hell and free all the captives. He also made a proclamation of freedom (*karah*),[56] essentially walking in and boldly declaring, in no uncertain terms, "Liberty! Freedom! You are now free!" This amounted to a release from bondage for those whom God owned, which was now possible because Abaddon no longer had any power over them through death because of their sin. On the other hand, contrary to the way this passage is often interpreted, Yeshua did not go down and preach or teach. Here's how the apostle Peter put it:

> [18]For Christ also died for sins once for all, the just for the unjust, so that He might bring us to God, having been put to death in the flesh, but made alive in the spirit; [19]in which also He went and made proclamation to the spirits now in prison, [20]who once were disobedient, when the patience of God

> kept waiting in the days of Noah, during the construction of the ark, in which a few, that is, eight persons, were brought safely through the water. (1 Peter 3:18–20)

When did all this happen? Chapter 12 of Revelation talks about a male child who was born with a dragon (Satan) waiting to consume Him. But the dragon wasn't able to consume Him; that is, he wasn't able to cause Him to sin during any part of His life on earth, as ultimately proved by Yeshua's victory over sin on the cross.

This brought on a war between Ha Satan and the archangel Michael, because Yeshua didn't succumb to Satan's temptations. Michael thus powered the righteous angelic hosts over the rebellious angelic horde, which meant that Satan lost His place in heaven and fell to earth (Revelation 12:7–9).

To help understand all this, remember that – prior to Yeshua's triumph over sin – Satan was still able to come before the throne of God, as he did back in the book of Job. However, in a post-resurrection world Satan has been able to function only upon the earth and within its atmosphere.

In other words, though we don't always clearly differentiate between these two devils – largely because the evil being we call Ha Satan has always been the front man – *Abaddon fell to earth with him and has been lurking behind the scenes ever since.* And, he has had a lot of power that we, for the most part, do not recognize and therefore do not acknowledge as we should. Abaddon has also been left free to roam around at will.

The key was then reclaimed by God when Yeshua took it back after His resurrection. This came about because of His victory at the Cross, plus the resulting authority He won back over death. As we are told very early in the book of Revelation:

> ¹⁷When I saw Him, I fell at His feet like a dead man. And He placed His right hand on me, saying, "Do not be afraid; I am the first and the last, ¹⁸and the living One; and I was dead, and behold, I am alive forevermore, and I have the keys of death and of Hades. (Revelation 1:17–18).

For many people, understanding all this should bring on a huge "Aha!" moment. Even so, for reasons known only to God, Yeshua then gave the key back to Abaddon, so that sometime in the future Abaddon would be able to unlock the abyss one last time. In other words, God has one final bit of work for Satan to do to bring on the end, and that's the release of the teraphim He locked up back in Genesis. So it's a "use one time only" kind of thing.

Who's in the Abyss?

- **Verses 3–11:** Before we even begin to discuss these verses, let's fill in some background. Teraphim are of the third and lowest form of angels and are able to appear as men. We are encouraged to be hospitable because – conceivably – at any time we might entertain "angels unawares" (Hebrews 13:2, to quote the familiar *King James Version*). However, not all of the teraphim allied themselves with God. Some fell under deception and joined ranks with Satan, perpetrating the sin of sexual union with the daughters of man, which then produced offspring called *Nephilim* (Genesis 6:4). The book of Enoch explains how these very same former angels were locked away in the abyss as punishment for their deeds, which is also referred to in the books of 2 Peter and Jude as referenced in our previous book, Volume 1 in this series.[57]

  Now . . . how does the paragraph above apply to verses 3–11? Well, what beings were locked up in the abyss? Undoubtedly, these would include all the fallen angels mentioned (but not specifically named) in Genesis 6, who were locked away in judg-

8 - The First Trumpets

ment for perpetrating the Nephilim upon the earth, meaning the abominable acts spoken of in Genesis 6, which involved fallen angels interacting with human women to produce the "giants" known as Nephilim. These are the ones who were largely responsible for bringing on the flood of Noah's time. Most of their names were given in chapter 7 of the book of Enoch, as also quoted in Volume 1 of this series.

But remember, though many Bible scholars seem to forget this verse and never mention or deal with it in any significant way, the book of Genesis tells us:

> The Nephilim were on the earth in those days, and also afterward, when the sons of God came in to the daughters of men, and they bore children to them. These were the mighty men who were of old, men of renown. (Genesis 6:4)

- **Verse 3:** Abaddon proceeds to open and release locusts from the pit. The Hebrew word for "locust" in this verse is *arbeh*.[58] The root for Arbeh means "to knot, to weave, to intertwine, to mingle, to lie in wait, to watch in ambush" and indicates an undergirding of craftiness and cunning, paralleling exactly what we see in the books of Enoch and Jude. A derivative of this root is *arbah*, which means "a pit, chimney, or smoke hole."

What Is This Nonsense About Helicopters?

Despite what many commentators have suggested over the years, the locusts that we encounter in the book of Revelation are not helicopters. Neither are they vertical takeoff aircraft or whirling dervishes on jet-propelled pogo sticks.

In other words, the apostle John is not struggling to interpret some future technology that was nonexistent in his day. Once again we must remember that this is a Hebrew book. Without looking at

> everything John said from a Hebraic perspective, we'll simply never understand. He's describing what he saw, in detail, from that perspective only.

In Revelation 9:3 these "locusts" (i.e., another group of fallen angels) are released and allowed to harm mankind for five months, but only those without the mark of God. These locusts are devils, not to be confused with demons who are the offspring of teraphim and mankind (see Volume 1). Men and women will wish to die from the pain of these creatures' stings, but death will elude them.

Even the descriptions of the locusts in these verses make more sense when you understand that these are fallen angels. When we are told that they have crowns of gold on their heads and have faces like the faces of men, the text is referencing fallen angels. They also have iron breastplates, and iron is a symbol for angelic activity in the earth.

The apostle John is seeing fallen angelic creatures in their physical form. Thus God is bringing us knowledge of a stark reality that our generation has never known about, which has been hidden for the last 1,500 years.[59] He is revealing "true truth" rather than the sanitized versions we've so often been taught. John is using terms that he is fully acquainted with. He was a student of the book of Enoch, and he was very familiar with all these creatures. Indeed, one of the most significant revelations in the book of Revelation is about the return of the Nephilim.

A Special Kind of Pain

- **Verse 3–5:** Many times the word *locusts* (verse 3) is used as a Hebraic reference to devils. For example, the book of Joel lists four different kinds – *gnawing, swarming, creeping,* and *stripping,* but these also symbolized something far more dangerous. In verse 5, the word for pain that the locusts/teraphim are in-

8 - The First Trumpets

structed to inflict on those with no seal on their foreheads (i.e., the pain that lasts five months) is the Hebrew word for pain that signifies *birth* or *labor* pains.

This brings up a fascinating yet horrific possibility. The "five months" in this verse could well refer to the minimum gestation time for a viable human fetus, which could also be the more-or-less "normal" gestation period of a Nephal – an offspring of a fallen angel and an earthly woman. Birth pains per se would not last this long, but the pain of carrying a Nephilim baby certainly could be felt during the entire pregnancy.

The following verses from Matthew could also be prophesying the same thing:

> ³⁷"For the coming of the Son of Man will be just like the days of Noah. ³⁸"For as in those days before the flood they were eating and drinking, marrying and giving in marriage, until the day that Noah entered the ark, ³⁹and they did not understand until the flood came and took them all away; so will the coming of the Son of Man be. (Matthew 24:37–39)

That "they were eating and drinking, marrying and giving in marriage" hardly seems like a sign that you could use to identify the second coming of Yeshua, yet here it is, listed among all the other signs in Matthew. The word interpreted "they" is a mischaracterization of the two words *Ba'al Nashim*. In English, those two words mean that devils/idols (Ba'al) and women (Nashim) will be eating and drinking and marrying in the days preceding the coming of Messiah. So, what Yeshua was really saying was that one of the signs will be fallen angels having relations with human women, and the result will be the return of the Nephilim.

Likewise, the well-known second chapter of the book of Daniel talks about iron (fallen angels) and clay (mankind), mixing their seed together:

> And in that you saw the iron mixed with common clay, they will combine with one another in the seed of men; but they will not adhere to one another, even as iron does not combine with pottery. (Daniel 2:43)

This is an end-times prophecy about the last kingdom that will be on the earth at the coming of Messiah. This also certainly seems to be another obvious allusion to devils having intercourse with women. Also, these locusts have breastplates of iron, which (as we indicated previously) is an image of angelic activity on earth. Likewise, Peter goes out of his way to identify what's coming, any or all of which could easily be referring to the same abominations:

> [9]The Lord knows how to rescue the godly from temptation, and to keep the unrighteous under punishment for the day of judgment, [10]and especially those who indulge the flesh in its corrupt desires and despise authority. Daring, self-willed, they do not tremble when they revile angelic majesties, [11]whereas angels who are greater in might and power do not bring a reviling judgment against them before the Lord.
>
> [12]But these, like unreasoning animals, born as creatures of instinct to be captured and killed, reviling where they have no knowledge, will in the destruction of those creatures also be destroyed, [13]suffering wrong as the wages of doing wrong. They count it a pleasure to revel in the daytime. They are stains and blemishes, reveling in their deceptions, as they carouse with you, [14]having eyes full of adultery that never cease from sin, enticing unstable souls, having a heart trained in greed, accursed children; [15]forsaking the right way, they have gone astray, hav-

8 - The First Trumpets

ing followed the way of Balaam, the son of Beor, who loved the wages of unrighteousness; [16]but he received a rebuke for his own transgression, for a mute donkey, speaking with a voice of a man, restrained the madness of the prophet.

[17]These are springs without water and mists driven by a storm, for whom the black darkness has been reserved. [18]For speaking out arrogant words of vanity they entice by fleshly desires, by sensuality, those who barely escape from the ones who live in error, [19]promising them freedom while they themselves are slaves of corruption; for by what a man is overcome, by this he is enslaved.

[20]For if, after they have escaped the defilements of the world by the knowledge of the Lord and Savior Jesus Christ, they are again entangled in them and are overcome, the last state has become worse for them than the first. [21]For it would be better for them not to have known the way of righteousness, than having known it, to turn away from the holy commandment handed on to them. [22]It has happened to them according to the true proverb, "A DOG RETURNS TO ITS OWN VOMIT," and, "A sow, after washing, returns to wallowing in the mire." (2 Peter 2:9–22)

In other words, it's certainly quite possible that once this evil horde has been freed they'll be perpetuating many of the same crimes they engaged in back in Genesis 6. This could then give Satan some of the extra manpower he might need to make the final moves in his grand plan, which he's been pursuing since the Garden of Eden. He intends to claim to be the god of the entire world, while sitting (however temporarily!) on the throne of the real God in Jerusalem.

- **Verse 11:** As we have already indicated, Abaddon is the very same angel of death who was allowed to destroy all the firstborn in Egypt of those who had not applied blood to their doorposts (Exodus 12:23).

As a former cherub of God, Abaddon could well be one of this first order of angels, who were given special authority and placement around God's throne. In partnership with Ha Satan, Abaddon fell from his place in heaven along with a third of the other angels. They succumbed to the deception of the one we now call "Satan," who was another of the six cherubs surrounding God's throne.

Most English versions of the Bible render the original Hebrew of Daniel 9:27 as follows:

> "And he will make a firm covenant *with the many* for one week, but in the middle of the week he will put a stop to sacrifice and grain offering; and on the wing of abominations will come one who makes desolate, even until a complete destruction, one that is decreed, is poured out on the one who makes desolate." (italics added)

In this context, "week" is understood to be the last seven years preceding the second coming of Messiah. However, the majority of Bible students think that the word "he" in this verse is the False Messiah (the Antichrist), who is making a covenant with the Jews to rebuild the temple. But on the contrary, the Hebrew word interpreted as "he" comes from the root word *gabar*, which means "a soldier" and also means "to be strong, to be powerful, to be mighty, to confirm, to act proudly; insolent." All of this suggests a much more likely allusion not to Satan but to Abaddon.

In other words, Abaddon will be making a "covenant with the many" that he will then break in the middle of the seven years. But who are the "many"? Revelation 9:1–11 gives us a detailed account – the "covenant with the many" could be between Abaddon and the teraphim from the pit, just as the book

8 - The First Trumpets

of Enoch described how they entered into covenant with each other to create new offspring in partnership with earthly women.

These teraphim have been locked away for nearly 5,000 years and will be *very angry* with Satan and Abaddon, so he *has* to give them something in return. This verse is *not* predicting a future contract between the Antichrist and the Jews; those who are entering into this contract are not Jews at all – they are teraphim.

Unfortunately, the Antichrist-Jew-covenant prediction is another example of how to build an interpretation on a false concept. In actuality, the temple will be rebuilt starting sometime after the second seal, and will be completed sometime before the sixth trumpet. When Gog and Magog come together and attack Israel at the sixth trumpet, that will cause a cessation of temple practices (see Joel 1:9), which means that the temple had to have been rebuilt and functioning sometime prior. In addition, our introduction to this chapter makes it clear that the trumpets describe a temple service. For additional information on this topic, see chapter 4 of Volume 1 in this *Lost in Translation* series.

To wrap this section up, it's good to be aware that the Hebrew equivalent for the English word "woe" also means "lamentation." A woe both "is" and "involves" a lamentation; thus it's even worse than everything that has come before. How much worse? Well, it includes the return of the Nephilim, in major force, and that's pretty bad indeed.

Think about it. Until now, God has allowed nature to reflect His anger and bring about His punishment. But now He is releasing Satan and his hordes, at which point Satan gets to play his own end game. And what does Satan therefore do? Well, he begins by creating his own race of people and corrupting and deceiving the rest of mankind, just as he did in Genesis. They will be causing additional pain and suffering – and remember, these devilish

Nephilim procreators have had 4,500 years to simmer and stew and figure out creative ways to be as nasty as they possibly can once they get the chance.

To review, then, in the fifth trumpet we get introduced to Abaddon, who releases thousands of teraphim out of the bottomless pit, who've been locked away for the better part of 4,500 years. They begin their retaliation by causing mankind to suffer in horrendous ways. But then, as we shall soon see, they themselves will make a covenant with the unrighteous to again attack God's chosen people, just as we saw in seal #2.

This ends the first woe, and now comes the second.

The Sixth Trumpet (Second Woe)

During the past few events, beginning with the second seal and continuing until the sixth trumpet, God's holy temple in Jerusalem has been under construction. Now it's complete, and the symbolism is unmistakable. God is saying very clearly, "Here are my temples, the original in heaven and now the rebuilt copy on earth. So now there's no more excuse; it's time to worship for real."

Meanwhile, the abyss has been opened and the devil's hordes are being released, to form a large army made up of a sinister combination of devils and humans. Here is how Revelation 9 describes the scene:

> [13]Then the sixth angel sounded, and I heard a voice from the four horns of the golden altar which is before God, [14]one saying to the sixth angel who had the trumpet, "Release the four angels who are bound at the great river Euphrates."
>
> [15]And the four angels, who had been prepared for the hour and day and month and year, were released, so that they would kill a third of mankind. [16]The number

of the armies of the horsemen was two hundred million; I heard the number of them.

[17]And this is how I saw in the vision the horses and those who sat on them: the riders had breastplates the color of fire and of hyacinth and of brimstone; and the heads of the horses are like the heads of lions; and out of their mouths proceed fire and smoke and brimstone.

[18]A third of mankind was killed by these three plagues, by the fire and the smoke and the brimstone which proceeded out of their mouths. [19]For the power of the horses is in their mouths and in their tails; for their tails are like serpents and have heads, and with them they do harm.

[20]The rest of mankind, who were not killed by these plagues, did not repent of the works of their hands, so as not to worship demons [devils], and the idols of gold and of silver and of brass and of stone and of wood, which can neither see nor hear nor walk; [21]and they did not repent of their murders nor of their sorceries nor of their immorality nor of their thefts. (Revelation 9:13–21)

The sounding of the sixth trumpet reveals that the devils who have been set free from the pit, described as horses with lions' heads, are now allied with mankind as symbolized by the men riding on their backs. Ironically, the description we are given here matches perfectly with that of an ancient mythical beast. In Persian mythology, this particular creature was known as a *manticore*. According to both written and pictorial records, it was a fire-breathing beast with a lion's head, a horse-like body, and a serpent's or scorpion's tail. Some had bat-like wings and some didn't, although the creatures referenced in Revelation definitely do. They were known as "consumers of men," which is certainly fitting because they are allowed to consume a third of mankind.

False Colors

The riders wear breastplates displaying colors of covenant – red, blue, and yellow. However, even though these three primary colors represent the covenants of servanthood, friendship, and inheritance, the human riders have not entered into covenant with their Creator. A closer look shows that these people have chosen instead to be governed and controlled via the behavioral bondages that result from relationships with Satan. They have entered into counter-covenant with God's primary adversary. These horse riders have chosen not to obey the real King but have joined ranks with the enemy instead, as symbolized by their position on the horse-beasts.

Together they are given the power to kill one-third of mankind by fire, smoke, and sulfur. In Revelation 9:20 we are reminded of the sons of Adam who were not killed but still did not repent of their deeds and continued to worship demons. The word interpreted as "demons" is actually *shedim* in Hebrew, which means "devils" or "destroyers." Teraphim are devils, not demons, and they obtain worship from those survivors who still will not repent of their deeds. In verse 20 these same devils are described as idols of gold, silver, bronze, and clay.

Obviously, this image refers back to Daniel 2:29–45, which contains Daniel's divinely inspired interpretation of Nebuchadnezzar's most famous vision. This vision described a layered statue of gold, silver, bronze, and iron, with feet of iron and clay. (Incidentally, clay is a combination of little pieces of stone, mixed with detrital material such as leaves and wood. All these are the same materials that make up the devil-idols of Revelation 9:20.)

This statue is commonly interpreted as a prophecy dealing with the four evil kingdoms that will attempt to rule over mankind by the power of evil. As most mainstream prognosticators teach, this prophecy has been largely fulfilled by the rise of the Babylonian,

8 - The First Trumpets

Medo-Persian, Greek, and Roman Empires. The Roman Empire is represented by the iron legs. The iron legs and the iron/clay feet of Daniel's statue suggest that two phases of Roman tyranny will occur. In AD 476 the first phase ended; we still await the final phase.

Likewise, just as the silver portion of the statue had two arms to represent the two national entities that were allied together (i.e., the Medes and the Persians), the two legs represent two different influences that the Romans had, and also *will* have. These were the capitals of the two divisions within the Roman Empire – the Western capital, Rome, which controlled the Western portion, and the Eastern capital, Constantinople, which controlled the Eastern portion.

In Old Testament Hebraic typology, iron represents angelic activity on earth, including that of devils, while clay represents mankind. Daniel 2:43 tells us that these two groups, as symbolized by iron and clay, will mingle their seed together. Thus this final phase of the Roman Empire will again usher in sexual union between teraphim and mankind, which is exactly what happened in the days of Noah (Genesis 6:2–4; Daniel 2:43; Matthew 24:38).

This fits perfectly into the overall scenario. Throughout time, Satan has attempted to control God's creation, especially mankind, by deceiving men into worshiping him and his cohorts, the other fallen angels. Here in Revelation we will now see one final attempt by Satan to complete and finalize his government and make it into an everlasting kingdom. This doomed kingdom will be a composite of all the other satanic attempts to rule creation.

The technique he's going to use, to deceive the whole world, will be coming to the Jews, the Christians, and the Arabs, and attempting to prove to them that he's the long-awaited messiah they've all been watching for. Their acceptance of him will allow him to sit on the throne, in the earthly temple, and claim to be

God. However, even Satan's best efforts will fail with the coming of the real King.

But meanwhile, even though his victory will be quite short-lived, Satan will have fulfilled the very goal that he first envisioned way back in the book of Genesis, in the Garden of Eden – which was to steal God's identity and authority. This identity and authority God actually gave to man, to whom God also gave authority to rule His creation. Because Satan has now "become man" by becoming a man-beast (he looks like man; he pretends to be God) he now believes he can claim to rule over creation as well.

In other words, Satan has finally achieved the goal he's always wanted . . . except that he will have only 3.5 years to enjoy it. God and Satan both had "plans" and both are being fulfilled at the same time. It's also no accident that both kingdoms are claiming to represent the Creator-God, with the corresponding right to rule all of creation. This is a battle for control, and it's finally coming to its ultimate conclusion. Sadly, most people don't see the long continuum, the whole panorama. And without a clear perspective on the whole thing it's impossible to really see how it's playing out.

This Isn't Armageddon Either

Unfortunately, right here at the sixth trumpet, some people confuse this war with the one that occurs in Revelation 6 at the second seal. But on the contrary, the text of Revelation is talking about two entirely separate wars. Here are two of the obvious proofs:

- In the first war, at the second seal, one-fourth of the population is destroyed, through sword, famine, plagues, and wild beasts.

- Here, at the sixth trumpet, one-third of the population is destroyed by fire, smoke, and/or sulfur brimstone.

8 - The First Trumpets

We should also recall that the previous, second-seal war is a great war caused by the sons of Esau, known in ancient days as the Edomites but now known as Arabs. The Arabs have always been opposed to Israel. We also know the result of the first war through prophecy – Israel wins! And her victory ushers in the period of time we referenced above, between the second seal and the sixth trumpet.

Now . . . at this point it's really important for you to take the time to read through the longest and clearest references in the Bible to this huge conflict between Gog and Magog. Ideally you would read the complete text of Ezekiel 38 and 39, for these two chapters are absolutely essential to an understanding of what's going on here in Revelation.

We would also urge you to read the entire book of Joel, which is only three short chapters long and focuses mostly on this same sixth-trumpet war. In Joel, the manticores are referenced as locusts, as in the book of Revelation. After you read all that we will continue our commentary. Meanwhile, we're including the first five verses of Joel 1 and the first ten verses of Ezekiel 38, directly below, to help you get started:

> ¹The word of the LORD that came to Joel, the son of Pethuel:
> ²Hear this, O elders,
> And listen, all inhabitants of the land
> Has anything like this happened in your days
> Or in your fathers' days?
> ³Tell your sons about it,
> And let your sons tell their sons,
> And their sons the next generation.
> ⁴What the gnawing locust has left, the swarming locust has eaten;
> And what the swarming locust has left, the creeping locust has eaten;
> And what the creeping locust has left, the stripping locust has eaten.

⁵Awake, drunkards, and weep;
And wail, all you wine drinkers,
On account of the sweet wine
That is cut off from your mouth. (Joel 1:1–5)

¹And the word of the LORD came to me saying, ²"Son of man, set your face toward Gog of the land of Magog, the prince of Rosh, Meshech and Tubal, and prophesy against him ³and say, 'Thus says the Lord GOD, "Behold, I am against you, O Gog, prince of Rosh, Meshech and Tubal.

⁴"I will turn you about and put hooks into your jaws, and I will bring you out, and all your army, horses and horsemen, all of them splendidly attired, a great company with buckler and shield, all of them wielding swords; ⁵Persia, Ethiopia and Put with them, all of them with shield and helmet; ⁶Gomer with all its troops; Beth-togarmah from the remote parts of the north with all its troops – many peoples with you.

⁷"Be prepared, and prepare yourself, you and all your companies that are assembled about you, and be a guard for them. ⁸"After many days you will be summoned; in the latter years you will come into the land that is restored from the sword, whose inhabitants have been gathered from many nations to the mountains of Israel which had been a continual waste; but its people were brought out from the nations, and they are living securely, all of them. ⁹"You will go up, you will come like a storm; you will be like a cloud covering the land, you and all your troops, and many peoples with you."

¹⁰"Thus says the Lord GOD, "It will come about on that day, that thoughts will come into your mind and you will devise an evil plan ¹¹and you will say, 'I will go up against the land of unwalled villages. I will go against those who are at rest, that live securely, all of them living without walls and having no bars or gates, ¹²to

8 - The First Trumpets

capture spoil and to seize plunder, to turn your hand against the waste places which are now inhabited, and against the people who are gathered from the nations, who have acquired cattle and goods, who live at the center of the world.' (Ezekiel 38:1–12)

Who Needs Walls Anymore?

As we indicated above, note in the passage from Ezekiel that Gog and Magog (Russia) are now attacking Israel in an environment of peace. They are literally attacking a country whose inhabitants are living in unwalled villages (Ezekiel 10:11). And the temple of those people has also been rebuilt, which means that the deterring influence of the Arabs must be gone. More than likely, after the war described in the second seal (and other Old Testament prophecies as well) between the Edomites (Arabs) and Israel, the Arabs are simply not there anymore in numbers sufficient to bother Israel.

This period of peace to which Ezekiel 38 refers will provide a time in which Israel will be able to recover from war. Literally, Israel will now live in "unwalled villages," in contrast to the current time period in which she's living, both metaphorically and literally, in walled villages. However, in that context, please note that the word "wall" refers here (1) to physical walls with heavily guarded entrances and exits and (2) to a shield of protection, based on radar and other advanced detection systems that warn the country of any imminent military attacks. The Israelis will now be able to rebuild the temple because, once again, they will have regained full control of Temple Mount.

But let's be clear. Here we are talking about the great Gog/Magog war. The teraphim/Nephilim are joining together with mankind to bring ultimate destruction to the Jews . . . except that it doesn't quite work out that way. Gog and Magog are incensed because the Jews have become "fat and happy" and are living in peace, with no walls around their cities and no one to prevent them from worshipping twice a day in their temple.

Once again God has blessed His people and has glorified His name through them, which Gog/Magog simply cannot stand. And thus they launch the second of the three wars in Revelation. This is *not* the war that brings about the final destruction of the enemies of God, but it certainly will be catastrophic. However, this will usher in the perfect political and economic environment from which the False Messiah will arise. Keep in mind, however, that all of this has to happen prior to His Second Coming.

A Quick Look Ahead . . .

At this point, in contrast to the way much of Revelation has been laid out so far, God deviates from His orderly presentation of the events brought about by the blowing of the seven trumpets. Right here in the middle of the 6th trumpet, after the description of the huge war we've just read about, chapter 10 of Revelation introduces us to the seven thunders. And momentarily at least, the seven thunders discussion can really seem to take us sideways.

Why God does so at this particular moment is not immediately clear, but if there's one thing we should remember about the divine workings of the Divine Mind it's this very simple rule. *He does not do such things without a divine purpose*, which we will do our best to explore in the final two chapters of this book.

Meanwhile, note at least one interesting "coincidence" that is most likely no coincidence at all. It's obvious that God has inserted the thunders between (1) His discussion of the cursed ones,[60] just completed, and (2) His discussion of the blessed ones that is yet to come. In other words, what we've completed so far amounts to the first five-and-a-half trumpets; what's yet to come is the remainder of trumpet number six, plus trumpet number seven. It's interesting to note that this follows the same general pattern we find in the

8 - The First Trumpets

seals, where we encounter six seals, then we insert a shamash passage, then we encounter the seventh seal.

This division corresponds to the way He divided His explanation of the blessings and curses into two distinct parts, as detailed in the book of Deuteronomy. First came the curses, corresponding to the way God commanded the people to proclaim forth the curses they would inherit for disobedience on Mount Ebal, in Deuteronomy 27. Next came the blessings they would inherit for obedience, which He commanded them to proclaim from Mount Gerizim, in Deuteronomy 28.

In that context, as we will further explain momentarily, in Revelation 10 we are about to encounter perhaps the most significant shamash chapter in all of Revelation, containing God's own yardstick by which those who will be cursed and those who will be blessed can be measured. What better place than in the very middle of the master menorah, the shamash, providing those who will be cursed with righteous judgment and those who will be blessed with a righteous foundation for joy and happiness?

But let us hold that discussion momentarily while we review what's happened in the trumpets, so far.

In Closing . . .

The first four trumpets will bring about some horrific physical changes on the earth. In many ways it will become almost instantly unrecognizable by comparison to its former glory.

- When the first trumpet sounds, one-third of the surface of the earth, one-third of the trees, and all the green grass will be burned up.

- When the second trumpet sounds, water in the sea will turn to blood. This will result in the death of one-third of the living creatures that dwell in the seas, plus the destruction of one-third of all the ships that are on those seas.

- When the third trumpet sounds, one-third of the earth's fresh water will become bitter, causing untold suffering and death.

- When the fourth trumpet sounds, one-third of the sun, moon, and stars will turn dark.

Beyond the above, one of the more noteworthy (and frightening) aspects of the seven trumpets is the way they seem to be organized and directed. The focus of these judgments seems to be our basic sources of life – the foundational building blocks on which the entire chain of life on our planet depends.

Without fresh water the plants can't grow, and without normal sunlight they couldn't grow very much no matter how much water they had. At the same time, without lots of plants our worldwide supply of oxygen will be severely depleted, and without either one the earth won't be able to sustain as many animals – and then not so many humans as well. Plus, without our normal harvests of both plant and animal life from the seas, millions more will go hungry as hundreds of additional links in the chain of life break apart.

Likewise, in a bitter, ironic sense we'll need to be cranking out as many hydrocarbons as we possibly can. Even if global warming really is a legitimate threat here in the early part of the twenty-first century (and there's far more evidence suggesting that it's *not* than there is to support the kind of panic we've gored ourselves with since the 1990s), the first four trumpets alone will result in significant global cooling. And this, of course, will be the precise opposite of what has occupied so much of our recent attention.

After God allows the partial destruction of the foundational blocks of life, He allows the same thing to continue but lets it be aimed directly at mankind. Man's life, spiritually and physically, will first be affected, in more "personal" ways, by the devilish/demonic relationships that are being re-established. Second, man's life will be further affected by the horrendous influence of those same devilish/demonic relationships on mankind as a whole, which will cause another huge war that brings death and destruction all over the world.

9

The Seven Thunders

NOW IT'S TIME TO EXAMINE one of the most misunderstood chapters in what often seems like the least understood book in the entire Bible. So let's be clear before we start. This is a defining moment.

You've heard of such "islands in time" before – those rare occasions in our lives when we suddenly see the truth and either run toward it or run away from it. This could be one of those moments when the words from Romans 1:20, to the effect that we are all "without excuse," suddenly become doubly relevant.

To help explain what we mean, let's go back to our short dissertation on those "three points that make a plane" idea back in chapter 2 of this book. In that discussion we said:

- **First**, the book of Revelation is a thoroughly Hebraic text and therefore communicates on four levels at the same time.

- **Second**, in terms of its actual construction, most of the book of Revelation arrays itself naturally onto a very simple, solid, and familiar structure – the *master menorah*.

- **Third,** as we took great pains to establish in Volume 1 of this series, an accurate understanding of Revelation requires an understanding of the basic forms of covenant. And though we haven't said it very often in this volume, *an understanding of ancient Hebraic marriage covenant is one of the single most important "bodies of knowledge" you can possess at this moment in history.* Because, everything in the book of Revelation – and therefore everything in your eternal future – revolves around that concept. Truly, it's the ultimate focal point of the entire message of the entire Bible.

In chapter 2 in this volume – and even more so throughout Volume 1 – we also tried to make it clear that God often uses multisensory methods and delivers His truths to us via our bodies, our spirits, and our souls – and especially through the three parts of our souls – our intellects, our emotions, and our wills. Most important, when it comes to those last three (on which a major part of our understanding of His Word ultimately rests), He often provides us with image upon image upon image, with which He hopes we will engage every single one of those magnificent faculties He has endowed us with, so that we will develop *maximum understanding of what He's trying to convey.*

Contrary to so much of what we've been taught by the society we now live in, especially here in the last half-century, He has given us the innate ability we need. But, *it's still up to us to work hard, pay attention, read carefully, think Hebraically, and truly endeavor to "get our minds around"* all He wants us to know.

To paraphrase Paul, we are still called upon both to "study to show ourselves approved" (2 Timothy 2:15) and to "work out our salvation [victory] with fear and trembling" (Philippians 2:12). Nowhere else in God's Word is this more true, for all these basic principles come into play at once here in chapter 10 of Revelation.

9 - The First Thunders

However, at the same time, this portion of Revelation is so filled with Hebrew idioms and symbols that it's not hard to figure out why it's so often misinterpreted. Likewise, within the structural metaphor (the master menorah) on which our understanding of Revelation rests, these verses also function in several separate ways at the same time, as separate parts of the master menorah. And finally, these same verses illustrate, uphold, and exemplify the basic principles of ancient Hebraic covenant to an interlaced and interlocking extent that very few other passages can match.

These verses also represent the third leg of that stool (i.e., the conceptual metaphor of Hebrew marriage covenant) we talked about earlier, by presenting to us the yardstick by which the ultimate Groom will identify the ultimate Bride. And here in Revelation 10, the book in His hand identifies His Bride as clearly and definitively as anything possibly could.

The Book of Life

In Hebrew thought – and also, incidentally, in American Indian (i.e., Native American) thought as well – our names alone represent something important about us.

This is true because our names were given to us and written down by God even as He conceived His individual plan for each of our lives – encompassing what we should do, what we should learn, how (and perhaps whom) we should love, what impact we should have on others during our lifetimes, and what lasting effect we should leave behind. Having thus identified us He will then look to these descriptions to see if there is anyone's life within His Book with which our set of accomplishments can be identified. Sometimes the only part of our life that is in the book is the record of our salvation. That's a major positive but that is not, however, God's entire end game plan for us.

Sound convoluted? Incomprehensible? Above your pay grade? Maybe Revelation 10 is really not as difficult as all that. Let's start with its construction.

As we have noted in several places already, each explanation of each of the mini-menorahs has been preceded in the text of the book of Revelation by at least one "shamash chapter." So far these have all been complete chapters amounting to brief textual "interludes" – if you prefer that word – that sometimes appear to be taking us sideways even as they highlight absolutely essential information.

But then, those batches of information often come together in a series of sudden-dawning revelations that flash inside the empty spaces of our minds with the power of thousand-watt bulbs. And those bulbs are set off by God Himself, the same One who designed and built the brains we comprehend with. Thus the shamash chapters, complete with themes and purposes, become so much more understandable when we see them unfolding as parts of a *separate, parallel story*. At the same time they are initiating groups of seven events, many of which amount to disasters (i.e., curses) on the earth brought about by our disdain for our Creator.

In other words, the shamash chapters often have two distinct yet interlaced purposes, which become more obvious the farther we get into Revelation. Later on, some of these shamash passages will occupy only short portions of certain chapters. But either way, each shamash passage provides basic information that we need to understand before we can then approach each separate development, laid out sequentially in each mini-menorah, with the proper perspective.

So far, in marked contrast to the mini-menorah chapters, most of these shamash chapters have provided us with insights into certain people and events, usually in heaven, that clearly represent divine preparations for the upcoming Wedding of the Lamb. For example, one after another they have introduced many of the main participants. However, here in Revelation 10 we find ourselves encountering seven thunders with no shamash passage at all to introduce them. Only the introduction to Yeshua Himself, coming with a book in His hand from which He proclaims the seven thunders, functions as anything remotely resembling a shamash. Why?

Well, oddly enough, the seven thunders have no shamash because they *are* the shamash of the entire master menorah! They're the real deal, the entire message of the entire Bible wrapped up in the tenth chapter of Revelation – one little passage of eleven verses.

But that's only half of the story. This chapter is also unique because it's a mini-menorah chapter as well. This is true because of its place on the diagram, where it acts as the central shamash even as it functions as the *absolutely central* mini-menorah with seven lights.

Shamash and Menorah All at Once

And what should the Grand Theme of that Grand Shamash be? Of course – it's the Messiah! The thunders identify the Groom Himself, in all His glory, presented in a way that may seem unusual and even out-of-place sequentially, but which is entirely consistent with the Hebraic context of this text.

The thunders identify Yeshua the Messiah as the Groom. Simple as that. And that is exactly what this chapter in Revelation starts with. Yeshua is coming down from heaven to explain the terms of the wedding covenant and define who will be His Bride.

Basically, then, the thunders represent the Torah – or "principles for righteous living" – by which Yeshua (and all of us as well, if we're paying attention) can identify the Bride. Because, that is what He will be doing. Remember we are told to look in the mirror of the Torah, and when we do we are supposed to look like our Maker. As James said:

> ²²But prove yourselves doers of the word, and not merely hearers who delude themselves. ²³For if anyone is a hearer of the word and not a doer, he is like a man who looks at his natural face in a mirror; ²⁴for once he has looked at himself and gone away, he has immediately forgotten what kind of person he was. (James 1:22–24)

Likewise, for the last time in the final moments leading up to the Wedding of the Lamb, the only person the entire Bible has ever called "The Word" – who also just happens to be the Groom Himself and the only person legally empowered to open the wedding ketubah and proclaim the absolute truth of that Word – is looking at our reflections in the same mirror.

At the same time, Yeshua is now summarizing what the entire Bible has been proclaiming ever since the first words in the book of Genesis. In effect He is saying, "Remember that scroll I was holding in Revelation 5, when it was still closed? Well, guess what! It's now open because, by my authority, I 'spoke open' the signatures. And now, every single one of my Bride's qualifications is right here, and it's laid out so clearly there's not a single one of you with a plausible excuse for not getting it. This is what my Bride will look like."

Remember, dear reader, before the ancient Hebrew groom could come to get his bride he had to identify her. So maybe the Harvest will be coming along pretty soon, eh?

The Angel and the Little Book

With all the above as preface let's back up, let's carefully examine the actual words of Revelation 10, and let's see how all this lays out. Here's the complete text:

> ¹I saw another strong angel coming down out of heaven, clothed with a cloud; and the rainbow was upon his

9 - The First Thunders

head, and his face was like the sun, and his feet like pillars of fire; ²and he had in his hand a little book which was open. He placed his right foot on the sea and his left on the land; ³and he cried out with a loud voice, as when a lion roars; and when he had cried out, the seven peals of thunder uttered their voices.

⁴When the seven peals of thunder had spoken, I was about to write; and I heard a voice from heaven saying, "Seal up the things which the seven peals of thunder have spoken and do not write them."

⁵Then the angel whom I saw standing on the sea and on the land lifted up his right hand to heaven, ⁶and swore by Him who lives forever and ever, WHO CREATED HEAVEN AND THE THINGS IN IT, AND THE EARTH AND THE THINGS IN IT, AND THE SEA AND THE THINGS IN IT, that there will be delay no longer, ⁷but in the days of the voice of the seventh angel, when he is about to sound, then the mystery of God is finished, as He preached to His servants the prophets.

⁸Then the voice which I heard from heaven, I heard again speaking with me, and saying, "Go, take the book which is open in the hand of the angel who stands on the sea and on the land."

⁹So I went to the angel, telling him to give me the little book. And he said to me, "Take it and eat it; it will make your stomach bitter, but in your mouth it will be sweet as honey." ¹⁰I took the little book out of the angel's hand and ate it, and in my mouth it was sweet as honey; and when I had eaten it, my stomach was made bitter. ¹¹And they said to me, "You must prophesy again concerning many peoples and nations and tongues and kings." (Revelation 10:1–11)

As with all the previous *shamash* passages in Revelation, the apostle John is witnessing an event that will have a great deal of significance almost immediately. The central figure in this particular vision is an unidentified angel – except that He will not remain unidentified very long. As we examine this divine being's characteristics, some intriguing insights and biblical "connections" begin to unfold.

For example, throughout the Bible we find numerous passages detailing incarnations of Messiah, yet in several cases these passages refer to Him as an angel. Abraham's visitation with three "men," Jacob's nighttime wrestling match with "an angel," Joshua's verbal interaction with "the captain of Adonai's armies," and Gideon's encounter with the "angel of the Lord" are all prime examples.

In each case, the Scriptures make it clear that the heavenly being who is called an "angelic visitor" is really the Lord Himself. In other words, what is actually described is Yeshua the Messiah coming in angelic fashion. Angels are messengers, and Messiah is coming conveying a message.

The Hebrew word for this angel is *malakh*, which means *one sent, a messenger, a messenger of God*. Many times malakh is used in reference to an angel, yet at certain times it has been used to refer to Yeshua himself. But this happens only when the term is accompanied by descriptions of qualifying characteristics utterly unique to Messiah.

Revelation 10 provides its own distinctive descriptions, as follows:

- He is robed in a cloud.

- He has a rainbow upon His head.

- His face is like the sun.

- His feet are like pillars of fire.

- He has an open book in His hand.

- He places His right foot on the sea and His left foot on the land.

These identifying markers clearly reveal our divine messenger, here in Revelation 10, as Yeshua. Even so, let's take the time to focus on a few more specific words to make our point crystal clear.

Coming on the Clouds

Though we could cite many more, let's look at just two or three passages from other Scriptures that parallel what we're told here, which clearly identify the divine messenger in Revelation 10:1 as Yeshua, Son of God:

- Matthew 24:30 tells us: "And then the sign of the Son of Man will appear in the sky, and then all the tribes of the earth will mourn, and they will see the SON OF MAN COMING ON THE CLOUDS OF THE SKY with power and great glory."

- In Genesis 9:16–17 God speaks of the rainbow as the sign of His everlasting covenant with all living creatures on the earth. In Revelation 4:3, the apostle John sees a rainbow surrounding the throne of God, above His head (AMP).

- Revelation 1:13–16 describes Yeshua the Messiah in detail: "And in the middle of the lampstands I saw one like a son of man, clothed in a robe reaching to the feet, and girded across His chest with a golden sash. His head and His hair were white like white wool, like snow; and His eyes were like a flame of fire. His feet were like burnished bronze, when it has been made to glow in a furnace, and His voice was like the sound of many waters. In His right hand He held seven stars, and out of His mouth came a sharp two-edged sword; and His face was like the sun shining in its strength."

All these Scriptures prove that this is Yeshua, the Messiah Himself. And He's coming as the Groom.

The Scroll

In Revelation 10:2, The Hebrew word for scroll is *sefer* which means "a book, a writing, a scroll." This is the same word used in Revelation 5:1, referring to the scroll sealed with seven seals – or "signatures" as we should now understand. Only the Lamb of God, Yeshua the Messiah, is found worthy to open this scroll.

We have also learned that this scroll is a *ketubah*, a Hebrew marriage contract written in five sections. And remember, one of those sections always records, in sometimes exhaustive detail, everything that the groom and everything that the bride have agreed to bring to the marriage itself, including both physical things and moral/spiritual obligations and accomplishments. At the very least these mutual agreements include absolute purity, total devotion to each other, and an eternal commitment to the union itself. Remember, also, that Torah is written in the form of a ketubah.

Keep all this in the back of your mind as we proceed. The ketubah for the Wedding of the Lamb has now been opened by the only person legally empowered to do so. Though He has been called by many other names and titles, His correct name is Yeshua and He is the intended Groom. Indeed, the scroll in Revelation 10:2 (again, the ketubah) now lies open in His hand, and *it is the Torah*.

The Land and the Sea

Revelation 10:2 also introduces more Hebraic symbolism when it tells us that "He placed his right foot on the sea and his left on the land." In Hebraic understanding the sea can signify *mankind*, while the land – or earth – can symbolize *death* or the *grave*.

9 - The First Thunders

Symbolically, then, this image tells us that this particular "strong angel" has authority over the living and the dead.

This has to be Yeshua for the simple reason that only One Person in all of history has ever earned that power and authority. Only Yeshua literally conquered Death, and He is not a mere angel. Yeshua is coming with power and authority to proclaim a message of great importance, holding the open ketubah in His hand and operating in the capacity of a groom.

Yet this particular picture symbolizes more than that. If He's straddling Jerusalem with his right foot on the sea, that sea is the Mediterranean and His left foot is therefore in Israel. This means that His back is turned toward the north, which is where Gog, the ones who have chosen to be cursed, live. He has turned Himself away from Gog, which is the same as disowning them. And, His face is now facing Jerusalem where He plans to dwell with His beloved. Later on, Jerusalem itself is metaphorically described as His Bride (see Revelation 21:2).

This image represents both life and death. Symbolically, it tells us that Yeshua has authority over the living and the dead. But in perhaps a more graphic sense, by its positioning it tells us who the living and the dead will be. This north-south orientation is exactly the orientation of the mountains on which the blessings and the curses were read. The "curse" mountain lay to the north while the "blessing" mountain lay to the south.

From the Mountaintop

As we mentioned earlier, in Deuteronomy 27 God commanded Moses that – once the Israelites had crossed over the Jordan River – they were to position six tribes on Mount Ebal and six tribes on Mount Gerizim. The tribes on Mount Ebal, to the north, comprising Reuben, Gad, Asher, Zebulun, Dan, and Naphtali, would begin by reciting the curses of Deuteronomy 27 and 28. The tribes on

> Mount Gerazim, to the south, comprising Simeon, Levi, Judah, Issachar, Joseph, and Benjamin, would then recite the blessings of Deuteronomy 28.

The Thunders Themselves

Revelation 10:3–4 tells us:

> ³"And he cried out with a loud voice, as when a lion roars; and when he had cried out, the seven peals of thunder uttered their voices. ⁴When the seven peals of thunder had spoken, I was about to write; and I heard a voice from heaven saying, 'Seal up the things which the seven peals of thunder have spoken and do not write them.'"

Before we can examine this passage we need to ask a fundamental question: What is a thunder? The word translated as "thunder" is *ra'am*, which means "to rage, to roar, to be angry, to tremble." It is the origin for our English word "rumble."[61]

It is also accepted in Jewish culture that the blowing of the shofar (the ram's horn trumpet) is itself a type of thunder. The concept here is that God breathes His Spirit into us and brings about a change in our souls. We then respond by breathing back His Spirit to Him, through the shofar. The shofar is used to celebrate, to announce the sacrifices, and as a call to war. The implication of Revelation 10 is that Yeshua the Groom is coming forth to defend His Bride against Gog, the ones who are cursed. He is angered by the atrocities being done to His beloved (Revelation 6:9–11), and He prepares to go to war against her assailant, the evil Ha Satan.

Thundering Forth the Oral Torah

The apostle John is about ready to write down what he heard spoken in the seven thunders, but then he is commanded not to write down anything at all. Instead John is told to "seal up the words." Ironically, in Revelation 1:19 John was instructed to do what appears to be just the opposite: "Therefore write the things which you have seen, and the things which are, and the things which will take place after these things." However, it is John himself who has not remembered his original instructions – to write down what he sees but not to write down what he only hears.

But that also brings up an obvious question. John did not actually see the thunders; he heard them instead. So, how can he "seal up" something that has been spoken audibly but cannot be written down?

Let's look once more at the original Hebrew words. The word used in this passage, translated "seal up," is the Hebrew word *khatam*. It does means "to seal up" but it also means "to complete, to lock up, or to hide away." And, by implication it means "to enclose for the purpose of protecting." How would John accomplish that?

The ancient rabbinic sages had a saying concerning the giving of Torah. "Moses received Torah from Sinai and handed it on to Joshua, and Joshua to the elders, and the elders to the prophets, and the prophets passed it on to the men of the Great Assembly. They said three things: 'Be deliberate in judgment, raise many disciples, and make a hedge [i.e., "seal up" via an enclosure of protection, to keep it safe] about the Torah.'"[62]

What many believers might not realize is that the Hebrew scholars quoted above were referring to both Written and Oral Torah. In other words, they were not referencing only the words that Moses wrote down. According to Mosaic tradition, God also gave him quite a bit of Oral Torah at Mount Sinai, which was not written down for thousands of years.

Indeed, when the Scriptures refer to God speaking to Moses, giving forth the Torah, the Hebrew word those Scriptures use is *kol,* which means "voice, sound, noise, thunder, thunderings." When God speaks He does so in the form of thunder. Also, as we've already indicated, when God gave the Torah it was accompanied by the blowing of the ram's horn shofar and God's thundering (kol), exactly as the following passage from the book of Exodus makes abundantly clear:

> [16]So it came about on the third day, when it was morning, that there were thunder [kol] and lightning flashes and a thick cloud upon the mountain and a very loud trumpet [shofar] sound, so that all the people who were in the camp trembled. [17]And Moses brought the people out of the camp to meet God, and they stood at the foot of the mountain. [18]Now Mount Sinai was all in smoke because the LORD descended upon it in fire; and its smoke ascended like the smoke of a furnace, and the whole mountain quaked violently. [19]When the sound of the trumpet grew louder and louder, Moses spoke and God answered him with thunder [kol]. (Exodus 19:16–19)

In Hebraic thinking, the passage from the rabbinic sages that we've quoted above, with respect to "placing a hedge" or "sealing up" Torah, specifically refers to Torah only. But it can also refer to Oral Torah, which literally *was* the hedge around Written Torah. And this Oral Torah, according to tradition that has come down to us through the centuries, is best honored, best "hedged in," and best protected from corrupting influences by being properly interpreted and "lived out."

In other words, we honor and "seal up" Torah, *first,* by carefully and consistently observing God's teachings and instructions. And then, *second,* we take the next step by literally *integrating* His divine wisdom into our very souls. By doing this we place a guard around our hearts even as we guard His Word, exactly as the apostle

Paul instructed us to do in Philippians 4:7: "And the peace of God, which surpasses all comprehension, will guard your hearts and your minds in Christ Jesus."

Now, in order to help them do everything we just identified, God's faithful people have further helped themselves accomplish all this by creating traditions that honor Him and His instructions. And that brings us to the most important question of all if we're going to truly understand this chapter in Revelation: What is the Oral Torah?

Oral Torah, according to the tradition explained in *Option #1*, below, amounts to additional commandments that God gave at Mount Sinai, which were not written down by Moses but were passed on orally down through the centuries. It was referred to as "Oral Torah" because the Hebrews did not want to honor it as highly as Written Torah. For that reason, for many centuries it was memorized but never written down for fear that it might replace Written Torah in its level of importance and observance.

For all those centuries, Oral Torah has also been known by the Jewish people as *The Mishnah*, which is a word that many believers in Yeshua have undoubtedly heard but which relatively few non-Jewish people fully understand. In fact, it probably makes sense to take a chance on one more minor "sideways discussion" here to ensure that what we're leading up to will make complete sense.

What Is Mishnah All About?

With respect to Mishnah itself there are at least two broad and somewhat divergent opinions – or options – that amount to two contrasting explanations as to what Mishnah truly consists of. Here they are:

- **Option #1:** The first view holds that God gave Moses additional law, besides the Written Torah, at Sinai. Following that, over the centuries the Hebrew scribes then added their own commentary – presumably to create that "hedge" and to make things more clear and more accessible to the people. Along the way, this aggregate body of God-given law and manmade commentary then became Mishnah. Many rabbis today view Oral Torah/Mishnah as equivalent to the written Word of God.

- **Option #2:** The second view holds that all of Mishnah is a compilation of commentary, accumulated over the centuries, on the Written Torah we know today as the first five books of the Tanakh. These are the same books that Christianity calls the "Pentateuch of the Old Testament." This view holds that Mishnah is commentary on the written Word of God. It is not equal to the written Word of God; it is commentary only. This view is certainly more ancient than the view in option #1, above. However, this view holds that Mishnah was not sourced from Moses and was never to be written down because it was never to be honored at the same level as Torah, which *was* written down.

In the Christian world today, a comparable example might be a copy of the Bible on a bookshelf by itself, juxtaposed against an entire wall of bookshelves at the opposite end of the room. Those bookshelves would then be filled with commentaries on the Bible, written by everyone from Augustine to Matthew Henry and hundreds of others as well, and often from widely divergent theological positions.

Basically, the latter position (Option #2) is the one we hold, except that Mishnah certainly does not represent a "world of commentary" as diverse as what has grown up around the Christian Bible. We believe that the majority of the modern Mishnah – the modern-day "Oral Torah" – is largely a *reflection of the heart of man to please God*. However, even as our Constitution here in the United States became the foundation of the body of law that established our American form of government, from that same Constitution came all kinds of precedent-setting additional law (called case law) that frequently amounted to additional explanations and interpretations of the underlying document.

The ultimate validity of Mishnah is the subject of an ongoing debate that has evolved over the centuries, with Hebrew scholars even debating with other scholars who had died long before, in many cases. Sometimes we do not agree with some of the ideas put forth as proper interpretations of the Written Torah. But even so, the majority of these "mishnaic ideas" represent very well the ideals for holy living as expressed by God in Torah.

To summarize, we believe that Mishnah evolved from the priestly and levitical rulings that were first brought forth in response to people's questions on various issues of God's Torah itself. As one rabbinic sage made clear, Oral Torah was largely a way "of clarifying biblical texts for their proper legal meaning."[63]

However, keep in mind that the Hebrews, when trying to build a hedge around the Torah, would often add extra layers of law to make sure that no one would violate Torah accidentally. How, for example, does a person properly observe the Sabbath? Mishnah developed as an attempt to answer questions like that. Unfortunately, as Yeshua Himself made clear, sometimes those rules went a bit over the top.

Beyond all that, another reason why we disagree with the strict Option #1 definition of Oral Torah is that more than once God told Moses to "write down everything I tell you; this is every thing that I said." So where's the room for additional Oral Torah?

Even so, none of our feelings about the precise origin of Mishnah negate the value of Mishnah itself. Many things in Mishnah are not only true but also quite valuable. Overall it's another case of not throwing the baby out with the bathwater, as was done with the book of Enoch.

What Did Yeshua Think of Mishnah?

The best way to figure out how Yeshua felt about Mishnah is to look at His own words. He literally quoted Mishnah all over the place. Remember, Yeshua was a rabbi from the school of Hillel. As we have mentioned before, Yeshua and the apostle Paul memorized both the Tanakh and the Mishnah.

As a result, the Mishnah is exactly what Yeshua was referring to when He said, "You've heard it said" (not "You've heard it written") as a prelude to many of His teachings. At the same time, Yeshua was so completely versed in Mishnaic concepts that he sometimes paraphrased both Mishnah and *similar teachings from some of the great rabbis who preceded Him*, including Hillel, without necessarily giving His familiar "You've heard it said" credit. Thus, those who are familiar with Mishnah see Mishnaic concepts in many of Yeshua's teachings. Here's a good example from a recent study guide to the book of Romans:[64]

> Paul was a student of Gamaliel, who was the grandson of Hillel and the one who continued Hillel's famous School of Hillel during Paul's lifetime. Hillel was famous for teaching the *Spirit of the Law* rather than the *Letter of the Law*, as Christ Himself also did. . . . Hillel was [also] the first to write down the seven ancient rules of scriptural interpretation, from the ancient Hebraic viewpoint, that are still in wide usage today. Indeed, many scholars believe that these rules were exactly what Paul meant when he mentioned "rightly dividing the Word of Truth" in 2 Timothy 2:15. These are the Hebraic rules of *biblical exegesis* (i.e., an explanation or an interpretation of something from the Bible)[65] that were also observed in the writing of much of both the Old and the New Testaments. For, on the other side of the equation (i.e., that of the writer), *these also correspond to* [Mishnaic] *rules*

9 - The First Thunders

of logic and orderly presentation that Christ Himself often followed in His parables and other teachings.

A good example, in fact, of the training Christ Himself received as a young boy in the temple would be this [Mishnaic] principle, taught by Hillel:[66]

> *What is hateful to you, do not do to your neighbor... that is the whole Torah ...*

which was later expressed by Christ as:

> *Therefore, whatever you want men to do to you, do also to them, for this is the Law and the Prophets.* (Matthew 7:12 NKJV)

Much of Hillel's thinking, and certainly his thoughts on orderly exegesis of the Scriptures, come from both Mishnah and *Pirke Avot*, the latter known in English as *Wisdom of the Fathers*.

How Does Mishnah Relate to the Thunders?

To tie all this directly into Revelation 10:4, it was understood from the time of Moses that Mishnah was not to be written down. It was not intended to take precedence over Written Torah but was only to be passed on orally from generation to generation. To compile it in a written form was expressly forbidden.

However, after the destruction of the temple in AD 70, the Jews found themselves exiled from Jerusalem and dispersed throughout the world. At that point, Mishnah's survival became problematic at best, for there were relatively few teachers and no longer a huge, homogenous Hebraic community in Jerusalem capable of continuing the oral tradition. So, fearing that this important body of knowledge would be lost forever, in the third century AD a rabbi named Yehuda HaNassi made a major decision. "A text would have to do as a better-than-nothing replacement. Yehuda prayed that he would be forgiven for his deed, and penned the first portion of the most important book in Judaism after the Bible."[67]

Now – what does all this mean to our discussion of Revelation 10? Just this: There are absolutely *amazing* parallels between the seven thunders in Revelation 10 and the Mishnah, beginning with these:

- Mishnah, like the thunders, was not to be written down but it was intended to be remembered. Therefore, devout Jews embedded Mishnah within their own body of tradition.

- Mishnah was to be sealed up or enclosed within a "hedge of protection" exactly as the thunders were.

- The concepts of Mishnah, as they properly represent written Torah, were originally thundered forth by God to mankind.

All these same parallels exist in Revelation, but the list doesn't end there. The structure of Mishnah itself provides even stronger validation of these parallels, for it is divided into six tractates as shown in the list below:

- **Zera'im** (seeds) deals with all the agricultural rules and laws for kosher (kashrut) foods, plus their respective blessings.

- **Mo'ed** (appointed times) delineates the rituals of the Sabbath and all the Jewish festivals.

- **Nashim** (women) examines issues between men and women, including marriage, divorce, and sexual relations.

- **Nezikin** (damages) summarizes civil and criminal law.

9 - The First Thunders

- **Kodashim** (holy things) deals with the laws of sacrifice and ritual slaughter.

- **Taharot** (purities) summarizes the laws of ritual purity and impurity.

If we overlay these six divisions of the Mishnah on the trumpets and bowls of Revelation (we'll deal with the bowls in Volume 3), and if we then compare the type of events with the focus of each of those six divisions (as in Table 8-1), we discover that they coincide almost exactly. However, there are only six divisions in Mishnah yet there are seven thunders. How do we reconcile this and get an exact correspondence?

Let's remember that the B'rit Hadashah (the New Testament), is written in the same literary style as Mishnah. Some Messianic rabbis believe that it could be added as another division to Mishnah. If we did so to complete this overlay, what heading and position would the B'rit Hadashah logically be placed under? As Table 8-1 shows, it would fall under the heading of "Messiah," and thus would take the fourth or *central shamash* position just as the shamash (servant light) of a menorah is the symbol of Messiah.

Let's now look at a slightly more detailed explanation of each of the six traditional Jewish divisions of the Mishnah, plus the B'rit Hadashah in the central position, as shown in both Table 8-1 and the extended explanation below.

- **Zera'im** (seeds). The first event to take place in the trumpets and bowls involves the destruction of specific percentages of the trees and the grass. Plus, these judgments also will involve sores in the genital area, which is where mankind's own seed comes from.

- **Mo'ed** (appointed times/seasons). Next, certain fixed percentages of the sea and all that is in it will be affected. The sea plays a major role in controlling the weather patterns and conditions that determine our seasons. So, everything that happens here, in effect, will affect our seasons.

- **Nashim** (women). The third event of both the trumpets and the bowls affects the springs of water. Hebrew understanding is that springs of water, from which the seas also originate, are the source of life. Women are likewise recognized as the source of *human* life. The Hebrew word for mother is *em*, which pictographically means "the strong or first water"[68] and correlates with the word for spring. All mankind springs forth from the first woman, known in the Bible as Eve (*Chava*). Poisoning of the fresh water is thus symbolic of the poisoning of humanity itself.

- **B'rit Hadashah** (Renewed Covenant of Messiah). The fourth event of the trumpets and bowls affects the sun, the moon, and the stars. One-third of the day and night will be left without light. Remember that Messiah is called the Shamash, the servant-light. The word for sun in Hebrew is *shamash*, the same word for the light that ignites all other lights on the menorah. The shamash is also known as the "plumb line" as in Zechariah 4:10:

    > For who has despised the day of small things? But these seven will be glad when they see the plumb line in the hand of Zerubbabel – these are the eyes of the LORD which range to and fro throughout the earth.

    This is the one distinctive light on the menorah by which all other lights are measured. Just as the sun lights the world, Yeshua *is* the Light of the world (John 8:12). However, now the sun is "burning" those who have been measured against the plumb line and found wanting.

Table 8-1: The Mishnah/B'rit Hadashah Correspondence with Thunders

Thunders/Mishnah Tractates	First	Second	Third	Fourth	Fifth	Sixth	Seventh
	Seeds (Agriculture)	Appointed Times (Seasons)	Women (Life givers)	B'rit Hadashah Shamash – The Son (Spiritual Light-Giver)	Damages (Penalties for violating law)	Holy Things (Brings life through covenant)	Ritual Purities (Purifies the temple)
Trumpets	Grass and Trees Destroyed (Plants that feed life)	Part of Sea Destroyed (Affects seasons)	Fresh Water Destroyed (Water supports life)	1/3 of Sun and Moon Darkened (Natural Light-Giver)	Abaddon Sent (Sinners tormented as penalty for sin)	Unholy Devil (Brings death through counter-covenant)	Purity (Earth purified through blood of sinners)
Bowls	Genital Sores (Place of reproduction; seeds)	Poisons the Sea (Turns to blood)	Poisons the Fresh Water (Water symbolizes humanity)	Burned by the Sun (Rash/Sunburn)	Darkness (Those who violate the law have no light)	Devils (Deceptive miracles)	Death (To be judged by what you have done)

- **Nezikin** (damages). This tractate of Mishnah is concurrent with the fifth events of the trumpets and bowls. The fifth trumpet reveals the releasing of the fallen teraphim from the abyss by their king, Abaddon the Destroyer, to torment unrepentant man (Revelation 9:1–11), just as the fifth bowl judgment brings damage/darkness upon the throne of the Beast and his unrepentant followers (Revelation 16:10).

- **Kodashim** (holy things). "Holy things" concerns laws of sacrifice and holy slaughter. This tractate of Mishnah identifies that which is righteous and that which is unrighteous. The sixth trumpet unveils the joining of teraphim with fallen man in a covenant that slaughters one-third of unrepentant mankind, all of them in unholy counter-covenant with Ha Satan. This results in an unholy sacrifice to Abaddon, the angel of death. The sixth bowl also shows us what this type of vile sacrifice to an unholy master really represents, as demonstrated by unclean, loathsome evil spirits (frogs) proceeding from the mouth of the Beast and the False Prophet who, at that time, are residing in the temple and defiling the most holy place of God.

- **Taharot** (purities). The climactic final events of the seventh trumpet and seventh bowl are multifaceted. The last trumpet leads directly to the seven thunders and the seven bowls. It also coincides with the mystery of God (1 Corinthians 15:51). At the last trumpet God comes to take His Bride, who has made herself ready to put on the pure white wedding garments. The last trumpet also initiates the bowls, which brings purity to God's creation by purging everything that is unholy.

Given all this, is it purely accidental that the divisions of Mishnah, with the B'rit Hadashah as its central interpretive standard, parallel the trumpets and bowls? We think not.

9 - The First Thunders

Raising Your Right Hand to Heaven

To continue on with the text, in order for us to explain the details of the seventh tractate more accurately, we must examine the following verses of Revelation 10:

> ⁵Then the angel whom I saw standing on the sea and on the land lifted up his right hand to heaven, ⁶and swore by Him who lives forever and ever, WHO CREATED HEAVEN AND THE THINGS IN IT, AND THE EARTH AND THE THINGS IN IT, AND THE SEA AND THE THINGS IN IT, that there will be delay no longer, ⁷but in the days of the voice of the seventh angel, when he is about to sound, then the mystery of God is finished, as He preached to His servants the prophets. (Revelation 10:5–7)

In verse 5, this divine being, whom we have identified as Yeshua, raises His right hand to heaven and swears by the Almighty. No angel in all of Scripture has ever done this. Recall these two passages from the books of Matthew and James:

> ³⁴"But I say to you, make no oath at all, either by heaven, for it is the throne of God, ³⁵or by the earth, for it is the footstool of His feet, or by Jerusalem, for it is THE CITY OF THE GREAT KING. ³⁶"Nor shall you make an oath by your head, for you cannot make one hair white or black. (Matthew 5:34–36)

> But above all, my brethren, do not swear, either by heaven or by earth or with any other oath; but your yes is to be yes, and your no, no, so that you may not fall under judgment. (James 5:12)

The first is a command from Yeshua Himself. Would an angel, in delivering a message to one of God's servants, violate his Master's commandment? Certainly not! Even more compelling, both of these scriptural references are also direct quotes from Mishnah, concerning the taking of an oath. As we have said, understand that

Yeshua and the apostles (as well as many of the rabbis of that time) quoted from Mishnah hundreds of times, even as many rabbis from that time to this have done and still continue to do.

Now consider the last half of Revelation 10:6 plus Revelation 10:7 as recorded below:

> [6] . . . there will be delay no longer, [7]but in the days of the voice of the seventh angel, when he is about to sound, then the mystery of God is finished, as He preached to His servants the prophets.

To understand this statement, we should read I Corinthians 15:50–52:

> [50]Now I say this, brethren, that flesh and blood cannot inherit the kingdom of God; nor does the perishable inherit the imperishable. [51]Behold, I tell you a mystery; we will not all sleep, but we will all be changed, [52]in a moment, in the twinkling of an eye, at the last trumpet; for the trumpet will sound, and the dead will be raised imperishable, and we will be changed.

Also I Thessalonians 4:16, 17:

> [16]For the Lord Himself will descend from heaven with a shout, with the voice of the archangel and with the trumpet of God, and the dead in Christ will rise first. [17]Then we who are alive and remain will be caught up together with them in the clouds to meet the Lord in the air, and so we shall always be with the Lord.

Hinting at the Harvest

The mystery of God that will be revealed is none other than the harvesting of the Bride.

9 - The First Thunders

In Revelation 11:15, after the death and resurrection of the two witnesses, the seventh trumpet sounds. Yeshua then comes as a Groom, paralleling Hebrew wedding customs, to snatch away His Bride. However, the snatching away of the Bride is just one of three separate Harvests (as opposed to "Raptures") that will occur here in the middle portion of the book of Revelation, all of which we'll discuss in greater detail in Volume 3 of this series.

Meanwhile, the seventh and last tractate of Mishnah deals with customs of ritual purities and impurities. What is the major promise that a bride in a Hebrew wedding is supposed to keep? Of course – it is the promise to keep herself pure. As Revelation 19:7–8 tells us:

> [7]"Let us rejoice and be glad and give the glory to Him, for the marriage of the Lamb has come and His bride has made herself ready." [8]It was given to her to clothe herself in fine linen, bright and clean; for the fine linen is the righteous acts of the saints.

Finally, let's move on to the last few verses in the 10th chapter of Revelation. Revelation 10:8–11 reads:

> [8]Then the voice which I heard from heaven, I heard again speaking with me, and saying, "Go, take the book which is open in the hand of the angel who stands on the sea and on the land." [9]So I went to the angel, telling him to give me the little book. And he said to me, "Take it and eat it; it will make your stomach bitter, but in your mouth it will be sweet as honey." [10]I took the little book out of the angel's hand and ate it, and in my mouth it was sweet as honey; and when I had eaten it, my stomach was made bitter. [11]And they said to me, "You must prophesy again concerning many peoples and nations and tongues and kings."

This is a misunderstood passage because it is based on an ancient Hebrew custom. In those times, when Jewish children first entered the classroom to learn Torah, the rabbi in charge would ask them to spread honey on a small corner of a page in their Torah. They would then tear the corner off and eat it, conveying in unforgettable imagery that in order to properly study God's Word we must consume it and make it a part of our bodies and souls.

Just as Revelation implies, Torah tastes sweet when it enters the mouth. But, when it reaches our inner parts – where our flesh resides – it then turns sour because our flesh is at war with God's holy and righteous commands.

This reference to ancient Hebraic customs, in Revelation 10, provides further evidence that the scroll laying open in Yeshua's hand truly is the Torah, the ketubah, the wedding contract that He made between Himself and His people.

This Scripture also proves one more vital point. One must make God's word a part of his soul to properly prophesy. Without having thoroughly ingested God's word first there is always the danger of prophesying falsely or incorrectly. And, all of this further validates the message of Proverbs 1 and 2. Both of these chapters admonish the reader to seek and revere wisdom, for it warns against calamity and provides its own measure of security by bringing understanding, something that those who fail to heed the book of Revelation will someday sorely lack.

In Closing . . .

When we overlay this portion of Scripture on the master menorah of Revelation we also discover another significant truth. Torah is the Word of the Almighty, spoken to Moses and recorded. It promises the blessing of God if we are obedient, but it also promises the curses if we are disobedient.

> [26]"See, I am setting before you today a blessing and a curse—[27]the blessing if you obey the commands of the

9 - The First Thunders

Lord your God that I am giving you today; [28]the curse if you disobey the commands of the Lord your God and turn from the way that I command you today by following other gods, which you have not known." (Deuteronomy 11:26–28 NIV)

As we have explained, we believe that the seven thunders of Revelation 10 are actually the Mishnah and the B'rit Hadashah. They are thundered forth by Yeshua Himself, identifying His Bride and also functioning as a call to war against all who would oppose her.

For those who will experience the Tribulation, their standing in relation to this war depends on their standing in relation to the Groom and His commandments. If we are disobedient, if we seek after our own pleasures, serve other gods, and refuse to repent, then we are under a curse and will partake in the judgments allotted for the Beast, the False Prophet, and those who follow them.

But if we obey His commandments we receive His spiritual protection and blessing. God's people can be identified by their fruit and the soundness of their relationships with others, and with their God.

10

The Final Trumpets

As WE HAVE ACKNOWLEDGED SEVERAL TIMES in this volume, much has been made of the so-called "Rapture of the Saints," which we prefer to call a *Harvest* in keeping with the actual words of Revelation. However, contrary to what many others might teach, we believe that the book of Revelation actually identifies *three separate* Harvests that include the one that so many people mistakenly identify as the ultimate, all-inclusive "Rapture" that the apostle Paul talked about in 1 Corinthians 15:51–58, as follows:

> [51]Behold, I tell you a mystery; we will not all sleep, but we will all be changed, [52]in a moment, in the twinkling of an eye, at the last trumpet; for the trumpet will sound, and the dead will be raised imperishable, and we will be changed. [53]For this perishable must put on the imperishable, and this mortal must put on immortality. [54]But when this perishable will have put on the imperishable, and this mortal will have put on immortality, then will come about the saying that is written, "DEATH IS SWALLOWED UP in victory. [55]"O DEATH, WHERE IS YOUR VICTORY? O DEATH, WHERE IS YOUR STING?" [56]The sting of death is sin, and the power of sin is the law; [57]but thanks be to God, who

> gives us the victory through our Lord Jesus Christ. ⁵⁸Therefore, my beloved brethren, be steadfast, immovable, always abounding in the work of the Lord, knowing that your toil is not in vain in the Lord.

This familiar passage truly does describe the last trumpet – but not the last Harvest. Three Harvests are delineated in the book of Revelation, and three specific, clearly described groups of people are harvested at each one. At the same time, neither the purposes for their selection nor their immediate destinations are the same in all cases.

However, in keeping with our commitment to treat the chapters of Revelation *in order*, let us wrap up this book (Volume 2 in our three-volume series) by closely examining what's going on in Revelation 11, which will bring us to the exact middle of Revelation itself. In the process we will look very carefully at the deeper implications of several aspects of this chapter, which are not usually dealt with in detail by most commentators.

The Sixth Trumpet

The events of the sixth trumpet are completed in Revelation 11 as follows:

> ¹Then there was given me a measuring rod like a staff; and someone said, "Get up and measure the temple of God and the altar, and those who worship in it. ²"Leave out the court which is outside the temple and do not measure it, for it has been given to the nations; and they will tread under foot the holy city for forty-two months. ³"And I will grant authority to my two witnesses, and they will prophesy for twelve hundred and sixty days, clothed in sackcloth."
>
> ⁴These are the two olive trees and the two lampstands that stand before the Lord of the earth. ⁵And if anyone

wants to harm them, fire flows out of their mouth and devours their enemies; so if anyone wants to harm them, he must be killed in this way. ⁶These have the power to shut up the sky, so that rain will not fall during the days of their prophesying; and they have power over the waters to turn them into blood, and to strike the earth with every plague, as often as they desire.

⁷When they have finished their testimony, the beast that comes up out of the abyss will make war with them, and overcome them and kill them. ⁸And their dead bodies will lie in the street of the great city which mystically is called Sodom and Egypt, where also their Lord was crucified.

⁹Those from the peoples and tribes and tongues and nations will look at their dead bodies for three-and-one-half days, and will not permit their dead bodies to be laid in a tomb. ¹⁰And those who dwell on the earth will rejoice over them and celebrate; and they will send gifts to one another, because these two prophets tormented those who dwell on the earth. ¹¹But after the three-and-one-half days, the breath of life from God came into them, and they stood on their feet; and great fear fell upon those who were watching them.

¹²And they heard a loud voice from heaven saying to them, "Come up here." Then they went up into heaven in the cloud, and their enemies watched them. ¹³And in that hour there was a great earthquake, and a tenth of the city fell; seven thousand people were killed in the earthquake, and the rest were terrified and gave glory to the God of heaven. ¹⁴The second woe is past; behold, the third woe is coming quickly. (Revelation 11:1–14)

First of all, John is instructed to "measure the temple of God and the altar, and those who worship in it." The measuring rod that he's given, in Hebrew, is *shebet,* a *scepter*, which is also a sign of authority or identity. He's told to measure the inner court and the Holy of Holies but to leave out the outer court.[69]

To look at this from a slightly broader perspective, let's examine one more meaning of the Hebrew word (*middah*) translated into English as "measure." In Hebraic understanding, that word also means "to measure a portion." What we're talking about here is a portion of the groom's inheritance, which he traditionally gives to the father of the bride to pay the bride's price.

The portion that John is asked to measure is the part of the tabernacle that was always covered. The rest of the sections of the tabernacle were not. This covering clearly represents the chuppah, under which the bride and the groom stand during their marriage ceremony. Therefore, we have here a picture of Yeshua, measuring or "separating out" those people who are actually His Bride. He's identifying those who "measure up" because they have lived their lives according to God's instructions in Torah, and therefore qualify to be part of His Bride. Indeed, this passage could just as well read, "A scepter was given to me to go identify those I have selected and purchased; those under the chuppah; those who are my Bride."

At the same time, John is told *not to measure the outer court*. That's where the servants and the guests of the wedding party stand (recall Revelation 7 and the great multitude before the throne), and they're specifically not being measured for this relationship. Recall from our discussion in Volume 1 (chapter 5) that the tabernacle structure, including the camp surrounding it, was laid out in four sections. Each one represented different levels of intimacy with God, and thus they each corresponded to one of the four levels of covenant, as follows:

- **The main camp** = servanthood covenant
- **The outer court** = friendship covenant

- **The inner court** = inheritance covenant

- **The Holy of Holies** = marriage covenant

Now let's go back and repeat what we said a moment ago, only this time a little more clearly:

> *The people who are believers, positioned in the outer court, are not being measured to see whether they qualify as part of Bride.*

Indeed, they're not even being allowed into that most intimate, private room, and the reason is quite clear. They are not part of the Bride; they are the friends and the servants, essentially the *guests* of the wedding party, standing where the guests traditionally stand. Because, as we have already explained numerous times, not everyone who attends an ancient Hebrew wedding is either the bride or the groom. And those who are not the bride or the groom are positioned anywhere else *except* under the chuppah. Simple as that.

Two Different Brides

In a moment we want to consider two more semantic points that might not seem significant at first glance, but which further corroborate what we've said so far. But first, we would be remiss if we did not point out the direct linkage, here in chapter 11 of Revelation, to what the apostle John introduced in chapter 8. Remember the obvious references in chapter 8 to the morning and evening services in the heavenly temple, corresponding to the same services that were once conducted in the earthly temple in Jerusalem? Remember, also, the silence in heaven, and what it represented?

This initial portion of Revelation 11 links directly to that passage. Again we are in the temple, except that this time we are being shown "who is where," with all the obvious implications as to why those people are where they are.

Now, back to semantics. The word translated as "those who worship" is *ha'mishtakhavim*. But these are not "regular" worshippers because they're inside the inner court and even the Holy of Holies. And as we know, only the priests are allowed into the inner court and only one priest at a time is allowed inside the Holy of Holies. And even then it happens on just one day a year – Yom Kippur. It is understood that the high priest, on Yom Kippur, dressed in white like a bride, represented the Bride. So, the implication is that these worshippers are His Bride, fully qualified to be "under the chuppah" in the inner court.

Meanwhile, the word for bride is *kallah*. This word also means "completion, perfection, finished, to be made whole" and "to be prepared." Incredibly enough, at the same time it also means "to be destroyed, to be consumed," or "to perish." So – how and why can one word mean both perfection and destruction at the same time? The answer is that there are two brides, as follows.

- The first Bride is the one who has been perfected by Yeshua's righteous work, complemented by her sincere and heartfelt response. By virtue of Yeshua's blood on the cross, plus her own righteous conduct, this Bride has been perfected and her works have been accepted. What distinguishes this Bride from all the others who have been saved is the acceptance of her righteous works, which equates to the highest level of covenant.

- The second bride, to whom we will be introduced in a few chapters (and which we have hinted about already) is the bride of Satan. Unlike the Bride of Yeshua, she will be consumed and destroyed by her vile groom because he won't need her anymore.

10 - The Final Trumpets

The Two Witnesses

Next we are introduced to the two witnesses, who are given the authority to guard God's people, the worshipers in His sanctuary, as described in Revelation 11:1. The word *measure* in this verse comes from the Hebrew verb *mahd*, meaning "to cover as with a garment, to measure, to extend protection."

Ever since this vision was given to John, thousands of people have speculated about the identity of these two men. Some believe they could be Enoch and Elijah; some say Moses and Elijah; others say they're modern-day prophets; still others believe they represent nothing more than a concept. But in reality they are two distinct individuals, and the way they're described in Revelation indicates that they are just like the prophets of old.

We believe that these two witnesses are actually Enoch and Elijah. The text of Revelation does not reveal their names but it does give us several major clues.

- The two witnesses are identified as "those who prophesy" in verse 3. There are three types of prophets in Hebrew understanding. First is the "dreamer of dreams." This prophet is usually sent to individuals and gives personal direction from God. Daniel, the servant of God sent to help King Nebuchadnezzar of Babylon, is an example of this type of prophet.

The *prince* or *hosea* prophet is the second type. This prophet is given authority to speak words of encouragement or instruction to communities and congregations, with the obvious example of this type being Hosea.

However, the most authoritative prophet, a *navi* (*navi'im* in the plural), is given the responsibility to minister to nations and kings, and this is the kind of prophet referenced in verse 3. A *navi* was always present whenever the temple existed in Jerusalem; indeed, the construction and dedication of the temple could not have been accomplished without a *navi*. Both Enoch and Elijah were *navi'im*. This certainly supports the idea that they might therefore be the two witnesses, although it's impossible to be absolutely sure.

- Scripture does not tell us that the two witnesses are modern contemporaries of the end times, nor does it specifically characterize them as Old Testament prophets returning to earth to take care of unfinished business. However, Hebrews 9:27 does tell us "it is appointed for men to die once and after this comes judgment." In other words, everyone (except those living at the time of the Second Coming) will die once.

    The Bible tells us that only two people have never died – Enoch and Elijah. The Scriptures further indicate that Enoch and Elijah were both taken straight to heaven in bodily form (see Genesis 5:24, Hebrews 11:5, and 2 Kings 2:11–12).

- In several places the Scriptures tell us that the prophet Elijah has to precede the coming of Messiah. Probably the most clear and dramatic passage would be Malachi 4:5, which says: "Behold, I am going to send you Elijah the prophet before the coming of the great and terrible day of the LORD."

- Enoch was the prophet God chose to judge the fallen teraphim, who created the perverted offspring called *Nephilim* via their union with human women (see Enoch VI–XI).

    Elijah was the prophet who opposed certain Nephilim in positions of power and authority – false prophets who led the people astray. Elijah opposed Jezebel and Ba'al, whose corresponding personifications in this prophecy are the whore of Babylon (Jezebel) and the Beast (Ba'al).

- All through the Mideast, ancient figurines have been found of Jezebel riding on top of a beast, usually in the form of a bull. That's exactly a picture of the relationship we see coming, the Whore and the Beast, as we'll discuss at length in Volume 3.

- Finally, we believe that the description of the supernatural power the two men have (shutting up the sky to prevent rain for three-and-one-half years; calling down fire from heaven; all sorts of plagues at will) identifies powers that both of these prophets had in their own lifetimes. And, the specific miracles the two witnesses perform further suggest that Enoch and Elijah might be the ones.

We also believe the two witnesses will be these two prophets because they both have dealt with Nephilim in the past, including creatures such as Jezebel, who are all returning. Essentially they're both coming back at the end of the story, to finish what they started so many centuries before. They represent what we believe is the best possible interpretation from an Hebraic perspective – they opposed the same problem in the past that we'll be dealing with in the end times. This whole episode will be like an end game from a war that's been going on since the beginning. All the players are lining up, literally, for one last "Hail Mary" pass.

In any case, whether the above is ultimately true or not, whoever these men are (and unlike what happened in the past) they eventually die at the hands of "the Beast." But they are not defeated by him. In Jerusalem their bodies lie unburied for three-and-one-half days. They are then resurrected and ascend into heaven in a cloud.

Of Times and Timing

These witnesses have been given authority to rule for 1,260 days, dressed in sackcloth. The wearing of sackcloth is a sign of mourning and repentance; they're mourning because so many people have not repented. The main sign of this is the judgments that they are allowed to pour out, from the hand of God, on those who continue refusing to repent, refusing to see the light that will bring them back to God.

The two witnesses are allowed to cause drought, to turn waters into floods, and to strike with every kind of plague as often as they want, which they do as judgments but also as part of one last, vast attempt to get the attention of man before the harshest judgments of all come. As with the prophets of old, God always warned people prior to their coming destruction, whether it was Ninevah or Israel, and often gave them numerous chances to repent. That's what we see occurring here with the two witnesses – these are God's last prophets, coming to warn mankind of their final doom.

Their 1,260 days just happen to be exactly three-and-one-half years as per the Hebrew calendar. It's interesting to note that, in Daniel 9, there is one final seven-year period yet to be fulfilled, the first half of which is separated from the last half by a huge event – the abomination of desolation. This will involve the False Messiah (Satan, the Beast), who desecrates the temple, thus ending the holy sacrifices while temporarily usurping God's position and claiming to be God Himself. The death of the two witnesses at the hands of Abaddon, who is the False Prophet claiming to be Elijah, comes exactly at the midpoint of this last seven-year period. Immediately to follow, in both the Daniel text and here in Revelation, are the last three-and-one-half years during which Satan, the False Messiah, will claim to be God and will initiate his short but brutal rule over the kingdoms of the world.

10 - The Final Trumpets

Our God has an incredible sense of timing and coordination, which He often exercises to help us understand certain things. As a result it's hard to overstate the importance – to God Himself but also to us – of the sacred feasts and of certain other "passages of time," many of which are referenced frequently in the Scriptures. For example, most of the Christian world seems to be unaware that the four major events connected to the death and resurrection of Yeshua (i.e., Jesus Christ) occurred on four of the God-ordained Jewish feasts. He died on *Passover*, was put in the grave on *Unleavened Bread*, rose on *Firstfruits*, and sent the Holy Spirit to indwell believers 50 days later, on *Shavuot*.

Also, God sometimes punishes His people in a "years-for-years" ratio. Thus the Israelites' exile into Babylonia, under Nebuchadnezzar, lasted for precisely 70 years because, for 490 years in the Promised Land, they refused to honor every seventh year as a Sabbath as God had ordained. If you divide 490 years by 7 you get 70 years, for which the Israelites were then punished on a one-for-one ratio.

Sometimes He also speaks through His prophets in a "years-for-days" or a "years-for-weeks" ratio. Thus Daniel's seventieth *week* is really a *seven-year period*, which brings us to an amazing non-coincidence here in the book of Revelation. Daniel's seventieth-week (i.e., seven-year) period starts on the Hebrew New Year, Rosh Hashanah, also known as the Feast of Trumpets. This is a period of self-inspection and repentance during which it's entirely appropriate to be wearing sackcloth. Thus the two witnesses are following God's timing and His seasons.

The time period could also be exactly three-and-one-half plus three-and-one-half years, for a total of seven. Thus, if the two witnesses start their reign on Feast of Trumpets, three-and-one-half years later they'd be killed on or near Passover. If they're resurrected three-and-one-half days later this would probably happen on Firstfruits, as it did for Yeshua. Likewise, the entire seven-year period starts on the Feast of Trumpets and ends seven years later on another Feast of Trumpets, which is the exact feast on which Messiah is to return.

For thousands of years, the rabbis have been arguing about which feast the Messiah will return on. Some believed that it would be Passover, while others were convinced that it would be Feast of Trumpets. In fact, they were both right. The first coming was fulfilled when Yeshua came to Jerusalem to die on Passover. His second return will occur when He comes with His army to re-establish His right to rule and reign over His creation, on Feast of Trumpets.

Reprehensible Disrespect

Finally, in Hebrew culture, when someone dies their body is not embalmed but is buried immediately. It's reprehensible to leave a body lying out on the street. So, God will judge the anti-Yeshua kingdom even more harshly than He might have judged it for rejecting His two witnesses, because they will also leave the bodies of those two witnesses lying outside for three-and-one-half days. And that punishment will endure, as in the years-for-days ratio mentioned above, for three-and-one-half years.

If we're correct that the two witnesses die near or exactly on Passover and are resurrected on Firstfruits, those events would signal the beginning of the kingdom of Satan without the interference of the two witnesses, who cause floods, famines, and various other activities that might be embarrassing to Ha Satan. In any case, when we add three-and-one-half years to the Hebrew calendar, starting at Firstfruits, that witness-free, pro-Satan time should end very close to the Feast of Trumpets. And this is the feast on which Yeshua comes back with His army to establish His eternal reign. Hmmmmm . . . .

After three-and-one-half days, God resurrects the two witnesses and they go up to heaven in a cloud, in full view of the whole world. In that very hour a great earthquake hits and a tenth of the city (Jerusalem) is destroyed. But many who survive will be awestruck and will give glory to God, proving that many believers are still on earth. And there are some who, through these signs and wonders, will actually be impressed enough to repent and worship God.

Meanwhile, fifty days later, on Shavuot, comes the Harvest of the best – but we'll talk about that in Volume 3. To conclude this portion, Revelation 11:14 reminds us that what we've just seen is the second woe, with the third one coming quickly.

The Seventh Trumpet (Third Woe)

The seventh trumpet is introduced in the last half of Revelation 11, as follows:

> [15]Then the seventh angel sounded; and there were loud voices in heaven, saying, "The kingdom of the world has become the kingdom of our Lord and of His Christ; and He will reign forever and ever." [16]And the twenty-four elders, who sit on their thrones before God, fell on their faces and worshiped God, [17]saying, "We give You thanks, O Lord God, the Almighty, who are and who were, because You have taken Your great power and have begun to reign.
>
> [18]"And the nations were enraged, and Your wrath came, and the time came for the dead to be judged, and the time to reward Your bond-servants the prophets and the saints and those who fear Your name, the small and the great, and to destroy those who destroy the earth." [19]And the temple of God which is in heaven was opened; and the ark of His covenant appeared in His temple, and there were flashes of lightning and sounds and peals of thunder and an earthquake and a great hailstorm. (Revelation 11:15–19)

When the seventh angel blows the seventh trumpet he ushers in the events of the last woe, with these words from verse 15: "The kingdom of the world has become the kingdom of our Lord and of His Christ; and He will reign forever and ever."

Given that description – used so powerfully by George Frederic Handel in the great "Hallelujah Chorus" from *Messiah* – we might be tempted to believe that the end has finally arrived. However, seven more catastrophic events still remain, which the earth and those who still dwell on her will suffer.

In Revelation 11:19 the doors of the temple are thrown open, revealing the ark of His covenant. Revelation 15:5 also describes the same phenomenon, thus allowing the seven bowls of the seven angels to pour out God's wrath upon the earth. We will discuss the bowls at length in Volume 3 in this series, but meanwhile it's interesting to note that, as also recorded in Mishnah, the temple veil was rent and its doors were thrown open in AD 30, just after the death of Yeshua. Predictably enough, Mishnah interpreted this opening of the doors to mean that the temple had become an abomination through the corrupt leadership of the Sadducees.

In any case, at the last trumpet in Revelation the temple doors are once again thrown open. The timing of this event comes at the exact point of the corrupting of the temple through the abomination of desolation set up by the False Messiah. In the temple he proclaims himself to be God (Dan. 9:27), which starts the last three-and-one-half years of Daniel's prophecy.

However, here in Revelation 11, the seventh trumpet is more of a major announcement than anything else. Via this trumpet call to the faithful, God is now proclaiming the coming marriage between Himself and His Bride.

Indeed, I Corinthians 15:51–52, which we quoted at the beginning of this chapter, tells us that the arrival of Messiah (i.e., Yeshua) for His Bride will occur at the sounding of the last or seventh trumpet. The Groom will come for His Bride just after the seventh trumpet and just before the first bowl of judgment is poured out on the remaining earthly inhabitants.

In Volume 3 we will get into much more detail about Yeshua's coming for His Bride (see text box "Amazing Parallels"), but for centuries the feast of Shavuot has been recognized, exclusively, as the feast on which God gave the Torah on Mount Sinai and made Israel His Bride, and it should also be recognized as the feast on which He will come back for His Bride.

> **Amazing Parallels**
>
> In Hebrew culture, the fifty days that elapse between the third and fourth annual feasts, better known as Firstfruits and Shavuot, have long been very special days indeed. In a custom called "Counting the Omer," each individual day is carefully (and often publically) counted, and all religious Jews look forward to the culmination of that count.
>
> Ironically, since most Orthodox Jews do not recognize Yeshua as their promised Messiah, they also do not recognize the amazing parallels in His life on earth and His impending return. Counting the Omer corresponds to counting up to the day of the coming of the ultimate Groom for His Bride. Indeed, the last trumpet sounds on the 50th day after the resurrection of the two witnesses on Firstfruits.
>
> On Firstfruits, the Israelites passed safely through the Red Sea and were saved from the Egyptians. Fifty days later, on Shavuot, they received the Torah, God's marriage contract with us amid the loud sound of the shofar and God's thundering voice.
>
> Yeshua was resurrected on the feast of Firstfruits. Fifty days later the Holy Spirit came on Shavuot. The two witnesses of Rev-

> elation 11 will be resurrected on Firstfruits; fifty days later the last trumpet will sound on Shavuot, and Yeshua will return in the clouds for His Bride.
>
> Also, on ancient Shavuot celebrations, the primary focal point of this feast was the celebration at the temple and the offering of two loaves of leavened bread. Here, the bread represented life, and the leavening in the bread – rather than representing the increase in sin as in the past – will one day represent a massive increase of righteousness, even as the Bride undergoes a huge cleansing and establishing of righteousness sufficient for uniting with her Groom.

Thus, from a larger perspective, the sounding of the last trumpet is a picture of the Groom coming with His groomsmen on the night before the wedding. The resulting all-night party is celebrated only by the Groom, the Bride, the bridesmaids, the groomsmen, and all their escorts, in anticipation of the wedding ceremony slated to occur on the following day.

On another level, this last trumpet also represents the last trumpet blown at the end of each day in the temple services. In this case we hear the equivalent of the last trumpet blown on Erev Shabbat, the day before a Shabbat. This Shabbat is Shavuot, the fourth feast. This trumpet would be blown very close to sundown, thus ushering in the hours of darkness that initiate the next day. And certainly, over the next three-and-one-half years, the darkest of all history for all of mankind will be recorded.

In contrast, all these horrific events that occur simultaneously with God's wooing of His Bride reveal an initial "setting apart" – or bifurcation – between the sheep (God's people) and the goats (Satan's followers). At God's right are His people, being honored and protected on earth, and on the left are the goats – those who by their own choices have entered into covenant with Satan.

10 - The Final Trumpets

So far, the letter, seal, and trumpet tribulations have occurred in the presence of the Bride on earth. However, the bowls of God's wrath will not be poured out until His Bride has been taken away by the Groom to the all-night wedding party. But once His Bride has been removed, those who are left will suffer the torments of the seven bowls – as we will detail in depth in Volume 3 of this series.

In Closing . . .

- The "measuring" that's done in chapter 11 of Revelation is not only of the inner court and the Holy of Holies within the temple itself; it's of the people who are there as well. And only those who are qualified to be part of the Bride of Yeshua will be in those areas when such measuring begins.

- The same measuring will be undertaken to determine that those who have been assembled under the chuppah truly "measure up" according to Torah. Have they been faithful, and have they done their best to live according to Torah's mitzvot?

- All who are not part of the Bride will be outside, in the outer court, where they will not be covered by the wedding chuppah and hence will not be measured. They qualify to attend the wedding as guests and servants, but they are not part of the Bride. Remember the group of palm-branch holders who were before the throne, back in chapter 7? That's who these people are.

- The Hebraic word for "bride" can also refer to someone who is precisely the opposite of Yeshua's Bride. Thus enters the concept of the bride of Satan, who will be used, abused, and eventually killed by Satan when he needs her no more.

- Many have tried to guess who the two witnesses will be. The likeliest possibilities, in our view, will be Enoch and Elijah, neither of whom ever actually died in a physical sense. And both have unfinished business to complete, started thousands of years ago under conditions that haven't been the same until . . . now.

- The last trumpet will herald the coming of Yeshua, with His groomsmen, on the night before the Wedding of the Lamb, to snatch His Bride away for the traditional party that comes before the wedding. The letter, seal, and trumpet tribulations have now occurred in her presence, but she will not be here on earth for what comes next.

We have not yet arrived at a description of this snatching away. It will come in Volume 3 in this series, at which point it will be discussed in detail. But it's coming!

11

Coming to a Close

THIRTY OR FORTY YEARS AGO it didn't seem very likely that any of the prophecies in the book of Revelation would come true in the lifetimes of most of the people who were alive then. Iran was still allied with the United States, Libya was not yet our enemy, and African countries such as Chad and Ethiopia were certainly not allied with Russia.

But despite all that – and perhaps somewhat under the radar – things were not exactly quiet in the Arab world. In terms of how events in the Middle East eventually affected the United States, one of the more visible signs of Iranian unrest reared its head in 1979 when a small band of local militants stormed the U.S. embassy in Tehran and took seventy hostages. They held them for a grand total of 444 days, releasing them only after Ronald Reagan became president. Many people believed that even though Jimmy Carter had tied himself in Gordian knots of indecision, Reagan would not hesitate to come to the aid of his fellow citizens with every weapon in the U.S. arsenal.

Since then, however, over the last two or three decades we've seen virtually all of the Middle Eastern nations re-aligning themselves in various ways, exactly as predicted in the Bible. Just about the only consistent theme has been their hatred for the United States, coupled with their eagerness to get behind the Arabs to support in any way they could the Arab world's perverse determination to destroy Israel.

But then, a little less than two decades ago, the Russian "experiment" in communism completely failed, largely due to the artful maneuverings of Ronald Reagan. At the time, to some people, it looked like a prophetic collapse, but for those who were aware of the long-term realities of prophecy it seemed more likely that Russia was just consolidating. And sure enough, that's exactly what's happened over the last few years. Russia herself is still opposing the U.S. in the UN; if anything, she is more antagonistic than ever toward Israel and her overall agenda is becoming more and more plain. Russia will ultimately lead an invasion of Israel, as prophesized in Ezekiel 38, but it won't be happening tomorrow.

Where Are We Now?

At this point we have explored the panoramic view given by the seven letters and we've worked our way through the seven seals and the seven trumpets. Inevitably, all of that brings up the obvious question: Where are we now?

As we move toward the second decade of the twenty-first century, we believe that the first horse rider is riding and the second and third are on his heels. That rider on the white horse – with the bow in his hand and the crown on his head – has been out there "conquering" for decades, riding over the earth, increasing deception and dumbing down virtually all of mankind so we will be more receptive to his not-so-secret and not-so-subtle machinations.

Has there ever been a time, in the United States of America, when our educational standards were as low as they are today – when what we expect of high school and even college graduates

11 - Coming to a Close

barely equals what we once required of seventh and eighth graders? When we were less connected to our Judeo-Christian heritage? When we were less willing to stand up in our businesses, our courts, our legislatures, our executive branch, our schools, and our local communities for the God we claim to worship?

We also believe that all the dominoes are now basically set up for seal #2 to take place, which we believe will be a devastating war between Israel and the Edomites, now known as the Arabs. In fact, we may already be experiencing the opening tensions of that war, which are certainly building up every day. Soon we could very well see an explosion of events, leading to a violent war that will bring about the deaths of millions of people and could very well spread to many other locations around the globe. To be followed, of course, by famine, economic upheaval, plague, and disruptions of every kind all over the world.

But let's be clear. This war will not involve Russia and is *not* Armageddon. On the contrary, it is the war that has to happen first, as prophesied, so that a complete victory by Israel can lead to a time of peace all over the Middle East. During the years after this war we'll see Israel become very wealthy, living in peace and not worried about security as they are now. The Arabs will be disorganized, defeated, and disillusioned, and their numbers will be vastly reduced.

Meanwhile, Israel will greatly expand her borders, for which she will no longer need to build walls and fences. They will reclaim the temple mount so they can begin rebuilding the temple. After that we will see the re-initiation of the temple services by the priests, at which point Russia will begin to covet everything Israel then has, probably including oil deposits on land that is just now beginning to be explored.

It is further prophesied that during this time period the wealth of Israel will be compounded and multiplied, and that's what Russia will be lusting after – this blessing that God will pour out on Israel. The state of affairs in Israel, just before Russia and her end-times allies make their final move, is described in Ezekiel 38 and 39. In particular, Ezekiel 38:8 describes Israel just before the next invasion, while the remainder of the following portion of chapter 38 describes how Russia and several other nations will react:

> [8]"After many days you will be summoned; in the latter years you will come into the land that is restored from the sword, whose inhabitants have been gathered from many nations to the mountains of Israel which had been a continual waste; but its people were brought out from the nations, and they are living securely, all of them. [9]"You will go up, you will come like a storm; you will be like a cloud covering the land, you and all your troops, and many peoples with you." [10]"Thus says the Lord GOD, "It will come about on that day, that thoughts will come into your mind and you will devise an evil plan, [11]and you will say, 'I will go up against the land of unwalled villages. I will go against those who are at rest, that live securely, all of them living without walls and having no bars or gates, [12]to capture spoil and to seize plunder, to turn your hand against the waste places which are now inhabited, and against the people who are gathered from the nations, who have acquired cattle and goods, who live at the center of the world.'
>
> [13]"Sheba and Dedan and the merchants of Tarshish with all its villages will say to you, 'Have you come to capture spoil? Have you assembled your company to seize plunder, to carry away silver and gold, to take away cattle and goods, to capture great spoil?'" [14]"Therefore prophesy, son of man, and say to Gog, 'Thus says the Lord GOD, "On that day when My people Israel are living securely, will you not know it? [15]"You will come from your place out of the remote parts of the north, you and many peoples with you, all of them riding on horses, a great assembly and a mighty army;

> ¹⁶and you will come up against My people Israel like a cloud to cover the land. It shall come about in the last days that I will bring you against My land, so that the nations may know Me when I am sanctified through you before their eyes, O Gog." (Ezekiel 38:8–16)

God's Hand on Israel

Certainly we are all aware that, on a per capita basis, the Jewish people have earned more patents, made more medical and scientific discoveries, invented more technological marvels, earned more Nobel prizes, Oscars, and Emmys, and made more significant contributions – *including the Bible itself* – to mankind as a whole than any other people group anywhere else on the earth – by far. Ezekiel essentially tells us that God will continue to expand Israel's wealth, until Russia and all her cohorts simply cannot stand to sit idly by and watch themselves being outclassed, out-hustled, and outpaced in every meaningful way while they themselves continue to reap nothing more bountiful than what they have planted in anger, sown in hatred, and reaped in sorrow.

At the end of the second war in Revelation, Russia and all her allies – who by this time will all be linked together with her – will be annihilated by fire and brimstone. The clear implication of Ezekiel 38:18–23 is that they get themselves destroyed in a miraculous way by the hand of God, in the area between the Mediterranean Sea and the southern tip of the Dead Sea. This, incidentally, was also the area that was originally given to Judah, plus additional territory that lay south of there.

These events will then usher in the fulfillment of Daniel's prophecy, of which those oft-mentioned seven years remain. That time period is divided up into two halves, the first of which will be dominated by the two witnesses, who will bring the judgment of God on those who are disobedient. They will also extend a level of protection to God's Bride, who – contrary to what so many now believe – will still be here.

The last half of those seven years, which we'll much more fully describe in the next volume, will then be dominated by the False Messiah . . . until God finally declares "Enough!"

A Bit of Perspective

Thirty years ago, the imminence of so much of this could not have been discerned via the events and the alliances of that era. The essence of the huge, end-times deception that's now beginning involves (1) the evil kingdoms that we've talked about briefly in Volumes 1 and 2 of this series, and (2) the obvious ripening of the crops (i.e., the evil) they've been planting since the creation of the world, to be reaped in the final days before the Second Coming.

That's why we've spent so much time in these two books talking about devils, demons, Nephilim, good angels vs. bad angels, and the spiritual war that's clearly going on right now even if it hasn't yet made itself obvious enough for everyone to see. Because, as the first few chapters in Volume 3 unfold, we will see with startling clarity that this conflict really has been joined in bold, unmistakable ways. In turn, in very literal, unambiguous ways we're about to see things that have been anticipated for thousands of years, sometimes eagerly and sometimes with a great deal of apprehension.

Some of the issues we will address in Volume 3 will include:

- How will the False Messiah manage to personify the real McCoy? We know he'll fool a lot of people, but how?

- What does 666 really mean?

11 - Coming to a Close

- What will be the most likely flashpoint for the Arab/Israeli conflagration that will bring about vast changes in the world?

- When does the Bride join her Groom?

- What will the Second Coming look like – Hebrew betrothal ceremony, or something else entirely?

- What is the sequence in which God restores mankind back to the Garden of Eden ideal?

- When will man get his new body? How does this restoration overlay the coming of the Son, the Holy Spirit, and the Father?

- When will the Father begin to dwell forevermore with mankind?

- Why does the book of Revelation describe His Second Coming in two entirely different ways – first coming in the clouds, then on a white horse with an army behind Him?

Things to Watch for Next

- Increased economic upheaval, as foretold in the third seal

- Increased difficulty in the feeding of earth's population (i.e., famine)

- Increased antagonism against the West, especially the United States

- Continued military aggression, by Russia

- Continued strengthening of friendships between Russia and the Arabs, plus increased supplies of sophisticated weaponry sent to Syria and Iran. Iran, by the way, is prophesied to assist the Arabs in the war between the Arabs and Israel.

- Decreased alliances between the U.S. and Europe. Europe will be part of the alliance of nations that gives the False Messiah his platform. Recent comments about the European Union's early demise are incorrect.

Where Does the United States Fit?

Ironically, the United States is never specifically mentioned in prophecy but it is alluded to in a few places. Those allusions typically refer to the U.S., and others, as "righteous goyim," or a righteous Gentile nation. We suspect that the reason why many nations are not specifically mentioned in end-times prophecy is that God has not fixed their destiny yet, but has given them the opportunity to choose which way they'll go. Here in the United States especially He's given us great latitude to make good or bad decisions. Who we will stand with will be extremely important to our final destiny. Will it be Israel, or those who completely reject the God of the Bible and join with the Beast?

In that context the United States is becoming more and more rejected by the world, but that is not a bad thing. Praise God – the people who hate us so vehemently are those who will continue to reject Him in an ever-more-massive way. If that's why they are rejecting us . . . great! Standing up for God is sometimes lonely work. If you've ever been in the stock market, you certainly understand that it's always a bad idea to run with the herd.

Was George Washington Right?

Let us conclude with a look at what could be one of the most amazing prophecies in American history, once familiar to thousands of Americans but now mostly forgotten.

11 - Coming to a Close

In 1859, a Revolutionary War soldier named Anthony Sherman gave a detailed account of an astonishing prophecy to a writer named Wesley Bradshaw, who then published Sherman's recollections in *The National Tribune* in 1880. According to Sherman, God did leave this country with a prophecy, via the Father of America. General George Washington received it at Valley Forge, Pennsylvania, during the winter of 1777, and conveyed it to Anthony Sherman who was then a young soldier serving as an aide to Washington.

George Washington's prophecy detailed three great events that would come upon this nation in the years ahead:

- The first was the Revolutionary War, which was going on at the time.

- The second was the American Civil War, which began shortly after Sherman's death.

- The description of the third war coincides remarkably with what the book of Revelation tells us about one final conflagration that will usher in the Second Coming.

These first two wars have now taken place precisely as prophesied. Beyond that, in George Washington's own words as reported by Sherman, the angelic being who delivered the vision to Washington ended his message this way:

> "Son of the Republic, what you have seen is thus interpreted: Three great perils will come upon the Republic. The most fearful is the third, but in this greatest conflict, the whole world united shall not prevail against her. Let every child of the Republic learn to live for his God, his land, and the Union."

Washington himself then concluded: "With these words the vision vanished, and I started from my seat and felt that I had seen a vision wherein had been shown to me the birth, progress, and destiny of the United States."

According to the details of Washington's vision, in that final conflict America will be invaded by many nations from all over the globe, and for all intents and purposes will be on the verge of defeat. Except that, at the very end, God reminds America of what He instructed us more than two hundred years previously, which amounted to three things that we should live for:

- God

- Our land

- The unity of purpose, effort, and respect for each other's God-given rights on which the United States was built

What Really Lies Ahead?

Down through the years, some people have suggested that what has become known as "George Washington's Vision," as referenced above, could be a fake. Sadly, those people miss the point entirely. Whether it really happened or not, the message it contains is appropriate, timely, and pretty much irrefutable. We've already survived the two wars it predicted, and both the Bible and any reasonable understanding of current events, taken together, strongly suggest that this country will someday face some times of testing unlike anything we've seen in the past. And those times are probably not too far away anymore. Meanwhile, things are not likely to be anywhere near as easy for most of us as they've been for the last fifty or sixty years.

By way of illustration, not long ago, via email to thousands of people, someone circulated a current picture of the actors who played the leads in a sitcom called *Leave It to Beaver* back in the early days of television. This 1950s/1960s show has since attained

11 - Coming to a Close

iconic status and still attracts a fair-sized crowd of people eager to watch reruns of the original episodes, marketed now on DVDs.

But imagine what a jolt it must have been for so many folks to see that picture of the three major actors as they now appear – perfectly normal and respectable-looking gentlemen, but *older* gentlemen with wrinkles, hair-loss, and aged faces that hardly resemble what they looked like fifty years ago.

In a sense, that could well be the story of our country. America is more than two hundred years old now, and sometimes we show signs of aging. In fact, some of our wrinkles have turned into fault lines, and some of what we once recognized as minor political differences have now become earthquakes and tsunamis.

Even so, God has not given up on us and therefore we'd be crazy to give up on ourselves. He blessed us when we started, He's stayed with us through some of the world's major upheavals, and He's there right now, still waiting with arms outstretched to welcome us back to His embrace . . . if we would simply reach for Him.

In the end – literally – this is what it's all about. Whether we have twenty years, thirty years, or even more before the final Judgment Day, to paraphrase Ecclesiastes 12:1 we have plenty of time to "remember our Creator" – perhaps no longer in the "days of our youth" but certainly in every day that passes from now on.

This is what will determine how God will deal with the United States of America in the end times. As we finalize the book you're now holding in your hands, and as we look toward Volume 3 in this series, we urge you to remember that. To tell it to others. And then to do whatever you can to revamp, revitalize, and renew the love, the respect, and the heartfelt devotion toward the God who created us that once characterized most of our country.

This country still calls itself the *home of the free and the brave*, but we are only free when we truly trust in God and maintain an ongoing relationship with Him. And if we are not willing to acknowledge, to trust, and to lean exclusively on Him we cannot possibly be strong and brave enough to remain triumphant through the rougher portions of the end times that we will eventually have to endure.

What's true for all of us as individuals is true for our country, too. Through a prophesy delivered to George Washington, at the very moment when this country was going through its birth pangs, God forewarned all of us of what would be our eventual destiny if we rejected Him.

May we all choose wisely. And may the contents of this book – along with those of Volume 1 (now finished) and Volume 3 (yet to come) – help each of you, our readers, not only to make wise choices but to form wise associations and wise alliances with our Creator.

Let us make what *He* wants what *we* want as well.

Afterword

We realize that some of our readers might not have a personal relationship with Yeshua and His Father, and therefore might not fully understand where we're coming from when we speak so often of divine covenant. To put it as simply as possible, salvation itself is the only possible foundation on which the godly covenants of which we speak so often in these first two volumes can be built. Everything starts with salvation – it's the ultimate beginning, the ultimate first step, the ultimate "moment of change" that will usher in everything else that God wants for you.

But at the same time, as we have said before, salvation is just salvation – nothing more and nothing less. It's the beginning and not the end; it's the first step toward God, not the entire walk; it's the moment of reconciliation but not the entirety of the relationship that will develop from there. In truth it's only the beginning . . . but wonderful things do lie ahead.

Because, as we have explained extensively in both of these volumes – and especially in volume 1 – God is interested in an intimate relationship with you through biblical covenant, just like the ones He had with Abraham, Isaac, Jacob, Isaiah, Ezekiel, Matthew, John, and all the rest of His covenant partners in the Bible.

It all starts with this simple prayer by which you can begin your personal relationship with God:

Dear Yeshua,

I believe that you are the Son of God and the only way to God. I believe that you died on the cross for my sins and rose again so that I might be forgiven and might receive eternal life. I confess my sins before you and hold nothing back. I repent of my sins, I accept your sacrifice on my behalf, and I turn to you for mercy and forgiveness.

May this truly be the ultimate *Day of New Beginnings* for you!

Appendix A
God's Incredible Consistency

The master menorah is built on one foundational menorah with seven mini-menorahs added. The end result features one "mini" centered on each of the original seven branches. In addition, each of the seven original branches represents one of the three primary colors, which are also the colors of the various biblical covenants.

At the same time, from a construction standpoint, since each branch goes through the shamash branch in the center and extends out to the other side, each of the six outer branches is really part of a pair, as shown in Figure 3-3, with each color in the same relative position on *both sides* of the center.

So, the two outer branches are red (service), the two middle branches are yellow (salt), and the two inner branches are blue (sandal), arranged from the outside to the inside. Likewise with each of the corresponding mini-menorahs.

Now, take a look at that well-known quotation from the book of Ezekiel:

> [4]As I looked, behold, a storm wind was coming from the north, a great cloud with fire flashing forth continually and a bright light around it, and in its midst something like glowing metal in the midst of the fire. [5]Within it there were figures resembling four living beings. And this was their appearance: they had human form.
>
> [6]Each of them had four faces and four wings. [7]Their legs were straight and their feet were like a calf's hoof, and they gleamed like burnished bronze. [8]Under their wings on their four sides were human hands. As for

Appendix A - God's Incredible Consistency

the faces and wings of the four of them, ⁹their wings touched one another; their faces did not turn when they moved, each went straight forward.

¹⁰As for the form of their faces, each had the face of a man; all four had the face of a lion on the right and the face of a bull on the left, and all four had the face of an eagle. ¹¹Such were their faces. Their wings were spread out above; each had two touching another being, and two covering their bodies.

¹²And each went straight forward; wherever the spirit was about to go, they would go, without turning as they went. ¹³In the midst of the living beings there was something that looked like burning coals of fire, like torches darting back and forth among the living beings. The fire was bright, and lightning was flashing from the fire. ¹⁴And the living beings ran to and fro like bolts of lightning.

¹⁵Now as I looked at the living beings, behold, there was one wheel on the earth beside the living beings, for each of the four of them. ¹⁶The appearance of the wheels and their workmanship was like sparkling beryl, and all four of them had the same form, their appearance and workmanship being as if one wheel were within another. ¹⁷Whenever they moved, they moved in any of their four directions without turning as they moved.

¹⁸As for their rims they were lofty and awesome, and the rims of all four of them were full of eyes round about. ¹⁹Whenever the living beings moved, the wheels moved with them. And whenever the living beings rose from the earth, the wheels rose also. ²⁰Wherever the spirit was about to go, they would go in that direction. And the wheels rose close beside them; for the spirit of the living beings was in the wheels. ²¹Whenever those went, these went; and whenever those stood still, these

stood still. And whenever those rose from the earth, the wheels rose close beside them; for the spirit of the living beings was in the wheels.

Vision of Divine Glory

²²Now over the heads of the living beings there was something like an expanse, like the awesome gleam of crystal, spread out over their heads. ²³Under the expanse their wings were stretched out straight, one toward the other; each one also had two wings covering its body on the one side and on the other. ²⁴I also heard the sound of their wings like the sound of abundant waters as they went, like the voice of the Almighty, a sound of tumult like the sound of an army camp; whenever they stood still, they dropped their wings. ²⁵And there came a voice from above the expanse that was over their heads; whenever they stood still, they dropped their wings.

²⁶Now above the expanse that was over their heads there was something resembling a throne, like lapis lazuli in appearance; and on that which resembled a throne, high up, was a figure with the appearance of a man. ²⁷Then I noticed from the appearance of His loins and upward something like glowing metal that looked like fire all around within it, and from the appearance of His loins and downward I saw something like fire; and there was a radiance around Him. ²⁸As the appearance of the rainbow in the clouds on a rainy day, so was the appearance of the surrounding radiance. Such was the appearance of the likeness of the glory of the LORD. And when I saw it, I fell on my face and heard a voice speaking.

Chapter 2

¹Then He said to me, "Son of man, stand on your feet that I may speak with you!" ²As He spoke to me the

Spirit entered me and set me on my feet; and I heard Him speaking to me. (Ezekiel 1:4–2:2)

This rather long quotation includes some of the most fascinating references in the entire Bible, all coming from a prophetic vision given to one of the Old Testament prophets. It has inspired innumerable flights of rhetorical fancy, even as it has been interpreted in many different ways.

But maybe it doesn't have to be "interpreted" at all. Rather than assuming that Ezekiel saw something symbolic, why not consider that he saw something absolutely real instead? Here's what we believe it could have been.

Building on Eternal, Universal Principles

Suppose that God sat on His throne in the middle of a gigantic menorah-like structure, with the colors of covenant built into the branches. Suppose that gigantic structure also included mini-menorahs, corresponding in colors and arrangement to the mini-menorahs on the master menorah we use to map the book of Revelation. Finally, suppose that – like everything else in the universe – that gigantic throne/menorah spun at incredible speeds just like all the structural components of God's creation.

What would be the result from a visual standpoint? And how would an ancient Hebrew prophet react to what he was seeing, given what he was familiar with in that era?

- **First,** the "wheels within wheels" description in Ezekiel 1:16 would be perfectly logical if he saw rotating mini-menorahs, spinning within the rotating master menorah, to create a wheels-within-wheels image. As is well known in physics, if you spin a light source around a center fast enough your eye can no longer perceive the individual source of the light, but now perceives a *circle* of light.

- **Second,** the primary colors of the foundational (master) branches, visually mixed and overlaid at the proper speeds with the primary colors of the mini-menorahs, could easily create the appearance of a rainbow, either surrounding the whirling objects or embodied within them, which Ezekiel saw in 1:28.

- **Third,** God's throne would most assuredly be in the very center (i.e., the shamash) of the master metaphor, exactly where Ezekiel saw it in 1:26.

What proof do we have that the above explanation is correct? Well, compare Ezekiel's vision to what we already know about God, and how he repeatedly relates to mankind.

- Let's consider all the *symbolism* inherent in the colors of covenant, the physical structure of the menorah, the placement and identity of the mini-menorahs, and the principles of the various forms of holy, biblical covenant that govern how we can establish and build true relationships with God Himself. Symbolism is one of the most obvious things that God uses to reinforce his messages to us, as we discussed at length in Volume 1 of this series. If you've been away from that book for a while, please go back and review it since much of Volume 1 touched repeatedly on this very subject.

- Let's consider the *physical structure* of what Ezekiel saw. No one can deny that God repeatedly brings together form, color, and other reinforcing elements to not only convey His personal messages to us on a symbolic level but also to establish and unify the structural integrity of His entire creation. Starting with the very smallest part of creation that man has been able to identify via incredibly powerful electron microscopes, and extending out to the farthest reaches of the cosmos that man has been able to see via incredibly powerful telescopes, the basic foundational *structure-of-creation* pattern is the same.

The pattern is 100% consistent throughout creation, whether at the atomic level, the planetary level, or the galactic level.

Thus the nucleus of each atom contains *protons* and *neutrons*, surrounded by smaller particles called *electrons* that zip around the center at astonishing speeds. As a result, most atoms are actually 99% empty space yet are surrounded by such incredible force fields that they function as though they were solid all the way through. Likewise at the other extreme – the universe is composed of unbelievably huge celestial bodies that are also surrounded by smaller bodies that rotate around the center of the larger body at astonishing speeds. And the same general construction is true of everything in between – lots of motion, lots of "emptiness," yet lots of solidity, balance, and stability created by super-hyper, seemingly endless activity. All of which would fly apart in a hot minute if someone could counteract the forces holding everything together, as we have learned to do on a relatively small scale via atomic weapons.

And all of this is controlled and created (and maintains its status quo) by the four elemental forces that we've described elsewhere in this volume: gravity, electro-magnetic attraction and the "greater" and "lesser" atomic forces that keep the atoms of creation from flying apart.

At the other extreme, all the galaxies we are familiar with (especially the spiral galaxies) are organized in the same way, featuring central light sources surrounded by other suns.

Is it possible that all of this might also be consistent at the human family level as well? Or, that it might all mirror the covenants that God offers to us?

- Finally, let's consider what we know about how God positions Himself on His own throne. Everything that we've mentioned above revolves around a center. In our own solar system that center is the sun, a huge light to which God has often been compared. In the same way we know that God sits on His throne in heaven, and it's perfectly logical to assume that both the throne itself and all its attendants also revolve in the same fashion, with God at or above the center exactly as Ezekiel saw Him. After all, God is the ultimate God of Consistency – and what arrangement would be more consistent with that central truth?

All of the above also parallels God's desired relationship with us on a metaphorical level. He is the shamash around which we circle, mirroring the ancient Hebrew marriage tradition in which the bride encircles her groom seven times during their wedding ceremony. He is also our source of light and direction, and therefore He should always be at the very center of our lives.

Appendix B
The Seven Rules of Hillel

The Seven Rules of Hillel[70] existed long before Rabbi Hillel (60 BCE – 20 CE?), but he was the first to write them down. The rules are so old we see them used in the Tenach[71] (Old Testament).

Rabbis Hillel and Shamai were competitive leading figures in Judaism during the days of Yeshua's youth. Hillel was known for teaching the Spirit of the Law and Shamai was known for teaching the Letter of the Law. Yeshua's teaching largely followed that of the School of Hillel rather than that of the School of Shamai (an exception being Yeshua agreeing with Shamai regarding divorce in Matthew 19:9).

For example, Yeshua's famous "golden rule": *Whatever you would that men should do to you, do you even to them, for this is the Torah and the Prophets.* (Matthew 7:12)

This reads very closely with Hillel's famous statement: *What is hateful to you, do not do to your neighbor that is the whole Torah ...* (b.Shabbat 31a)

Upon Hillel's death the mantle of the School of Hillel was passed to his son Simeon. Upon Simeon's death the mantle of the school of Hillel passed to Gamliel. This Gamliel spoke in defense of the early Nazarenes (Acts 5:34-39). He was the teacher of Sha'ul/Paul (Acts 22:3).

In 2 Tim. 2:15, Paul speaks of *"rightly dividing the word of truth."* What did Paul mean by this? Was he saying that there were right and wrong ways to interpret the scriptures? Did Paul believe there were actual rules to be followed when interpreting (understanding) the Scriptures? Was Paul speaking of the Seven Rules of Hillel?

Paul was certainly taught these rules in the School of Hillel by Hillel's own grandson Ganliel. When we examine Paul's writings we will see that they are filled with usages of Hillel's Seven Rules (several examples appear below). It would appear then that the Seven Rules of Hillel are at least part of what Paul was speaking of when he spoke of *"rightly dividing the Word of truth."*

These are the Seven Rules of Hillel:

1. Kal Vahomer *(Light and Heavy)*

The *Kal vahomer* rule says that what applies in a less important case will certainly apply in a more important case. A kal vahomer argument is often, but not always, signaled by a phrase such as *"how much more..."*

The Rabbinical writers recognize two forms of kal vahomer:
- *kal vahomer meforash* – In this form the kal vahomer argument appears explicitly.
- *kal vahomer satum* – In which the kal vahomer argument is only implied.

There are several examples of kal vahomer in the Tenach.
For example: *Behold the righteous shall be recompensed in the earth: much more the wicked and the sinner.* (Proverbs 11:31)

And: *If you have run with footmen and they have wearied you, then how can you contend with horses?* (Jeremiah 12:5a)

Other Tenach examples to look at: Deuteronomy 31:27; 1 Samuel 23:3; Jerermiah 12:5b; Ezekiel 15:5; Esther 9:12. There are also several examples of kal vahomer in the New Testament. Y'shua often uses this form of argument.

For example: *If a man receives circumcision on the Sabbath, so that the Law of Moses should not be broken, are you angry with me because I made a man completely well on the Sabbath?* (Jn. 7:23)

And: *What man is there among you who has one sheep, and if it falls into a pit on the Sabbath, will not lay hold of it and lift it out? Of how much more value then is a man than a sheep? Therefore it is lawful to do good on the Sabbath.* (Mt. 12:11-12)

Other examples of Y'shua's usage of kal vahomer are: Matthew 6:26, 30; Luke 12:24, 28; Matthew 7:11; Luke 11:13; Matthew 10:25; John 15:18-20; Matthew 12:12; John 7:23.

Paul especially used kal vahomer. Examples include: Romans 5:8-9, 10, 15, 17; 11:12, 24; 1 Corinthians 9:11-12; 12:22; 2 Corinthians 3:7-9, 11; Philippians 2:12; Philemon 1:16; Hebrews 2:2-3; 9:13-14; 10:28-29; 12:9, 25.

2. G'zerah Shavah *(Equivalence of Expressions)*

An analogy is made between two separate texts on the basis of a similar phrase, word or root – i.e., where the same words are applied to two separate cases, it follows that the same considerations apply to both.

Tenakh example: By comparing 1 Samuel 1:10 to Judges 13:5 using the phrase *"no razor shall touch his head"* we may conclude that Samuel, like Samson, was a Nazarite.

New Testament example: In Hebrews 3:6-4:13 Paul compares Psalms 95:7-11 to Hebrews 3:7-11 to Genesis 2:2 to Hebrews 4:4, based on the words "works" and "day"/"today" ("today" in Hebrew is literally "the day"). Paul uses this exegesis to conclude that there will be 6,000 years of this world followed by a 1,000 year Shabbat.

3. Binyan ab mikathub echad *(Building up a "Family" from a Single Text)*

A principle is found in several passages: A consideration found in one of them applies to all. Hebrews 9:11-22 applies "blood" from Exodus 24:8=Hebrews 9:20 to Jerermiah 31:31-34.

4. Binyab ab mishene kethubim *(Building up a "Family" from Two or More Texts)*

A principle is established by relating two texts together: The principle can then be applied to other passages.

For example: *You shall do no unrighteousness in judgment, in measures of length, of weight, or quantity. Just balances, just weights, a just ephah, and a just hin, shall you have; I am the Lord your God, which brought you out of the land of Egypt.* (Leviticus 19:35-36)

By use of the fourth rule of Hillel we can recognize that the provision of *equal weights and measures* applies also to how we judge others and their actions.

In Hebrews 1:5-14, Paul cites the following to build a rule that the Messiah is of a higher order than angels:

>Psalms 2:7 = Hebrews 1:5
>2 Samuel 7:14 = Hebrews 1:5
>Deuteronomy 32:43/Psalms 97:7/(Neh. 9:6) = Hebrews 1:6
>Psalms 104:4 = Hebrews 1:7
>Psalms 45:6-7 = Hebrews 1:8-9
>Psalms 102:25-27 = Hebrews 1:10-12
>Psalms 110:1 = Hebrews 1:13

Binyan ab mikathub echad and *Binyab ab mishene kethubim* are especially useful in identifying biblical principles and applying them to real life situations. In this way Scripture is given a renewed context so that it remains relevant for all generations.

5. Kelal uferat *(The General and the Particular)*

A general principle may be restricted by a particular usage of it in another verse – or, conversely, a particular rule may be extended into a general principle. A Tenach example: Genesis 1:27 makes the general statement that God created man. Genesis 2:7, 21 particularizes this by giving the details of the creation of Adam and Chava (Eve). Other examples would be verses detailing how to perform sacrifices or how to keep the feasts. In the Gospels, the principle of divorce being allowed for "uncleanliness," is particularized to mean for sexual immorality only.

6. Kayotze bo mimekom akhar *(Analogy Made from Another Passage)*

Two passages may seem to conflict until compared with a third, which has points of general though not necessarily verbal similarity.

Tenach examples:
- Leviticus 1:1, *"out of the tent of meeting"* and Exodus 25:22, *"from above the ark of the covenant between the cherubim"* seem to disagree until we examine Num. 7:89 where we learn that Moses entered the tent of meeting to hear YHWH speaking from between the cherubim.
- 1 Chronicles 27:1 explained the numerical disagreement between 2 Samuel 24:9 and 1 Chronicles 21:5.
- Exodus 19:20, "YHWH came down upon Mount Sinai" seems to disagree with Deuteronomy 4:36, *"Out of Heaven He let you hear His voice."* Exodus 20:19 (20:22 in some editions) reconciles the two by telling us that God brought the heavens down to the mount and spoke. (m.Sifra 1:7)

An example from Romans: Paul shows that the following Tenach passages SEEM to conflict:

The just shall live by faith (Romans 1:17 = Habakkuk 2:4) with *There is none righteous, no, not one ...* (Romans 3:10 = Psalms 14:1-3= Psalms 53:1-3; Ecclesiastes 7:20). Paul does the same here: *[G-d] will render to each one according to his deeds.* (Romans 2:6 = Psalms 62:12; Proverbs 24:12) with *Blessed are those whose lawless deeds are forgiven, and whose sins are covered; Blessed is the man whom YHWH shall not impute sin.* (Romans 4:7-8 = Psalms 32:1-2)

Paul resolves the apparent conflict by citing Genesis 15:6 (in Romans 4:3, 22): *Abraham believed G-d, and it was accounted to him for righteousness.* Thus Paul resolves the apparent conflict by showing that under certain circumstances, belief/faith/trust (same word in Hebrew) can act as a substitute for righteousness/being just (same word in Hebrew).

7. Davar hilmad me'anino *(Explanation Obtained from Context)*

The total context, not just the isolated statement, must be considered for an accurate exegesis. An example would be Romans 14:1, *"I know and am convinced by the Lord Yeshua that nothing is unclean of itself; but to him who considers anything to be unclean, to him it is unclean."* Paul is not abrogating the kosher laws, but pointing out to Gentile believers in the congregation at Rome (within his larger <u>context</u> of Romans) that: 1) things are unclean not of themselves but because God said they are unclean, and 2) they must remember the higher principle, that their "freedom to eat what is unclean" is secondary to the salvation of unsaved Jews who are observing their behavior, as they are looking for "Gentiles coming into the faith of Israel" to be acting in an "appropriate manner" as a truth test of Paul's ministry (and Yeshua's Messiahship).

Endnotes

Chapter 1 — Revelation Revealed

[1] The book you hold in your hands is Volume 2 in a projected series of three. So, every subsequent reference to Volume 1 in this series, including these footnotes, will refer specifically to *Lost in Translation: Rediscovering The Hebrew Roots of our Faith*, by John Klein and Adam Spears, with Michael Christopher (Knoxville, TN: Selah Publishing Group, 2007). The ISBN number of Volume 1 is 978-1-58930-199-3.

[2] A ketubah is a Hebraic/Jewish marriage contract; see "What Is a Ketubah?" in this chapter.

[3] From both biblical and extra-biblical sources. Also known as the "Nazarene sect," it referred to those who adhered to the Torah but also accepted Yeshua's divinity and His virgin birth. See also Volume 1 in this series, and other reference works in the Bibliography and the Recommended Reading section at the end of this volume. The history of what later became known as "the church" during the first few centuries AD has been well-documented and is fascinating reading, but is beyond the scope of this volume.

[4] The name "Jesus Christ" is derived from Greek and Latin sources; the name given to Him at birth, by His Hebrew parents, was *Yeshua*.

[5] See Volume 1, chapter 3.

[6] See Volume 1, chapter 4.

[7] Alfred Edersheim, *Sketches of Jewish Social Life* (Peabody, MA: Hendrickson, 1994), p. 137. Additional information can also be found in: George Robinson, *Essential Judaism: A Complete Guide to Beliefs, Customs, and Rituals* (New York: Simon & Schuster/Pocket Books, 2000), p. 160.

[8] "Tanakh" is a Hebrew transliteration for the acronym "TNK," which stands for Torah (law), Navi'im (prophets), and Ketuvim (writings). The tanakh is also called the "Book of Covenants"; our non-Jewish name is the Greek-derived designation, "Old Testament." "B'rit Hadashah" is Hebrew for "Renewed Covenant," which is the correct name for what most Christians call the "New Testament."

[9] See Volume 1, chapter 1.

¹⁰ David Biven and Roy Blizzard, Jr., *Understanding the Difficult Words of Jesus* (Shippensburg, PA: Destiny Image Publishers, 1994), p. 111-115.
¹¹ Matthew 5:21-26 is the first of five examples given by Jesus to illustrate his method of interpreting Scripture. The commandment "Do not hate your brother in your heart" is found in Leviticus 19:17. The commandment "Do not murder" is found in Exodus 20:13 and Deuteronomy 5:17. (Note: This footnote taken directly from bottom-of-page commentary from *Understanding the Difficult Words of Jesus*, p. 114.)
¹² Gesenius, H. W. F., *Gesenius' Hebrew-Chaldee Lexicon to the Old Testament* (Baker Books: Grand Rapids, MI, 1979), p. 473–474.
¹³ See Volume 1, chapter 5.
¹⁴ See Volume 1, chapter 1.
¹⁵ Ibid.
¹⁶ For additional examples, see Volume 1 – for example, the Matthew 11 passage on the "breaker" (i.e., *peretz* in Hebrew) coming forth (i.e., the shepherd releasing the sheep from the fold), in Volume 1, chapter 1.
¹⁷ Acts 26:14 and Acts 21:40 are often interpreted correctly, as saying that Paul was speaking (or being spoken to by God) in the "Hebrew dialect." But again, we find some scholars saying that this has to be incorrect: "They must have meant Aramaic." See also *Understanding the Difficult Words*, p. 7.
¹⁸ The word "Hebrew" was purposely mistranslated as "Aramaic." Some of the translations that do so are the KJV, the NIV, the NASB, the RSV, the ASV, the NLT, the ESV, and the NKJV.
¹⁹ Dr. Daniel ben Gigi, a noted Hebrew authority who has spent a lifetime studying the so-called "Greek writings" of the New Testament, said this in a seminar at the Messianic Jewish Northwest Regional Conference in Portland, Oregon, in February 16–19, 2001.
²⁰ This is a common expression among Bible translators.
²¹ See Volume 1, chapter 6.
²² Go to www.baonline.org, then click on "Study the Books of the Bible, then "Rev.pdf."
²³ *Ethics of the Fathers*, from *Pirkei Evot*. This is the second-to-last tractate of Mishnah; for further discussion of Mishnah, see chapter 9 in this volume.

Endnotes

Chapter 2 — The Master Menorah

[24] In the Old Testament, God is referred to in the Hebrew context as (1) *Elohim* or *Yahweh*, (2) *Mashiach*, or (3) *Ruach*. In the New Testament those three concepts get interpreted as *Father*, *Son*, and (Holy) *Spirit*. *Elohim* is used as a title, *Yahweh* is His personal name, and *Mashiach* is the Hebrew word for *Messiah*. *Christ* is an English word taking the place of the underlying Hebrew word. To pull all this together, we actually *do* get the Trinity concept in the Old Testament (Genesis 1:2; Exodus 15:1–3; Isaiah 49:26), but the text is seldom interpreted that way. Meanwhile, in the New Testament the Hebrew word is still *Mashiach* but is translated as "Christ" or "Savior." Thus *Yeshua* (Jesus), as *Messiah*, is clearly in both the Old and the New Testaments, all of which is meant to make just one point. In each of these cases, no new God is being introduced! It's always the same God. The issue is translational preferences that change from the Old Testament to the New Testament. The underlying verbiage is the same, and so is the divine Creator-God.

[25] The following comes from Volume 1, chapter 5:

> In the first chapter of Ezekiel, in his first recorded vision, the prophet encountered something extraordinary. He described what he saw as a brilliant light encircled by a rainbow of colored fire and concentric "wheels within wheels." Centuries later, as recorded in Revelation, the apostle John saw something equally baffling – seven shining golden lampstands with someone standing in their midst, glowing as brightly as molten metal.
>
> Between these two accounts we read of shining rainbows, sapphire seas, winged creatures circling and shouting, thunders roaring, and lightning flashing. And in the center of all this frenzied activity, God stands alone like the nucleus of an atom, while everything glows and spins and whirls around Him.
>
> What are Ezekiel and John trying to convey? Like the blind men feeling an elephant in the familiar story, could both of these men be describing the very same thing, but from their own unique perspectives?
>
> Our research indicates that the throne of God described in Ezekiel 1:15–28, and the seven lampstands of Revelation 1:12–20, are one and the same. The seven branches on the lampstand seen by John all had a unique feature. Each separate branch was also an entire seven-branched menorah unto itself, like the "wheels

within wheels" described by Ezekiel. As flames crown the wheels and angels fly in and out, we get the impression of a spinning menorah.

Ezekiel also says that this object is God's throne, which corresponds to the throne/menorah description in Revelation 4:1–6 . . .

Even before the above, in Revelation 1:11, John is instructed to write letters to seven churches in Asia Minor. These are also represented as seven golden menorahs. Again, the foundation for understanding Revelation can be found right here, among all this evidence taken from vastly separated portions of the Bible yet interwoven together, in the Lord's own inimitable "multisensory" style, into a multi-reinforced, unmistakable image.

This configuration is the master pattern for the entire book of Revelation. The seven menorahs become a massive superstructure for organizing all the details that follow, all the way through to the end of the Bible. However, to appreciate what we're saying you first have to sort, arrange, coordinate, and then study the events of Revelation.

You do this, first, by positioning them on the master menorah, then by examining them from that perspective, carefully considering them in context as they relate to each other. At that point, the individual events begin to fit together, within the overall scenario. And then they "suddenly" make far more sense than from any other viewpoint.

[26] We have used the term "master menorah" throughout this volume. However, when we teach this subject in person we often use the term "compound menorah" as well. These are interchangeable terms, although one refers, perhaps, more to the *essence* of the concept and one refers more to the *structure* of the concept.

[27] Let us not forget that the original text of the Bible was not broken up into chapters and verses. It was one continuous document; chapter/verse breakdowns were inserted later, by various translators, and sometimes seem entirely arbitrary.

[28] *The New Testament in Hebrew and English, 3rd Edition* (Middlesex, England: The Society for Distributing Hebrew Scriptures, 2000), p. 490.

[29] This was exactly the purpose of the ancient menorah itself. Inside the tabernacle where God dwelt it was the only implement providing light for those individuals who were there to serve Him. The obvious implication is that, to be a light for God (which is what

we're supposed to be) we have to work with a sense of order, within a definite structure.

Chapter 3 — Meat on the Bones
[30] Indeed, Adam's very name derives from *Adama*, meaning "soil" or "of the earth."
[31] Gesenius, p. 695a.
[32] See Volume 1, chapter 7.

Chapter 4 — The Seven Letters
[33] David H. Stern, *Jewish New Testament Commentary* (Clarksville, MD: Jewish New Testament Publications, 1989), p. 785.
[34] See chapter 1 of this volume.
[35] Joseph Free, rev. by Howard Vos, *Archaeology and Bible History* (Grand Rapids: Zondervan, 1992).
[36] Biven and Blizzard, *Difficult Words*.
[37] Frank Seekins, *Hebrew Word Pictures* (Phoenix, AZ: Living Word Pictures, 1994).
[38] Isaac E. Mozeson, *The Word* (New York: SPI Books, 2000).
[39] The biblical Hebrew custom (and the forerunner of modern Christian baptism) is perhaps more commonly known as *mikveh*, although this word refers more specifically to the body of water itself. However, in Volume 1 we have used *mikveh* in its more common association and continue to do so in many of our teachings.
[40] *Letters of Aegenius*, Gnostic Library, Constantinople.
[41] By the time Paul wrote the book of Romans [i.e., between AD 55 and 58], the Nation of Israel (i.e., Judea and Samaria) had been part of the Roman Empire for a number of years. However, largely because of their strong national identity and their own robust legal code, the Jews had been given several rare privileges within the Roman Empire itself since the time of Julius Caesar. These included: (1) The right to govern and tax themselves; (2) The right to establish and enforce their own codes of discipline, to a point just shy of the right to carry out their own executions; (3) The right to enjoy common meals; (4) The right to hold real property; (5) The right of exemption from service in the Roman military machine; (6) The right not to worship the Roman Emperor; (7) The right to assemble together in orderly meetings, on their own schedules.

Perhaps the most significant benefit of all—and closely linked to the Jews' right to gather together—was that Judaism was the

Endnotes

only non-pagan religion allowed within the Roman Empire. Partly for this reason, most new believers in Christ, for several years after Christ's death, met in the synagogues with "regular" Jews. The Jews retained this privilege because Judaism had been well-established when the Romans conquered Israel. Perhaps the civilizing influence of Judaism seemed like a secure source and the Romans considered them safe, non-rebellious citizens.

In other words, by letting the Jews be Jews, the Romans apparently felt secure in believing that the Jews would never be a serious threat to the sovereignty of Roman authority. Unfortunately, in A.D. 70, forty years after the crucifixion of Jesus Christ, they were proven wrong. But Paul did not live to see either the Jewish uprising or the resulting destruction of the temple—plus the expulsion of all Jews from Jerusalem—that were finalized in that year.

At the same time, absolutely no new religions were allowed by the Romans in the years leading up to A.D. 70. This, in fact, partially explains why the early Christian church eventually had to go underground, into the catacombs, to survive the wanton persecutions of that era, once it began to split off from established Judaism and could no longer find shelter under Judaism's protective umbrella. Indeed, after the destruction of the temple and the expulsion of the Jews, those followers of "The Way" (an earlier name for the sect within Judaism that became Christianity) who stayed on in Jerusalem no longer had any such "umbrella" to hide under at all! They were no longer part of a protected or "allowed" religion—indeed, all known Jews had been forbidden to live in Jerusalem—and thus the early believers in Christ dared not openly identify themselves as Jewish in any way—or even as Jewish sympathizers. (Taken from *Romans: The Power of God*, by Michael Christopher. Nashville, TN: Thomas Nelson Publishers, 2004).

Chapter 5 — Shamash to the Seven Seals

[42] See http://www.askelm.com/doctrine/d760201.htm for a good introduction to this whole subject, which has also been examined exhaustively in a number of books available from many sources.

[43] The emerald crystal forms naturally into an elongated, six-sided shape, which explains why so many emeralds are cut in the rectangu-

lar "emerald cut." Ezekiel's reference (Ezekiel 1:22–28), cross-referenced against Revelation 4:3, could suggest that the rainbow around God's throne is six-sided, suggesting both the six-sided shape of an emerald and of a multi-dimensional menorah, since His throne is the master menorah.

[44] Dionysius (also known as "pseudo-Dionysius") was a Christian Neo-Platonist ("Neo-Platonism" is really "Platonism," or adherence to the ideas put forth by Plato) from the late fifth or early sixth century AD. Dionysius is given credit for transposing pagan Neo-Platonism into a distinctly new Christian context.

[45] Gesenius, p. 413.

[46] *The New Testament in Hebrew and English,* p. 496.

Chapter 6 — The Seven Seals

[47] Gesenius p. 156a–b.

[48] Money from three different sources circulated in the biblical lands during Yeshua's time – Roman coins, Greek coins, and local coins minted by the Jews themselves. Of these, the denarius was a commonly accepted Roman coin worth a day's wages.

[49] *Pirkei Avot (Ethics of the Fathers)*. This Mishnah tractate talks about war, famine, plague, and tells why each one comes on the earth as a result of violations of Torah.

Chapter 7 — Shamash to the Seven Trumpets

[50] Gesenius, p. 411a.

[51] "Code of Jewish Law" refers specifically to the *Shulchan Arukh* (literally: "Set Table"), which is a written manual – or codification – of Jewish law. It was composed by Rabbi Josef Karo in the 16th century.

[52] Gesenius, p. 773b.

Chapter 8 — The First Trumpets

[53] Reuven Prager is the man referred to here; the organization he founded is known as *Beged Ivri*. You can find him at www.begedivri.com.

[54] Alfred Edersheim, *The Temple: Its Ministry and Services* (Peabody, MA: Hendrickson Publishers, 1994), p. 128.

[55] This is the traditional Aaronic blessing, from chapter 24 of the book of Numbers:

> The Lord bless you, and keep you;
> The Lord make His face shine on you,

And be gracious to you;
The Lord lift up His countenance on you,
And give you peace. (Numbers 6:24–26)

[56] *The New Testament in Hebrew and English.*

[57] See Volume 1, chapter 4.

[58] Gesenius, page 75b. The Hebrew word *arbeh* also refers to *Nephilim*; related words are *arav* and *Anak*. The Anakites were the people descended from Cain, many of whom interbred with devils and thus created Nephilim.

[59] Volume 1, chapter 4, tells us:

> The book of Enoch gives us incomparable insight into the difference between "devils" and "demons." That clear difference is one of those major, seldom understood concepts that reappear throughout Scripture but are almost never talked about in modern Christian churches. And yet, Yeshua clearly acknowledged it in Matthew 17:21 ("But this kind does not go out except by prayer and fasting") and Mark 9:29.
>
> This understanding – of a definite difference between devils and demons – is many thousands of years old. In Yeshua's time it was a common understanding among the Jewish people, and among rabbis in particular. Hence He felt no need to over-explain Himself in the Scriptures cited above. It is still understood by Hebrew people today who are educated in such matters.
>
> In fact, the notion that devils and demons are the same is the *newer* concept. It was arbitrarily introduced into the Christian Church in AD 553 by the Council of Constantinople, as noted above. The leaders of that convocation ruled that any written opinion that distinguished between devils and demons must be destroyed. Or, to be accepted by the Church it must be altered in line with the "new thinking."
>
> This ruling was an expansion of the anti-Jewish laws initiated in AD 327. It meant that *Mishnah, Talmud* (rabbinical commentaries on the Bible), and more ancient books, such as the book of *Enoch,* were immediately outlawed – but only because they couldn't be completely destroyed. Officially, the Roman Church claimed that those books no longer had any value in providing insight into Scripture, and they were even declared "heretical." Indeed, the same ruling *almost* succeeded in deleting the books of I and II Peter and Jude, because of their agreement with (and

Endnotes

references to) the book of Enoch.

[60] The cursed ones are those who allied themselves and entered into covenant with the beast that came out of the pit. They are now in covenant with evil, riding on the backs of the beasts, to slaughter a third of mankind. Conversely, we're about to learn about another group of individuals who are being marked out to be protected and guarded, right in the center of God's temple. Metaphorically, since the temple represents covenant, these people represent those who have been saved and have done the needed training of their own minds to accomplish God's will in their lives, thus earning the right to wear the white bridal garments that we'll learn about later.

Chapter 9 — The Seven Thunders

[61] Mozeson, p. 136.
[62] Judah Goldin, *The Living Talmud—The Wisdom of the Fathers* (New York: New American Library, 1957), p. 43.
[63] Rabbi Benjamin Blech, *The Complete Idiot's Guide to Jewish History and Culture* (New York: Macmillan, Inc., 1998), p. 128.
[64] Christopher, *Romans: The Power of God*, p. 49.
[65] See Appendix B.
[66] Ibid.
[67] Goldin, p. 129.
[68] Gesenius, p. 55a.

Chapter 10 — The Final Trumpets

[69] For a much more complete and detailed look, please read Ezekiel 40–42. The prophecies in Ezekiel that precede this measuring, as well as those that come after it, are the same prophecies being described in Revelation 11. Likewise, Ezekiel does his measuring in a "prophetic order" that is identical to what's contained in the book of Revelation.

Appendix B — The Seven Rules of Hillel

[70] James Trimm, Society for the Advancement of Nazarene Judaism, and Herbert Bateman IV, "*Early Jewish Hermeneutics and Hebrews 1:5-13,*" Chapter 1, 1997, American University Studies, Peter Lang Publishers.
[71] We have spelled this word as *tanakh* elsewhere in this book, but this spelling (i.e., *tenach*) is not incorrect. It simply demonstrates

that various Hebrew words are often spelled differently when they are transliterated into English. Indeed – please note that we have preserved the original spelling of most Hebraic references in Appendix B, even if somewhat different than our own spellings elsewhere in this volume.

Bibliography

Biven, David and Blizzard, Roy Jr. *Understanding the Difficult Words of Jesus.* Shippensburg, PA: Destiny Image Publishers, 1994.

Blech, Rabbi Benjamin. *The Complete Idiot's Guide to Jewish History and Culture.* New York: Macmillan, Inc., 1998.

Christopher, Michael. *Romans: The Power of God.* Nashville, TN: Thomas Nelson Publishers, 2004.

Edersheim, Alfred. *Sketches of Jewish Social Life.* Peabody, MA: Hendrickson, 1994.

Edersheim, Alfred. *The Temple: Its Ministry and Services.* Peabody, MA: Hendrickson Publishers, 1994.

Gesenius, H. W. F. *Gesenius' Hebrew-Chaldee Lexicon to the Old Testament.* Baker Books: Grand Rapids, MI, 1979.

Goldin, Judah. *The Living Talmud—The Wisdom of the Fathers.* New York: New American Library, 1957.

Klein, John; Spears, Adam and Christopher, Michael. *Lost in Translation: Rediscovering The Hebrew Roots of our Faith.* Knoxville, TN: Selah Publishing Group, 2007.

Mozeson, Isaac E. *The Word.* New York: SPI Books, 2000.

The New Testament in Hebrew and English, 3rd Edition. Middlesex, England: The Society for Distributing Hebrew Scriptures, 2000.

Robinson, George. *Essential Judaism: A Complete Guide to Beliefs, Customs, and Rituals.* New York: Simon & Schuster/Pocket Books, 2000.

Bibliography

Seekins, Frank. *Hebrew Word Pictures.* Phoenix, AZ: Living Word Pictures, 1994.

Stern, David H. *Jewish New Testament Commentary.* Clarksville, MD: Jewish New Testament Publications, 1989.

Recommended Reading

Aharoni, Yohanan. *The Land of the Bible.* Philadelphia: Westminster Press, 1962.

Aharoni, Yohanan & Avi-Yonah, Michael. *The MacMillan Bible Atlas.* New York: MacMillan, 1968.

Backhouse, Robert. *The Kregel Pictorial Guide to The Temple.* Grand Rapids: Kregel, 1996.

Black, Naomi (Ed.). *Celebration: The Book of Jewish Festivals.* Middle Village, NY: Jonathan David Publishers, 1989.

Brown, William. *The Tabernacle, Its Priests and Its Service.* Peabody, MA: Hendrickson Publishers, 1996.

Byers, Marvin. *The Mystery: A Lost Key.* Miami: Hebron Press, 2000.

Church, J. R. & Stearman, Gary. *The Mystery of the Menorah.* Oklahoma City: Prophecy Publications, 1993.

Cohen, Abraham A. *Everyman's Talmud: The Major Teachings of the Rabbinic Sages.* New York: Schocken Books, 1995.

Cohen, Shaye J. D. *From the Maccabees to the Mishnah.* Philadelphia: Westminster Press, 1987.

Crossan, John D. & Reed, Jonathan L. *Excavating Jesus.* New York: Harper, 2001.

Donin, Rabbi Hayim Halevy. *To Be a Jew.* Jackson, TN: Basic Books, 1982.

Donin, Rabbi Hayim Halevy, *To Pray as a Jew: A Guide to the Prayer Book and Synagogue Service.* Jackson, TN: Basic Books, 2001.

Recommended Reading

Dunn, James D. G. *Jews and Christians, the Parting of the Ways.* Grand Rapids: Eerdmans, 1992.

Edersheim, Alfred. *The Life and Times of Jesus the Messiah.* Peabody, MA: Hendrickson Publishers, Inc, 2000.

Finto, Don. *Your People Shall Be My People.* Ventura, CA: Regal Books, 2001.

Free, Joseph and Vos, Howard. *Archaeology and Bible History.* Grand Rapids: Zondervan, 1992.

Friedman, David. *They Loved the Torah.* Baltimore: Lederer Books, 2001.

Frydland, Rachmiel. *What Rabbis Know About the Messiah.* Columbus, OH: Messianic Literature Outreach, 1991.

Frymer-Kensky, Tikva, Novak, David, Ochs, Peter, Sandmel, David F., & Signer, Michael A. *Christianity in Jewish Terms.* Boulder, CO: Westview Press, 2000.

Homer, Lattimore, Richard. *The Odyssey of Homer.* New York: HarperCollins, 1991.

Howard, Kevin, and Rosenthal, Marvin. *The Feasts of the Lord.* Orlando: Zion's Hope, Inc, 1997.

Kasdan, Barney. *God's Appointed Times: A Practical Guide for Understanding and Celebrating the Biblical Holidays.* Baltimore: Messianic Jewish Publishers, 1993.

Kenyon, E.W. *Blood Covenant.* Lynnwood, WA: Kenyon's Gospel Publishing Society, 1981.

Kohlenberger, John R, III. *The Interlinear NIV Hebrew English Old Testament.* Grand Rapids: Zondervan, 1979.

Lamm, Maurice. *Jewish Way in Love and Marriage.* New York, NY: Jonathan David Publishers, 1980.

Recommended Reading

Lash, Jamie. *The Ancient Jewish Wedding and the Return of Messiah for His Bride*. Ft. Lauderdale: Jewish Jewels, 1997.

Laurence, Richard. *The Book of Enoch the Prophet*. Kempton, IL: Adventures Unlimited Press, 2000.

Levy, David M. *The Tabernacle: Shadows of the Messiah*. Bellmawr, N J: The Friends of Israel Gospel Ministry, 1993.

Martin, Richard P. *Bulfinch's Mythology: The Age of the Fable, The Age of Chivalry, Legends of Charlemagne*. New York: HarperCollins, 1991.

Mason, Steve. *Josephus and the New Testament*. Peabody, MA: Hendrickson Publishers, 1992.

Murray, Andrew. *The Two Covenants*. Fort Washington, PA: CSC Publications, 2001.

Nanos, Mark D. *The Mystery of Romans*. Minneapolis, MN: Augsburg Fortress Press, 1996.

Nanos, Mark D. *The Irony of Galatians*. Minneapolis, MN: Augsburg Fortress Press, 2002.

Neusner, Jacob. *The Mishnah: A New Translation*. New Haven, CT: Yale University Press, 1988.

Olitzky, Rabbi Kerry M., Judson, Rabbi Daniel, editors. *The Rituals & Practices of a Jewish Life*. Woodstock, VT: Jewish Lights Publishing, 2002.

Philips, Neil. *Myths & Legends: The World's Most Enduring Myths and Legends Explored and Explained*. New York, NY: DK Publishing, 1999.

Richmond, Barbara. *Jewish Insights into the New Testament*. Woodland Park, CO: For Your Glory, 1996.

Rosen, Ceil & Rosen, Moishe. *Christ in the Passover.* Chicago: Moody Press, 2006.

Scott, Bruce. *The Feasts of Israel.* Bellmawr, NJ: Friends of Israel Gospel Ministry, 1997.

Shanks, Hershel. *Understanding the Dead Sea Scrolls.* New York: Random House, 1992.

Stern, David H. *Restoring the Jewishness of the Gospel.* Clarksville, MD: Jewish New Testament Publications, 1990.

Trumbull, H. Clay. *The Blood Covenant.* Kirkwood, MO: Impact Christian Books, 1975.

Trumbull, H. Clay. *The Salt Covenant.* Kirkwood, MO: Impact Christian Books, 1975.

Trumbull, H. Clay. *The Threshold Covenant.* Kirkwood, MO: Impact Christian Books, 1975.

Vernes, Geza. *The Religion of Jesus the Jew.* Minneapolis, MN: Augsburg Fortress Press, 1992.

Wilson, Marvin R. *Our Father Abraham.* Grand Rapids: Eerdmans, 1989.

Winkler, Gershon. *The Way of the Boundary Crosser: Introduction to Jewish Flexidoxy.* North Vale, NJ: Jason Aronson, 1998.

Young, Brad H. *The Parables.* Peabody, MA: Hendrickson Publishers, 1998.

CPSIA information can be obtained at www.ICGtesting.com
Printed in the USA
BVOW11s2005100614

355975BV00029B/877/P